ADAM AND HEPPLEWHITE
AND OTHER NEO-CLASSICAL
FURNITURE

A   Drawing by Robert Adam. The State Bed at Osterley Park, Middlesex

ADAM AND HEPPLEWHITE
and other neo-classical
FURNITURE

by

CLIFFORD MUSGRAVE

TAPLINGER PUBLISHING CO., INC.
New York

First American Edition published by
TAPLINGER PUBLISHING CO., INC., 1966

Library of Congress Catalogue Card Number: 66–11302

Made and printed in Great Britain

For

ALICE AND EDWARD ALEXANDER
of Colonial Williamsburg,
Virginia, U.S.A.

ACKNOWLEDGEMENTS

In the preparation of this book I have met with unfailing kindness and help. I am deeply indebted to the following for the opportunities given to study their collections, and to take and reproduce photographs: H.R.H. the Princess Royal and the Earl of Harewood, the Duke of Bedford, the Duke of Northumberland, the Marquess of Bute, the Earl Spencer, the Viscount Scarsdale, the Viscountess Gage, the Lord Faringdon, the Lord Methuen, the Lord St. Oswald, the Hon. Andrew Venneck, Mrs. Dorothy Hart, Mr. David L. Styles, Mr. John Aspinall, Sir Trenchard Cox, C.B.E., F.S.A., F.M.A., Director of the Victoria and Albert Museum; Mr. Ralph Fastnedge, F.M.A., Curator of the Lady Lever Art Gallery; Mr. Alister Campbell, F.M.A., Curator of the Iveagh Bequest, Kenwood; and Mr. G. L. Conran, F.M.A., Director of Manchester City Art Gallery and Heaton Hall; Mr. Geoffrey Beard, Curator of Cannon Hall, Barnsley, Yorkshire; The Trustees of Sir John Soane's Museum, and the Trustees of the Earl of Chichester.

The work would have been impossible without the generous help of Sir John Summerson and Miss Dorothy Stroud in allowing me to study and to take photographs of the Adam drawings at the Soane Museum on many occasions.

For providing photographs and giving permission for their reproduction grateful acknowledgements are made as follows:

Mr. Norman Adams, for no. 175; Biggs of Maidenhead, for nos. 153, 154; H. Blairman and Sons, for nos. 72, 76, 77, 78, 88; Brighton Corporation, for nos. 13, 113, 168; The British Museum, for no. 3; Christie, Manson and Woods, Ltd., for no. 128; *Country Life, Ltd.*, for no. 121; English Life Publications, Ltd., for plate D; Fine Art Engravers, Ltd., for nos. 1, 4, 8, 11, 33, 34, 37, 38, 40, 41–55, 57, 59, 60, 62, 64, 65, 68, 69, 70, 71, 83, 92, 93, 94–99, 107, 108, 111, 112, 117, 120, 122, 126, 136–140, 146, 149, 155–158, 163, 164, 166, 167, 177; The Greater London Council, for nos. 80, 119; Mr. Leslie Harris, for nos. 2, 6, 35; M. Harris and Sons, Ltd., for nos. 89, 91, 129, 135; Hotspur, Ltd., for nos. 134, 143, 159, 169, plate B; Mr. A. F. Kersting, for nos. 132, 176; the Iveagh Bequest, Kenwood, for nos. 80, 119; the Lady Lever Art Gallery, for nos.

7

79, 125; Mallett and Son, Ltd., for nos. 84–87, 104, 105, 106, 127, 130, 131, 147, 160, 162, 173, 178; Manchester Corporation, for no. 171; the Metropolitan Museum of Art, New York, for nos. 63, 102; Tom Molland, Ltd., for nos. 100, 101, 142, 145; the National Museum of Wales, for nos. 133, 141; the National Trust, for nos. 132, 176; Frank Partridge, Ltd., for nos. 148, 161; the Philadelphia Museum of Art, for nos. 61, 82; Philips of Hitchin, for nos. 74, 165; the Royal Academy of Arts, for nos. 151, 152, 174; Sir John Soane's Museum, for nos. 15, 16, 17, 19, 20, 21, 22, 23, 24, 25, 26, 27; Sotheby and Co., for nos. 57, 81, 90; Trevor Antiques, for no. 75; the Victoria and Albert Museum, for nos. 18, 30, 31, 32, 39, 66, 67, 109, 110, 123, 144, plate C; Temple Williams, Ltd., for no. 170.

Photographs numbered 5, 7, 9, 10, 12, 14–17, 19–32, 36, 56, 58, 80, 103, 114–116, 118, 124, 150 and 172 are by the author.

For much valuable help and advice I am deeply grateful to Mr. F. J. B. Watson, C.V.O., F.S.A., Mr. H. D. Molesworth, Mr. John Hayward, Mrs. Helena Hayward, Mr. Anthony Coleridge, Mr. David du Bon, Miss Edith Standen, Mr. David Bland, Mr. L. G. G. Ramsey, F.S.A., Editor of the *Connoisseur*; Mr. Ralph Edwards, C.B.E., F.S.A.; Mr. John Fleming; Mr. Sidney Hutchinson, F.S.A., Mr. John Adams, Editor of *Country Life*, Mr. N. M. Neatby, Mr. I. O. Chance, Mr. Richard Timewell, Mr. M. Harris, Mr. R. G. Kerr, Mr. Francis Egerton, Mr. Elydr Williams, Mr. Leslie J. Godden, Mr. H. S. Evans, Mr. Charles M. Wood, Mr. John Herbert, Miss W. Burford, Mr. D. P. Graham, Mr. J. A. Kenworthy-Brown, Mr. A. T. Walker, Mr. Godfrey Thompson, Mr. E. H. Jermy, Mr. J. Barton.

I am particularly grateful to Mr. John Harris and Mrs. Eileen Harris for important information, and for permission to quote from their works, and to Mr. John Lowe and his successor as editor of this series of furniture monographs, Mr. Peter Thornton, for their invaluable suggestions and helpful criticism. I am indebted for much help to Miss E. V. Baird, B.A., F.L.A., Miss B. Greenhill and other members of the staff of Brighton Reference Library, Mr. H. F. Brazenor, F.R.N.S., Mr. Derek L. Rogers, Miss Patricia Ranger and Miss Rosemary Fraser; and above all to my wife for her helpful advice, and her infinite forbearance and encouragement.

CONTENTS

ILLUSTRATIONS

COLOUR PLATES

MONOCHROME PLATES
at the end of the book

INTRODUCTION

Since the days of its inception the Adam style has never ceased for more than a few years at a time to exercise its fascination for designers and patrons. Its influence in architecture, decoration and furnishing persisted right through the early nineteenth century, and after only brief periods of disfavour was revived from time to time in the Victorian and Edwardian periods. Indeed, some highly convincing Adamesque interiors were created even as late as the 1930's.

In this respect the Adam style has more in common with the Louis Quatorze vogue, which has experienced revivals of popularity from the days of its origin until recent years, than with the Regency style, which suffered an almost complete eclipse for the greater part of a century.

Even in houses where the scheme of decoration owed little to the Adam inspiration, furniture in that style has often been found to accord agreeably with decorations and furniture of other periods, and even of modern times.

Although much has been written on the subject during the present century, the furniture of the Adam period has remained less thoroughly understood than that of almost any other period in the history of the decorative arts. Much confusion has existed over the question of the extent to which Robert Adam himself designed furniture, and on the subject of his relationship with various craftsmen, above all with Thomas Chippendale.

A contribution of profound significance was made in 1944 in *Georgian Cabinet-makers* by Ralph Edwards and Margaret Jourdain with their assessment of the marquetry furniture produced by Thomas Chippendale's firm in the neo-classic manner as constituting the masterpieces of his career, exceeding in richness and quality even the finest articles of his *Director* period. Practically no systematic study had however been devoted to the furniture of the Adam period until the publication of *The Furniture of Robert Adam*, by Mrs. Eileen Harris, in 1963, which provides the first concise, coherent and scholarly account of the origin, development and character of Adam furniture.

While acknowledging the significance of James 'Athenian' Stuart's drawings for Kedleston and Spencer House in the formation of Adam's early neo-classical style, the writer has devoted some attention to a hitherto much neglected factor, the influence of traditional English classicism, and early manifestations of neo-classicism in the furniture of William Kent, and in the small number of classical designs found in Chippendale's predominantly rococo *Director*. The recent researches and discoveries made in connexion with French influences on Adam's work by such scholars as Mr. F. J. B. Watson, Mr. Geoffrey de Bellaigue and Mr. Svend Eriksen are also closely examined in relation to the long-standing conviction of some authorities that, in certain furniture designed by Adam, he anticipated characteristics embodied years later in the Louis Seize style.

In the present work an attempt has been made to survey the whole field of neo-classical furniture up to about 1790, and to illustrate its evolution not only in the designs of Robert Adam himself, but in the independent work of the great craftsmen of the day, the Chippendales, John Cobb, John Linnell, Ince and Mayhew, Samuel Norman, William France, Peter Langlois and others who were quick to seize upon the new style and to contribute to its development. Attention has been paid especially to the evolution of the principal types of furniture during the Adam and Hepplewhite periods as expressed in the work of the principal cabinet-makers.

A great advantage to the student and lover of Adam furniture is that it may be found in a comparatively small number of great houses for which it was originally made, and which are open to the public, as well as in various collections in national and provincial museums. It is hoped that this book will be of some service not only to those who visit these houses and collections, but also to the connoisseurs, collectors, decorators and dealers whose efforts in bringing to light and cherishing this gloriously beautiful body of furniture have been the means of bringing so much delight to the devotees of a remarkable age in the history of art.

CLIFFORD MUSGRAVE

Brighton
1965

THE ADAM REVOLUTION

Few changes of taste in decoration and furnishing have been so sensational in character, or so far-reaching throughout many different levels of society, as the revolution in fashion brought about by the Adam brothers between the years 1760 and 1790.

Thomas Malton, the topographical water-colourist, in his volume of views, *A picturesque tour through the Cities of London and Westminster*, published in 1792, referred to 'the Messrs. Adams, four brothers, by whose labours Great Britain has been embellished with many edifices of distinguished excellence. To their researches among the vestiges of antiquity we are indebted for many improvements in ornamental architecture; and for the introduction of a style of decoration, unrivalled for elegance and gaiety; which in spite of the innovations of fashion, will prevail as long as good taste exists in the nation.'

Robert Adam himself was not overcome with false modesty when he declared, in the volume that recorded *The Works in Architecture of Robert and James Adam*, in 1773, that 'the skilful . . . we doubt not, will easily perceive, within these few years, a remarkable improvement in the form, convenience and arrangement and relief of apartments; a greater movement and variety in the outside composition and, in the decoration of the inside, an almost total change.'

So radical a departure was there in the scale, proportions, 'projection' and motifs of the decorative schemes devised by the brothers from almost anything known before, that the architect Sir John Soane spoke of their achievement as 'a revolution of electric power'.[1]

The interiors of the great Palladian mansions of the early eighteenth century, like Moor Park, Houghton and Holkham, were based on the design of antique temples. Indeed, Colin Campbell himself, one of the foremost Palladian architects, spoke of having introduced at Houghton 'the temple beauties in a private building',[2] but in those days before the discovery of Herculaneum and

[1] J. Soane, *Lectures in architecture*. (Full titles of authorities quoted, and other details, are given in the Bibliography on page 175.)
[2] C. Campbell, *Vitruvius Britannicus*, III, p. 55.

Pompeii almost nothing was known regarding the furniture of antiquity. The provision of furniture for the new houses thus made special demands upon their designers.

For the furniture of the new interiors of the 1730's and '40's, for such great houses as Moor Park and Ditchley, for Houghton and Holkham, for Wolverton and Chiswick, William Kent and his followers like Thomas Ripley took as examples the baroque furniture of the late seventeenth and early eighteenth century villas and palaces of Italy, in default of more truly ancient models. It is a curiosity of artistic psychology that the baroque style that had been proscribed for the external architecture should thus have been tolerated for the contents.

The furniture designed by Kent and his followers, though limited in the range of types, is widespread and familiar, especially the side-tables and console-tables with marble tops and friezes worked with the wave-form 'Vitruvian scroll' moulding, and supported by the carved figures of eagles, dolphins, satyrs, nymphs or tritons, or by heavy S-shaped scrolls with scale decoration or coin-moulding. His chairs, too, had scroll-shaped legs and back rails.

This furniture, although grand and impressive, was to become looked upon more and more as clumsy and ponderous, although even small-scale furniture of similar character was made for houses like Stourhead in Wiltshire and Firle Place in Sussex and found more lasting favour. Here also, as at Longford Castle in Wiltshire, and in a table made for Coleshill, Berkshire (now in the Victoria and Albert Museum) figures of English animals like foxes and hounds, denizens of a credible everyday world, were used as furniture supports and were more easily acceptable than the fabulous creatures of classical legend.

What Adam was later to anathematize as the 'massive entablature, the ponderous compartment ceiling . . . the tabernacle frame' of Palladian character were being thought intolerably weighty and oppressive by the mid-century, and the mouldings 'of bold projection' and the heavily ribbed mouldings of ceilings in deep coffers, or huge geometrical rectangles, circles and ovals, gave place, not once more to the blowsily fulsome scrolls and cornucopias of the interior plaster-work of the baroque age, but to the delicately nervous foliage, shell-work and rock-work of the French taste of the *Régence* period. The Dining-Room at Stanmer Park, near Brighton, and rooms at Nettlecombe Court, Somerset, both of a date about 1735, display this lively early-rococo taste which in its perfect symmetry retains a sense of delicacy, formality and refinement that admits of no reversion to baroque licence and ponderousness. This was a development in which there was to be no conflict between the architecture and the furnishing.

The rococo style was welcomed as a relief from the oppressiveness and solemnity of Palladian decoration, but the new fashion affected the interior modelling of comparatively few houses, such as Chesterfield House, built in 1749 (and demolished in 1937), where 'the light fanciful manner of the French' was admitted by Izaac Ware, one of the strictest of the Palladians. Here, although frothing profusely over the walls and ceilings of the rooms, the new decoration was confined in a classical frame. At Hagley also it is seen in a charmingly restrained form.

The rococo designs of Boffrand, Oppenordt and Meissonnier, anglicized and applied in the realm of furniture by such English designers as Matthias Lock, Edward Darley, William Halfpenny and above all by Thomas Johnson,[1] advanced a vogue that reached its fullest expression in this field in 1754 with the first edition of Thomas Chippendale's *Gentleman and Cabinet-maker's Director*. Articles in the rococo taste such as Chippendale depicted were in general demand — even among the smaller houses of early Georgian, Queen Anne and William and Mary type, where the interior ornament consisted chiefly of simple classical mouldings and walls of painted panelling. The naturalistic ornament of tree and plant-forms, of rock-work and shell-work was retained, but a new disorder now invested all the parts of furniture, creating a fresh sense of liveliness and gaiety, and although all the earlier symmetry of design was abandoned, a satisfying balance of form was nevertheless achieved by the skilful opposition of masses and tensions.

It is extraordinary that such a fantastic, extravagant, and in many respects unpractical fashion, so alien to the English instinct for stability, reticence and sobriety, should have excited such a sweeping influence in furniture design as it did over so long a period, although in the decoration of interiors it commanded so much less popularity. The rococo style persisted in favour until as late as 1790, and indeed in the days of Hepplewhite attained its highest pitch of beauty and elegance (Figs. 40 and 165).

Robert and James Adam, at the onset of their career as architects, were eager to show their facility in the rococo style when they completed the building of Hopetoun House in West Lothian for Lord Linlithgow, which had been begun by their father and interrupted by his death in 1748. William Adam, the leading Scottish architect of his day, had imparted sound Palladian principles to his sons and it is evident in much of their later work, but the fact that Robert Adam,

[1] H. Hayward, *Thomas Johnson and English rococo*, Tiranti. London, 1964.

always avid for fresh novelties of style, was intrigued by the gay and lively spirit of the rococo as he had seen it expressed in the design-books of Halfpenny, Batty Langley and Robert Morris, is apparent in the assymetrical rococo ornament of the ceilings, and in the cartouches of the covings of the Yellow and Red Drawing Rooms of the South Wing at Hopetoun. Robert made use of the rococo style also in the decoration of Dumfries House, which he designed in 1754 in conjunction with his elder brother James, who eventually became the business partner of the famous architectural trio. Dumfries was in fact the first important country house that Robert carried out independently of his father.

Within a very few years the brothers were to dominate the architectural scene in Britain with an immense repertoire of new motifs of entirely different character, based neither upon the naturalistic themes of the rococo, nor upon classical forms and motifs as used in the florid, powerful and individualistic manner of the baroque era, but upon a new vision and interpretation of antiquity — the neo-classical — a body of architecture and ornament that aimed at re-creating 'the pure spirit of the ancients'.

The profound changes brought about by the Adam brothers could not have been the result only of fresh whims of fashion. All changes in art are the reflection, indeed sometimes the anticipation, of new patterns of social existence and human relations. The society of the latter half of the eighteenth century moved along different currents of thought and behaviour from earlier generations.

Society in the age of Adam formed itself into coteries and 'bands of initiates', knowledgeable in theories of art as well as of politics, and their cult of conformity within these circles was again something that made the success of the neo-classical style possible. Such uniformity would have been intolerable to the romantic, emotional 'man of sensibility' in the Regency, some forty years later, for whom the multiplicity of styles was essential for the full expression of his individuality.

The manners of late eighteenth century society may have been somewhat stilted, and their conventional artificiality was something that was eventually to give place to the studied casualness of the Regency, but these were the tendencies that shaped the furniture of the time. It was a period in which the new elegant arts of conversation and letter writing flourished, and the sofa had not yet come to be used merely for casual lounging, but was a focus for the formal conversational social group as well as being part of the architectural wall-decoration. But the social and psychological patterns which precipitate change in the arts do not complete themselves without the material factor of the wealth that makes patronage possible.

The signing of the Treaty of Paris that brought the Seven Years War with France to an end in 1763 ushered in a new era of prosperity and expansion. The immense fortunes accumulated in England during the long administration under the Whigs which had begun with Marlborough's successful wars against the French were not yet dissipated, and the full economic effects of the disastrous war of American secession under Lord North's inept leadership were not to be felt for some years.

The time that was one of the most favourable in our history for the cultivation of the arts, for the patronage of craftsmen and painters, for the fostering of all the interests that went towards the creation of the great houses of England as embodiments of all that was most excellent in the arts of architecture, decoration, furniture, painting, silverwork, and a host of other creative activities, was still at its zenith. The fresh element that made possible the development of a new attitude to antiquity was the emergence of more scientific methods of scholarship and of direct archaeological investigation. Hitherto knowledge of the classical past had been gained very largely from literary sources, too often not even from the ancient authors themselves, but from the writings of scholiasts and commentators. In Britain, especially during the sixteenth century and later, when traffic with Italy was limited by the religious wars and disputes, the knowledge of ancient architecture had derived not always from the actual monuments of antiquity, but from illustrations of Renaissance buildings in volumes of designs published in the Netherlands, or at best from not always well-produced editions of the first century Roman architect Vitruvius, whom Palladio took as his master five centuries later. Vitruvius himself was frequently inaccurate in his delineation of the architectural orders and of the details of ancient buildings, and some passages in his works are quite incomprehensible. Classical details often of a crude and inaccurate character, which appeared in furniture of the sixteenth and seventeenth century, derived from similar sources.

Beginnings of a new spirit of artistic thought based on the archaeological study of antiquity, are discernible in France as early as 1683 in the investigations of the French academies of art and architecture founded under Louis XIV by his chief minister Colbert, and the French academies, in both Paris and Rome, continued to be the chief power-houses of the neo-classical movement in Europe until the Revolution.

The French decorative artist J. N. Servandoni (1695–1760) was a pupil of G. P. Pannini (c. 1692–1765/8) whose paintings of Roman ruins and the Campagna were later to be framed upon the walls of Adam's interiors at Harewood and Osterley. Servandoni's design for the Church of St. Sulpice in 1733, intensely Roman in character, was a revelation of the vitality of the classical inspiration. Four years later the architect J. G. Soufflot (1713–81) designed the Hotel Dieu on advanced classical lines.

In 1748 the Roman architect and artist G.-B. Piranesi (1720–78) produced the *Antichita Romane*, a volume of engravings proclaiming the splendour of the Roman buildings. From 1755 onwards, when the German scholar Winckelmann published his treatise on *The imitation of Greek works of art*, a battle of books was waged over the relative merits of Roman and Greek architecture, a contest in which Piranesi attempted to demonstrate the superiority of the former in 1761, with his folio of engravings *Della magnificenza ed architettura de romani*. In subsequent volumes, however, Piranesi came to admit the excellence of Greek art, and in his *Diversi maniere d'adornari i cammini* of 1769, recommended the application not only of Greek and Roman themes, but also of Etruscan, Tuscan and Egyptian motifs to the decoration and furnishing of houses. Piranesi was thus himself less an originator of neo-classical ideas than one who reflected the changing attitudes of his time, provoked on the one hand by the propaganda of Winckelmann, and influenced on the other by the advanced ideas of his friends in the French *Académie des Beaux-arts* in Rome.

In 1749, Abel Poisson, the marquis de Vandières, later created Marquis de Marigny, was sent by his sister Madame de Pompadour on a visit to Rome lasting nearly two years with the object of preparing him for the post of *Directeur des Bâtiments, Jardins, Arts et Manufactures Royaux* to which he was appointed in 1755 through her influence. The visit was made by the marquis in the company of Soufflot; C.-N. Cochin, the artist and engraver, and a famous art critic of his day, the Abbé Leblanc, as mentors and travelling companions. It was a tour that heralded, if it did not actually precipitate, the ending of the rococo era and the beginning of the neo-classical.

Some two years after Adam's return from Rome Cochin made devastatingly ironical attacks on the extravagances of rococo designers, in two articles published in the *Mercure de France*, and upon the appointment of Marigny to the *Bâtiments Royaux*, Cochin was placed by him in charge of 'tout le détail de l'administration des arts'. In 1755 Marigny chose Soufflot as architect of the new church of St. Geneviève in Paris, which was modelled upon the Pantheon in Rome, and eventually became known by that name. Soufflot was also appointed by Marigny to the post under him of *Directeur de la Manufacture des Gobelins*. Marigny, Soufflot and Cochin thus became the leaders of the neo-classical movement in the early days of Louis XVI.

From 1752 onwards the comte de Caylus was publishing a series of volumes describing his own and other important collections of classical antiquities, the *Recueil d'antiquités égyptiennes, étrusques, grecques et romaines*, a work which served for many years afterwards as a rich mine of neo-classical inspiration for innumerable designers including eventually Robert Adam himself. De Caylus had indeed been advocating a return to classical inspiration since his election in 1731 as *Conseilleur honoraire* of the *Académie de Peinture*.[1]

Between 1757 and 1768 the architect J. F. Neufforge published his *Recueil d'Architecture*, the first general collection of purely neo-classical designs not only for buildings but for interior decoration, furniture, ironwork and decorative appurtenances like *torchères*, picture-frames and mirrors. A Supplement to the nine volumes appeared in thirty parts between 1772 and 1777, and Robert Adam drew upon the work for a number of details in his own designs (see page 70).

In England as early as the 1720's and '30's, Lord Burlington at the Assembly Rooms, York, and at Chiswick Villa, and William Kent at Holkham Hall in Norfolk, and at 44 Berkeley Square, London, embodied in the form and arrangement of those interiors the principles of Roman planning they had themselves studied at first hand in the buildings of that city. Their work was to provide a model for Robert Adam's own early neo-classical projects on a grand scale at Kedleston, and in miniature in the tiny domed and barrel-vaulted apartments of the Adelphi.

Adam seems almost certainly to have taken Kent's staircase at 44 Berkeley Square (1742–4) as the model for the staircase at Home House (1775–7), and Kent's compartment ceiling at the former house as the inspiration for his ceiling of the Red Drawing Room at Syon (1761–9). In the furniture also designed by William Kent, much of it based on drawings made by him in Italy, are many classical features that were to be adopted years later by Robert Adam in his first neo-classical exercises. Among these features are strings of husks or bell-flowers (Fig. 10); acanthus leaf-tip mouldings (Fig. 11); leaf-ornamented scrolls at the top of table-legs (Fig. 15); and supports shaped as human or mythical figures (Figs.

[1] F. J. B. Watson, *Catalogue of Furniture in the Wallace Collection*, 1956, p. xxxviii.

24 and 104). Indeed for Devonshire House, Piccadilly, designed by William Kent in 1734–5, a hall settee was provided in the style of this architect, having straight, turned baluster legs of slender proportions, and ornamented with acanthus leaf carving,[1] of a type not otherwise seen in English furniture until the 1770's (see also page 68).

While Kent had been inspired largely by Italian baroque furniture of the sixteenth and seventeenth centuries, in designing the massive pieces for Holkham, Houghton and Chiswick, features such as those now mentioned in Kent's furniture, almost fully neo-classical in their purity and fine proportion, must have been the result of direct observation and study by Kent of authentic ancient models.

In France there were isolated instances of advanced neo-classical furniture design as early as 1765 such as a chair with an oval back and straight legs appearing in a *gouache* drawing by P. A. Baudouin (see page 61) but even this is anticipated in certain features by the chair-designs made by Sir William Chambers about 1759 (see page 61). Although the sources that he used have not been traced in France, his designs were unquestionably made during his visit to France at that time.

In 1756–7 the French decorator Louis-Joseph Le Lorrain had designed some furniture in antique style for A.-L. La Live de Jully, the *chef de protocol* at Versailles, and two or three years later Horace Walpole and the Baron Grimm were reporting that to be fashionable in Paris everything must be 'à la grecque' (see page 58).

Among the early signs of the waning of the rococo in this country and of renewed enthusiasm for the ancient world was the publication in 1754 of *The Ruins of Palmyra* by Robert Wood. This work was one of the earliest to foster the conviction that 'the true style of the ancients' was to be found in the buildings of Imperial Rome rather than in the work of Palladio and other Italian architects which had inspired the Burlingtonians.

In the following year Robert Adam, who was then twenty-six, was given the opportunity of making the Grand Tour in the company of Lord John Hope, and being filled with ambitions to create a career in a wider sphere than his native Scotland, was able by this means to fulfil a long-cherished desire to visit Rome for a period of architectural study that was to last four years.

It is tempting to surmise that he had been fired with eagerness to study the architecture of antiquity by Robert Wood's work, but it appears that he was also

[1] R. Edwards, *The shorter dictionary*, p. 463, Fig. 2.

very strongly influenced by the desire to achieve the social prestige which resulted from having made the Grand Tour, 'to be received as a polished and accomplished young man of the world, able to make a leg with Parisian grace, ready to let the names of Italian artists and Roman buildings trip off his tongue without that sense of inferiority from which, according to Dr. Johnson, every man suffered who had not been to Italy'.[1]

In order to make the most of the social possibilities of the tour, he commissioned a sketch for a coat-of-arms, and gave instructions that letters were not to be addressed to him as 'Robert Adam, Architect', for in Rome such people were regarded, if not exactly as rogues and vagabonds, at least as socially inferior. Although Adam met Robert Wood frequently in Rome, he records no conversations with the investigator of Palmyra on the subject of the ruins there, but only his disappointment in his hopes of obtaining introductions into Roman society through that author. On his way to Rome, in November 1754, Adam spent nearly three weeks in Paris visiting churches, museums and royal palaces. At this time he met the French engraver C.-N. Cochin, who had recently returned from that visit to Rome in company with the marquis de Vandières and the architect Soufflot that has already been mentioned, and that was to have so far-reaching an influence in the development of the neo-classical movement in France.

Cochin was just about to publish his articles in the *Mercure de France*. Again it is tempting to imagine that at the time of his meeting with Adam, the French engraver was burning with enthusiasm over his ideas, and must have shown the Scotsman drawings and engravings revealing the possibilities of the new approach, including even designs that were soon to form part of the picture of *le goût grec*. It seems no less likely that Adam could have seen at the same time a copy of the volume which Cochin also published then, the *Observations sur les fouilles d'Herculanum*, or at least some of the material for it. Before many weeks Adam was himself to visit this site, the first of the buried cities to have been excavated. Adam's letters however tell us nothing of this encounter beyond having discussed the names of engravers suitable for engraving the various books which he and Cochin had it in mind to produce.

Continuing his journey towards Rome, Adam spent several weeks of gaiety in Florence, but there, after having danced some five hundred minuets and country-dances in a single night of Carnival, 'with all the greatest Quality and with some of the greatest Whores'.[2] Robert became disgusted with the meaningless life of the

[1] J. Fleming, p. 106.   [2] J. Fleming, p. 131.

English aristocrat abroad, who devoted most of his waking hours to inane gossip, dancing and gaming, and resolved to devote himself more wholeheartedly to study.

The essential architect in Robert Adam was thrilled electrically by the overwhelming panorama of antiquity that Italy presented. 'I already feel' he wrote[1] 'a passion for sculpture and painting which I before was ignorant of, and I am convinced that my whole conception of architecture will become much more noble than I could ever have attained by staying in Britain.' His resolution to make better use of his time was also fortified, perhaps, by the realization that while his companion, Lord John Hope, was willing to use his carriage and to let him bear more than his fair share of expenses, he was not so anxious to take Robert with him to the parties and receptions given by the aristocracy of the city. His conversion was complete, and he had discovered enlightenment, if not 'between the saddle and the ground', then, as it were, between the faro-table and the Forum.

If this revelation had any attendant angel, it appeared in the unprepossessing person of Charles-Louis Clérisseau, a French architectural draughtsman, who was passionately devoted to the study of antiquity. Adam found him at a loose end in Florence and engaged him as a drawing-tutor and travelling companion. Clérisseau 'would stay in the same house with me, would serve me as an antiquarian, would teach me perspective and drawing, would give me copies of all his studies of the antique, bas-reliefs and other ornaments; . . . and I shall furnish him a chamber and pay his meltiths and think it one of the luckiest circumstances could have happened.' He went on '. . . in Rome I must apply to drawing, I must walk about and sketch after the antiques. I must resolutely resolve to lay aside the fike-faks of company . . . I am conscious that hitherto, while I have dedicated my time to Gay Life I have done nothing else.'[1]

In Rome, guided by Clérisseau, Adam studied and made drawings of the ancient monuments, the great Baths of Caracalla and Diocletian, the basilicas, the vaulted temples, tombs and catacombs, the decorations of Hadrian's Villa at Tivoli, and of the lesser buildings and columbaria with their delicate stucco ornaments. He made drawings also in the churches and other buildings of the Renaissance and Baroque architects, and of the grotesques painted in imitation of Graeco-Roman decoration by Raphael and his pupils at the beginning of the sixteenth century in the loggias of the Vatican, and in the Villas Madama and Caprarola.

An immensely powerful influence must have been his friendship with Piranesi,

[1] J. Fleming, p. 140.

who later dedicated his book on the *Campus Martius* to Adam, and engraved four of the plates in *The Works* for him. It may well have been Piranesi's artistic freedom in combining the elements of antiquity into fresh and striking compositions, as was exemplified in the monuments and fragments of the classical world that he heaped up in his engraved title-pages, that gave Adam the key to the creation of new decorative groupings with ancient motifs.

Soon after his arrival in Rome Adam encountered William Chambers who was later to become his chief rival in the architectural profession, and whom even then he sensed as being a possible competitor. 'Chambers, who has been here six years', Adam wrote, 'is as superior to me at present as I am to Deacon Mack for greatness of thought, and nobility of invention, drawing and ornamenting. But damn my blood I will have fair trial for it and expect to do as much in six months as he has done in as many years.' Later, Joseph Wilton, the sculptor, also then in Rome, told Robert that Chambers 'owed all his hints and notions to Clerisseau',[1] from whom he had purchased drawings of Roman antiquities.

In 1754, Robert visited the ruins of Herculaneum, which had been excavated from 1738 onwards, and his brother James went to Pompeii, which was opened up in 1748, during his own visit to Italy after his brother's return. The excavations of the two buried cities provided an undreamed-of revelation of the domestic life of the ancients and of the decorations and furnishing of their houses. It now became possible to escape from temple architecture indoors and to adapt the style of Pompeiian interiors to modern needs. Adam was later to make much use of Pompeiian themes in his planning and furnishing, especially of the type of painted decoration in the buried cities which was then believed to be Etruscan, but which was in fact of late Greek origin.

A particular feature of Roman and Pompeiian houses which Adam adopted for many of his finest rooms, as at Osterley and Harewood, was the idea of wall-panels painted with imaginary landscapes, ruins and architectural fantasies, which were intended to give a sense of the enlargement of space in a room.

Adam's imagination and enthusiasm must have been greatly stimulated by contact and conversations with the pioneers of the neo-classical movement then in Rome — Pompeo Batoni, the portrait painter, and the French architects Marie-Joseph Peyre, Moreau-Deproux and De Wailly. Although the German painter Mengs did not begin to practise neo-classicism until several years later, about 1770, the spirit of the new approach must have been in the air, and his

[1] J. Fleming, p. 138.

pupil Gavin Hamilton, a fellow-countryman of Adam, later became a practitioner of it. It was another pupil of Mengs, Pannini, who executed for Adam years afterwards the paintings of imaginary ruins mentioned above.

On his return, Adam established himself in London with his brother James and two sisters. His almost immediate success was due to his having influential friends and patrons amongst his fellow-countrymen, such as Lord Bute, Admiral Boscawen and Lord Mansfield, and very largely also to his own genius for publicity and for exploiting the eagerness of patrons for a change in fashion.

While in Rome Robert had conceived the idea of producing a new edition of a work by the French architect Desgodetz, *Les Edifices Antiques de Rome*, first published in 1682, which had been out of print for many years. This he was convinced 'with a smart preface, a clever print of the author's head . . . could not fail to be of great authority and introduce me into England with an uncommon splendour'. It was, however, with a more original work that he eventually established his reputation as an investigator of antiquity.

Emulating the example of Robert Wood, in 1764 he published the folio volume of drawings entitled *The ruins of the palace of the Emperor Diocletian at Spalatro*, a production that was the fruit of a six weeks' expedition he made to Dalmatia during his Roman visit. This venture, however, provided him with little material for his own subsequent decorative work; in practice he made much greater use of the classical detail in Wood's *Palmyra*.

Through Lord Bute, Adam was appointed Architect of the King's Works, in company with Sir William Chambers, and after executing an important official commission to design the new arch and screen to Admiralty House, he embarked on a dazzling career of designing and re-modelling a series of great country houses, and later, of town houses, in the new style he had devised on the basis of the immense repertoire of classical ornament he had acquired in Rome.

While Robert Wood and his friends had been planning their expedition to Palmyra in Rome, as far back as 1748, they had met James Stuart, an artist who was said by Horace Walpole to have 'attended Lord Burlington in Italy'. Stuart was then making plans to visit and delineate the buildings of Athens, a project which he and Nicholas Revett (1720–1804), an artist and architectural draughtsman, carried out between 1751 and 1755. The first volume of the measured drawings which they produced, *The Antiquities of Athens*, was not published, however, until 1762, two years after the appearance of a less accurate study of Greek buildings, *Les ruines des plus beaux monuments de la Grèce*, although its author, J. D.

le Roy, had not made his own visit to Athens until some time after the expedition of the two Englishmen.

James Stuart had himself, however, created an early monument of neo-classicism that was the first building in Greek style to be erected in England, when in 1758 he built the little Doric temple which still stands in the grounds at Hagley.

The publication of the *Antiquities of Athens* had little immediate practical effect. As Mr. H. M. Colvin has pointed out, it was to be more influential for the Greek Revival of the early nineteenth century.[1] However, the work created a furore among scholars and connoisseurs and inspired Horace Walpole to bestow upon Stuart the nickname of 'Athenian'.

About the year 1757 Stuart was making drawings for Sir Nathaniel Curzon at Kedleston, and from 1759 up to about 1765 was designing decoration and furnishings for the interior of Spencer House, St. James's, London, for Lord Spencer. Stuart's design for the decoration of the Painted Room at Spencer House, dated 1759 (Fig. 3), with grotesques, panels and medallions, and pilasters painted with a 'flowing *rainceau*', anticipated in a striking fashion Adam's decorations of a few years later. The furniture that he designed for Kedleston and for Spencer House was to be influential in the development of Adam's neo-classical furniture in a way that has not been recognized until recently, and will be considered more fully in another chapter (see page 40).

The suggestion has been made that Stuart's neo-classicism derived from French sources, especially from the works of Caylus (1752 onwards), from Cochin's book on Herculaneum (1754) and from direct contact with the circle of French architects in Rome. Much of his inspiration may have been due, none the less, to his direct examination of Roman antiquities, for it can hardly be imagined that he devoted to such remains a less penetrating eye than he cast upon the monuments of Greece. Furthermore, it cannot be without significance that Stuart, in the company of Gavin Hamilton, the Scottish neo-classical painter, Michael Brettingham the Palladian architect, and his own colleague Nicholas Revett made a visit to Naples in 1748, the year that Pompeii was first excavated. It is difficult to believe that they did not then visit the excavations. There are important details of furniture presumed to have been designed by Stuart that closely correspond with those of ancient furniture at Pompeii (see page 183).

What the Adam brothers achieved in the realm of architecture and decoration

[1] H. M. Colvin, p. 582.

was admirably expressed by themselves in the first volume of *The Works in Architecture of Robert and James Adam* which they published from 1773 onwards.

'The massive entablature, the ponderous compartment ceiling, the tabernacle frame, almost the only species of ornament formerly known in this country are now universally exploded, and in their place, we have adopted a beautiful variety of light mouldings, gracefully formed, delicately enriched and arranged with propriety and skill. We have introduced a great diversity of ceilings, friezes, and decorated pilasters, and have added grace and beauty to the whole, by a mixture of grotesque, stucco, and painted ornaments together with the flowing *rainceau*, with its fanciful figures and winding foliage . . . we flatter ourselves, we have been able to seize with some degree of success, the beautiful spirit of antiquity, and to transfuse it with novelty and variety, through all our numerous works.'

In place of themes and motifs of the rococo age, the swirling curves, proliferating foliage, fantastic grotto-like shell-work, and rock-work dripping with water and icicles, — Adam's decorative schemes displayed within a framework of geometrical figures, circles and ovals, half-circles and half-ovals, rectangles and octagons, a precisely ordered array of formally disciplined leaf-scrolls, strings of bell-flowers or husks, swags, garlands and festoons, paterae and medallions, trophies of weapons, vases, urns and tripods, sphinxes and gryphons from the world of classical antiquity. These were modelled in plasterwork of light relief, or painted in colours of a variety rarely adopted in earlier decorative work.

In a sense Adam's efforts were contrary to the true spirit of neo-classicism, to the extent that they were not directed to the discovery of the 'purest style of the ancients', but to the realization of a personal vision of classical beauty that was hardly closer to the realities of the ancient world than were the classical scenes of Alma Tadema and Lord Leighton in the last century. Robert Adam's greatest contribution to decorative art was the sense of delicacy and refinement he imparted to classical forms, whether Etruscan, Roman, Renaissance, Palladian or Greek. Although so different in form from the naturalistic motifs of the rococo, Adam's classical elements were used by him with a delicacy that owed not a little to the slender intensity of the rococo line, and was thus acceptable to the devotees of the rococo as well as to the admirers of the puritan severity of Palladian classicism, because it retained the sense of formality and refinement that was essential to the ease of the mid-eighteenth century artistic mind.

The new decorations made fresh and exacting demands in respect of the furnishings. Adam himself aimed at a perfect harmony of style in his interiors, and as Sir John Soane[1] remarked years later, 'the light and elegant ornaments imitated from the ancient works in the Baths and Villas of the Romans, were soon applied in designs for chairs, tables, carpets and in every other species of furniture'. Soane went on to say 'However Mr. Adam may occasionally, in his flights of fancy, have descended to trifles, and given an elegance and an importance to a Sedan Chair, or the Keyhole of a Lady's Escritoire, let us in candour and justice to departed merit, remember that in the preceding age, the great . . . Kent . . . was likewise consulted for designs for State Coaches, City Barges and Children's Cradles.' These remarks by Soane have often been taken as indicating that Adam 'insisted' upon designing every article of furnishing in an interior, but the extent to which he did in fact personally design all the furniture in his rooms has been exaggerated.

Soane's reference to the great Palladian designer is significant. It was true that fifty years earlier William Kent had to a considerable extent created a harmony in the furnishings of the Palladian interiors of Chiswick, Houghton and Holkham by designing, in addition to the decorations of wall and ceilings, the details of door furniture and fire-grates, and such movables as settees, chairs, stools, pedestals and writing-tables. During a tour of English houses in 1749 to 1750, Robert Adam studied the work of Kent in a number of his important buildings, and greatly admired his achievements. In his first experiments in furniture design, before consolidating a workable classical style of his own, Adam made considerable use of Kentian forms. William Kent's tables with eagle supports, and similar ones by his colleague Thomas Ripley, possessed a tautness of design quite different from the sprawling abandon of more truly baroque furniture that was found in the Palladian era, like certain side-tables with tritons or river-gods as supports, and in this they anticipate the preciseness and tightly integrated design of Adam's neo-classicism.[2]

Like Kent, Robert Adam aimed at achieving a complete unity in the furnishings of his rooms to bring them into consonance with the architectural and decorative treatment, but in practice he rarely concerned himself with ordinary movables, paying greater attention to decorative pieces like pier-tables, side-tables, sideboards and sofas, forming units of a wall decoration, or appurtenances like tripods and pedestals that formed decorative accents in an interior composition.

The ideal of a completely unified interior was rarely realized in practice where

---

[1] J. Soane, *Lectures on architecture*.
[2] See *The Connoisseur*, May, 1965, p. 4, and R. Edwards, *Shorter dictionary*, Figs. 25, 27, 29, 30.

the movable furniture was concerned, except perhaps at Syon and at Osterley. It was certainly attained to a considerable extent at Nostell and Newby, and completely at Harewood, but in these instances the achievement of a neo-classical interior harmony was due more to the efforts of Thomas Chippendale working directly with the owners, and not, it seems, through direct collaboration with Adam.

The early developments in the revival of classicism had little immediate or general influence upon furniture. A third edition of Chippendale's *Director* was published in 1762, but with one or two classical exceptions, the designs were no less rococo than those of 1754. The only sign of a waning in this vogue was the omission of references to the Chinese and Gothic styles upon the title-page, although both of these fashions continued to be represented in the designs.

The Adam innovations were in a sense a 'palace revolution', worked out in a few great houses devoted to what the architect himself spoke of in *The Works* as 'the parade of life', but so closely did these improvements correspond with some of the most deeply felt needs in the designing of houses that eventually they became disseminated from the upper classes down to the middle and lower levels of society, transforming even many of the smallest dwellings and their contents.

Among those who lived in the humbler houses, who had never aspired to the richness of the French taste, there must have been a growing desire for furniture less heavy in form and sombre in colour than the mahogany articles of the 'pre-Director' period, or the old-fashioned oak and walnut furniture of even earlier date, that still furnished the majority of smaller houses even after the middle of the eighteenth century.

The Adam revolution was not merely a fashionable craze, or a passing phase in artistic philosophy. The delicacy and lightness that distinguished its productions were the mark of a new refinement and sensibility in human intercourse. The people of the 1780's and '90's who quietly promenaded and took tea in the Adamesque ballrooms of Brighton, Bury St. Edmunds, Shrewsbury, Salisbury and Newcastle were less uncouth than those who had footed it so grossly in the Assembly Rooms of Bath fifty years earlier, and who had called down upon themselves the strictures of Beau Nash.

The elegant and delicately proportioned furniture of Robert Adam, of Chippendale, Hepplewhite, Sheraton and Shearer likewise expressed a new sense of refinement and seemliness in domestic and social life.

ADAM'S FURNITURE DESIGNS
AND THE DEVELOPMENT OF HIS STYLE

The vast collection of nearly nine thousand drawings by Robert Adam which is preserved at the Soane Museum is a unique memorial to his talents as a designer of furniture as well as to his genius in architecture and decoration. The drawings were painstakingly gathered together in fifty-three volumes by Robert's youngest brother William, and were eventually bought by Sir John Soane in 1833 for £200 from Robert's niece, to whom they had been bequeathed.

The collection contains several hundred designs for furniture, and a number of other surviving drawings by Adam are preserved at various houses, including Croome Court, Kedleston, Corsham Court, Osterley and Harewood, and in the C. J. Richardson collection at the Victoria and Albert Museum. Not all the drawings are necessarily from the hand of Robert Adam, but most of them bear an inscription in his writing and are signed or dated from the Adelphi. In many instances very rough preliminary sketches exist as well as more highly finished designs for the same pieces. Many of the drawings must rank among the great masterpieces of architectural draughtsmanship, and among them some of those for furniture are also supreme of their kind.

While the Adam drawings throw a remarkable light upon the development of his furniture, to a great extent they are not conclusive in the evidence they provide. Comparatively few of them relate directly to actual articles of furniture that are known to exist. Far more of the architectural and decorative designs survive which correspond exactly to executed pieces. This is probably because such works were supervised directly by the architect, who would have retained the drawings.

The surviving furniture drawings must be regarded mostly as preliminary designs, the final versions of which were sent to the craftsman and apparently never returned. In the few instances where a design as executed exists, as in the case of the Saloon pier-tables for Nostell (Fig. 97), it is possible that they are duplicates intended for the approval of clients, or office copies, as suggested by

Bolton,[1] though if this was the case, it is strange that more of them are not preserved. Several entries in the Croome accounts refer to Adam's charges for 'drawings at large' or 'parts at large' of various articles of furniture 'at full size for the execution', and there is an entry for December 1764 which mentions a drawing of a detail for a bed 'at full size given to Mr. France'. These references make it clear that Adam was accustomed to providing such designs for the craftsmen, but hardly any drawings of this kind survive. A number of designs as executed for furniture in some important Adam houses like Syon, Kenwood and Luton Hoo, were reproduced as engravings in *The Works* (Figs. 27 and 28). In some cases they correspond to existing designs, in others the originals have been lost or modified in the execution, or they were carried out eventually for a different client.

As already mentioned, it has too often been supposed on the basis of Sir John Soane's remarks (see page 33) that Robert Adam 'insisted' upon his interiors forming a harmonious unity of architecture, decoration, fittings and movables. There is no evidence that he himself ever aimed at designing the entire contents of his interiors, but only such permanent decorative essentials as pier-tables, side-tables, looking-glasses and other important features of a room.

The drawings made in the 1770's for Sir Watkin Williams Wynne's house at 20 St. James's Square, London, give evidence of the scope of his intentions. There are designs for ceilings, friezes, doors, grates, chimney-pieces, mirrors, girandoles, silver plates, door-locks, and even for a sedan-chair. There are however hardly any drawings for ordinary movables, beyond those for a sideboard, a bookcase and a table. Furthermore, the drawings for different types of furniture do not exist in the collection in proportions representative of their predominance in the Adam period. Side-tables and chairs are two types of article in which the Adam spirit found its fullest expression, yet while there are about a hundred drawings for the former, there remain only about thirty of the latter. Nevertheless, the drawings for furniture may be seen to follow a pattern of development that corresponds to the evolution of his architectural and decorative style, and this will be examined in the following pages.

Several distinct phases of development are discernible in Adam's interior decorative schemes in the course of the twenty-five years when he was active in house design. The early period, from 1753 to 1759, covers the phase when, at Hopetoun in 1752 and at Dumfries in 1754, he was designing ceilings in pure

[1] A. T. Bolton, Vol. 1, p. 172.

rococo fashion. Even after his return from Rome he continued to make use of rococo elements at Shardeloes, Hatchlands and Croome Court, all begun in 1759.

From about 1760 to 1770 he was chiefly engaged in building or remodelling great country houses. In them there is much evidence of his Palladian training and even more of the influence of William Kent's anticipations of neo-classicism earlier in the century. The planning is based on Roman models; the structural form is strongly evident and three-dimensional in character.

In the entrance hall at Syon House, near Isleworth in Middlesex, Adam's first completely neo-classical interior (1761), he made use of tabernacle frames and Palladian mouldings, though of modified 'projection'; and in the drawing-room there, and in the gallery at Croome Court a year earlier, even used compartment ceilings of the kind he was later to decry, though as he himself wrote, no longer of 'the most enormous weight and depth'. His stucco ornaments of this early period, although displaying a new refinement and elegance, were bold in scale, modelled in deep relief, and broadly disposed over the surfaces they occupied, as at Syon in the ante-room (Fig. 95) and dining-room.

During the period from 1769 to 1777 his mouldings were of much finer character, the plasterwork of his ceilings and wall-panels in lighter relief, as in the gallery at Syon (Fig. 40), and in the eating-room at Osterley (Fig. 92).

His ornaments, however, still remain simple and bold, and are emphasized by being set in ample areas of space. This is the time of ceilings designed with round painted medallions set at wide intervals around a centre circle, or oval, also painted with classical scenes or figure groups as in the bedroom at Osterley (Fig. 109). Other bold and simple forms such as that of the Greek cross used in later ceilings at Osterley are characteristic of this period. Adam's enormous repertoire of decorative motifs was now at its fullest and richest extent, and was being used by him with complete assurance and perfect judgement, the containing spaces being so carefully proportioned as to set off his designs most effectively. Although the motifs are as familiar as the harmonies and cadences of Mozart's music, they are used with unfailing freshness and variety, no decorative scheme ever being exactly duplicated.

Between 1778 and about 1785 Adam's style became increasingly slight and superficial in conception. His ceilings and wall surfaces became more crowded with geometrical forms, executed in low relief, and with all available spaces crowded with ornament as in the gallery ceiling at Harewood (Fig. D). Although the decoration of the music room at Home House (the Courtauld Institute)

(1775–7) expresses this extreme tendency, and aroused the indignation of Walpole, nevertheless it possesses great beauty, but it represents a change from a plastic conception to a purely superficial and linear style.

The evolution of Adam's furniture style may also be divided into several main periods, which conveniently hinge upon the main turning-points of his general architectural and decorative evolution, though with something of a time lag. The four principal phases in the development of Adam's furniture style have been conveniently designated by Mrs. Harris[1] as Early (1762–4), Transitional (1765–8), Mature (1769–77) and Late (1778–92).

In the beginning, at least, Adam's instinct seems to have been much less sure in furniture design than it was in room decoration. The Early phase was a tentative, experimental one, in which Adam was feeling his way towards a formula for furniture appropriate to the interiors he was devising. Although as early as 1759 he had arrived at a workable solution, in his sideboard design for Kedleston (Fig. 2, and see page 40), he did not at first realize its full potentialities, and for a while continued to indulge in variations upon baroque and rococo themes.

The Transitional period, from 1765–8, is in many respects one of the most satisfying in the whole of Adam's development. It offers the promise of his maturity, but in it he has not yet acquired the mannerisms, the facility and the excessive sophistication of his later phases. Neo-classical form is now established in the early seat-furniture at Croome Court (Fig. 16), and at Osterley and Nostell, as well as in the noble group of square-legged side-tables at Syon (Figs. 8, 11, 15 and 93). Some initial experiments are made with baluster legs for sideboards and pier-tables, of robust and elaborate form, that are to lead the way for the later more delicate and elegant shapes (Fig. 18). Structural form is still vigorous and simple, and the ornament is of bold scale, though a wider variety of motifs is now coming into use, and there are signs of classical decorative motifs developing into structural forms, as in the instance of chair-backs being shaped as lyres (Figs. 60 and 62). The range of different types of furniture is still limited.

During the years of his Mature Period, 1769–77, the range of types of furniture that he designed was at its greatest, being extended especially to include articles of French character such as sofas and *confidantes*, as well as a greater variety of arm-chairs, hall-chairs and stools. Adam still concentrated upon the principal decorative articles, and never embarked upon certain more ordinarily domestic types such as the simpler articles of bedroom and dressing-room furniture for

[1] E. Harris, pp. 15–20.

which designs had been provided in Chippendale's *Director* and which were to be catered for again in Hepplewhite's *Cabinet-Maker and Upholsterer's Guide*.

As never before, decoration now becomes identified with the form of his furniture and seems to be a continuance of it. The forms themselves, although they have become much lighter than in the earlier phases, are still vigorous, vital and satisfying, as in the beautiful side-tables of Nostell and Osterley (Figs. 98 and 99). The element of colour assumes a fuller importance, culminating in the adoption of the 'Etruscan' scheme of colour combinations and contrasts.

During the Late Period, from 1778 until Adam's death in 1792, the form of his furniture becomes more attenuated, feminine and simplified, and tends to become overwhelmed with small-scale ornament in low relief. In place of carved or modelled ornament, the decoration is almost exclusively painted, or cast in composition. The fluency of his style in this late phase weakens into mere facility, and all his work seems to have lost its earlier vitality and to have become nerveless and standardized.

Adam's earliest surviving furniture design of all is for a chair, and is neither neo-classical nor traditionally classical but Gothic, and belongs to that early romantic Gothic episode in Adam's architectural work, which although little remarked upon in the past, is shown by Mr. Fleming[1] to have been one of the most original and interesting phases of his career. The design is dated 1761, and intended for Croome Church, but was eventually executed for Alnwick (Fig. 56) probably between 1777 and 1780, when Adam was producing other designs for the chapel there as part of the complete Gothic interior he created in the 1770's, but which was regrettably replaced in 1855 in neo-Renaissance style.

Although Adam's early decorative work, such as his interiors at Hatchlands, executed in 1758–61, did not show his fully formed manner, it possessed his unmistakable personal impress. This is not the case with his early furniture designs, particularly two designs for sofas in the Soane Museum. One of them, dated 1762 (Fig. 29), is inscribed 'for Lord Scarsdale & also executed for Mrs. Montagu in Hill Street'. The second drawing may relate to a sofa now in the Philadelphia Museum.[2]

These designs have some resemblance to sofas designed by William Kent for Palladian houses, modelled upon late seventeenth century and early eighteenth century baroque Italian models, with their outward curving ends and high backs,

[1] J. Fleming. Adam Gothic: article in *The Connoisseur*, October 1958.
[2] E. Harris, Figs. 99 and 100, and p. 90.

but Adam has altered the centre crest, which often originally took the form of a shell or plume of feathers, into what became the characteristic neo-classic Adam feature of a circular medallion containing a painted or modelled scene or group. This was a feature he presumably took from Neufforge, whose designs (of about four years earlier) abound with the medallion motif.[1] Both drawings, with the arm-supports shown in the form of syrens with scaly tails, are usually regarded as embodying preliminary ideas for the great 'mer-folk' sofas at Kedleston (see page 85), but these, which were executed, it is believed, by Linnell, have a baroque boldness of form and large scale far exceeding Adam's hesitant suggestions (Figs. 30–34).

Although Adam's style is still uncertain, these pieces show the attempt to give furniture the lightness and delicacy that was to become one of the principal distinguishing characteristics of his work.

A firmness and conviction absent in these early sofa drawings is found in the design made also in 1762 of a sideboard group for the dining-room apse at Kedleston which is preserved at the house (Fig. 2). This drawing of side-tables with square tapering fluted legs, and friezes decorated with half-paterae and swags, is the first completely neo-classical furniture design by Robert Adam that is known to exist. It would be tempting to place this drawing later than those for the sofas, and to suppose there was a logical development from baroque to neo-classical forms. However, separate drawings at the Soane Museum for the wine-cooler, the tripod candelabra, and the urns and basins that appear in the sideboard group suggest that they were drawn 'for Sir Nathaniel Curzon, Baronet' before 9 April 1761, and it would thus appear that the neo-classical sideboard design was conceived before those for the baroque sofas.

Mrs. Harris[2] has suggested that this is because Adam had not yet arrived at a satisfactory formula for classical seat-furniture, although he had found a solution for table design in the early neo-classical furniture designed by James Stuart for Spencer House, London, as early as 1759.

A drawing believed to be by James Stuart, for the Painted Room at Spencer House, shows a side-table with straight tapering legs of square section, of a type closely resembling Adam's sideboard-tables at Kedleston (Fig. 3). This drawing, which is preserved at the British Museum, is dated in a tablet above the door of the room in the drawing 'MDCCLVIIII', a date at least two years earlier than that of Adam's sideboard design. The drawing is important also in that it sets the begin-

---

[1] J.-F. Neufforge, Vol. 1, 1757, plates 64, 65, 66.   [2] E. Harris, p. 63.

nings of Stuart's designs for the interior of Spencer House at least a year earlier than has hitherto been supposed. The wall-decoration is of grotesques, with painted medallions containing figure-groups, in a manner similar to that adopted by Adam for the eating-room at Osterley, although not until 1767 (Fig. 92). The work at Spencer House was completed about 1765.

The side-table indicated by Stuart does not appear to have survived, if ever it was executed as designed, but there are tables from Spencer House preserved at Althorp, Northamptonshire, which have similar square-section tapered and fluted legs, and other furniture in a mature neo-classical idiom that we must now recognize could have been designed as early as 1759. Of this kind are the gilt pier-table in the Marlborough Room, and the pair of gilt pier-tables in the Great Room (Fig. 5), both from Spencer House. Two pairs of tripods from Spencer House are possibly of similar early date, and are of even greater importance, both of them fully neo-classical in spirit. One pair are the famous gilt tripods having bases painted with female classical figures and carrying ormolu tripod candelabra of the type often thought to have been made by Matthew Boulton and used by Adam at Kedleston and elsewhere (Fig. 9). Stuart's primacy in the design of these candelabra is demonstrated again by the British Museum drawing, where one of them is seen standing on the pier-table. The second pair of tripods are less spectacular, but probably earlier than the first, and interesting in that the inward-canted, square, fluted legs with lion-paw feet (Fig. 7), have a resemblance to those of the side-tables in Adam's gallery at Syon (Fig. 8), the designing of which occupied the years from 1762 to 1769. The classical tripod motif, adapted by Adam from a solid object to a linear decorative ornament, also appears in the Syon gallery as a feature of the stucco wall-decoration in low relief. This is also to be seen in the Northumberland House panelling, dating from 1773 to 1774 (now in the Victoria and Albert Museum), and in many of Adam's other later creations.

It seems not improbable that the designer of the Syon tables (whether Adam or a craftsman) was at this early stage endeavouring to arrive at a satisfactory neo-classical formula, by attempting to adapt the tripod-form to a console-table.

An unsigned drawing for a wall-pier at Kedleston (Fig. 6) which is preserved in the house must also be attributed to Stuart and is equally significant in showing a straight-legged side-table and a classical tripod. A letter from Robert Adam to his brother James published by Mr. Fleming[1] establishes the fact that Stuart was employed by Sir Nathaniel Curzon to make designs in 1756 or early 1757 for

[1] J. Fleming, p. 258.

Kedleston, and that Adam had seen them in December 1758. 'Sir Nathaniel brought me out a design of the Great Athenian's for his Rooms furnishing, which he beg'd me for Godsake not to Mention to any Body. They are so excessively and so ridiculously bad that Mr. Curzon immediately saw the folly of them & said so to some people which so offended the proud Grecian, that he has not seen Sr. Nathaniel these 2 years, and he says he keeps the Drawings Sacred in Self defence . . .'.

The opinion that Robert Adam had privately confided to his brother did not prevent his doing better justice to Stuart's gifts when years later in *The Works* he wrote[1] 'Mr. Stuart with his usual elegance and taste has contributed greatly towards introducing the true style of antique decoration'.

Adam's description of Stuart's drawing exactly corresponds with the sketch for the hall at Kedleston, which shows a pair of pedestals for busts similar to the tripods which Stuart designed for Spencer House (see page 41), as well as the table of the type which Adam later designed for the dining-room alcove at Kedleston. Not only did Adam have access to Stuart's designs; it is known also that he visited Spencer House, for he made a sketch of a 'Cornice in the South Dressing Room of Mr. Spencer's House by Mr. S(tuart)' (Soane: Vol. 54, No. 40). The conclusion that he took Stuart's furniture designs as a point of departure for his own neo-classical furniture is thus inescapable. A statement of A. T. Bolton's[2] that Stuart was believed to have designed the huge wine-cistern of Sicilian marble in the diningroom alcove at Kedleston (Fig. 1) is also strengthened by this evidence. A question that arises, however, in connexion with the classical design for tables is that of the extent to which Adam was inspired by classical elements in earlier Georgian furniture, especially in certain articles designed or influenced by William Kent. Although much of Kent's furniture has a ponderous baroque character, in many articles associated with him the classical elements — eagles, mouldings of classical frets, Vitruvian scrolls, straight tapering legs, all copied no doubt directly from antique models in Italy — were integrated with a tautness of design that anticipated Adam's neo-classicism as truly as did Kent's Roman planning at Holkham and Chiswick.

At Rousham, Oxfordshire, where Kent was making additions from 1738–41, there are side-tables and chairs almost certainly designed by him, having straight, tapering legs of square section, narrow 'therm' necking, block-feet, and strings of husks as ornament (Figs. 10 and 12). These are all of a kind frequently found

[1] *The Works*, Vol. 1, No. 1, 1773, p. 5.   [2] A. T. Bolton, Vol. 1, p. 241.

in Adam's early furniture, and could easily have served as the inspiration not only for him, but even for Stuart's first neo-classical experiments. In one of the tables, as well as fret and wave mouldings, there is seen the *pelta*, the Roman shield-ornament that became one of Adam's dominant decorative motifs but which was rarely if ever seen in other furniture at that date.

Up to 1764 Adam apparently had still not assimilated neo-classical forms to seat-furniture, but was obviously more confident when designing quite frankly in fully baroque style. This was clearly so in the instance of the sofas (Fig. 81) and chairs (Fig. 57) he designed for Sir Laurence Dundas in 1764.

The form is strongly early Georgian, with outward curving scroll arm-supports to the sofas, cabriole legs and massively proportioned frames. Following the general pattern of the development of style, in which novelties of design influence decoration before affecting changes of form, neo-classical elements appear in this design only as a superficial decoration composed of motifs of honeysuckle, sphinxes and scrolls of foliage modelled in light relief on the surface of the members of each piece. A set of two sofas and four chairs was executed for Sir Laurence at Moor Park, and later the articles were at his London house, 19 Arlington Street. Two of the sofas and a number of the chairs are today at Aske Hall, Yorkshire, the seat of the Marquess of Zetland.

At Woburn Abbey there are to be seen so many examples of baroque and neo-classical design of the type that Adam later made use of in his furniture designs, that one is led strongly to believe that Adam must himself have visited the house. In the state saloon are several large gilt sofas and armchairs of a baroque form similar to those already mentioned which Adam designed for Moor Park (Fig. 81). Between the windows in one of the rooms are a pair of large gilt pier-glasses displaying the terminal figures at the sides which later appear in Adam's pier-glasses in the dining-room at Syon (Fig. 155). Some oval mirrors have crestings in the form of female figures reclining upon the curve of the frame in a manner adopted by Adam years later for the girandole mirrors in the gallery at Osterley (Fig. 163), and other mirrors. The pair of massive gilt console-tables in the state dining-room, with their Vitruvian-scroll friezes and curved supports are of a form that might well have inspired Adam's early console-table design (Fig. 21). Furthermore, the ceiling of the state bedroom at Woburn, designed by Flitcroft about 1761, closely resembles the remarkable ceiling which Adam designed for the drawing-room at Osterley, both of them deriving from an engraving of a ceiling of the Temple of the Sun in Robert Wood's *Ruins of Palmyra*.

All these circumstances suggest that while Adam was still depending upon baroque models, he could have found a valuable source of inspiration for his early furniture in the decoration and furniture of Woburn Abbey.

A remarkable leap forward into the application of neo-classical form to seat furniture is made with the drawing inscribed 'Sopha for Sir Laurence Dundas, Bart', of 1764 (Fig. 16). This is for a small upholstered stool or window-seat with eight round-section tapered and fluted legs with knob- or top-shaped feet. The frieze also is fluted, with acanthus leaf ornaments above the legs, which have block capitals ornamented with paterae. The outward-curving scrolled ends still retain vestiges of Kentian influence, however. The design was apparently not accepted by Sir Laurence, but was later executed for Lord Coventry for Croome Court.[1] This appears to be Adam's first design for a round, tapered and fluted leg, and is linked with chairs made by Cobb about the same time for Croome Court (see page 63 and Fig. 58).

Adam was still however under the sway of early Georgian forms. This is apparent in the design of 1765 for the console-table with semi-circular top, inscribed 'Table frame for Sir Lawrence Dundas, Baronet' (Fig. 21). The robust proportions, the Vitruvian scroll of the frieze and the scale-moulding of the legs are typical of Kent's style, although the form derives from the Louis Quatorze French taste popular early in the century, or from English examples, like those at Woburn, deriving from the same source. The ram's-heads, festoons, and lion-paw feet infuse the neo-classical spirit into the design.

Adam's process of lightening the ponderous early classical forms and thus giving them elegance and refinement seems to have been deliberately carried by him experimentally to the ultimate extreme as early as 1768 in the design of a 'Glass and table frame for the ante-room at Shelburne (later Lansdowne) House.[2] In this the curved supports have been whittled down to a degree of attenuation hardly approached even in Adam's last phases of refinement. It was Thomas Chippendale who was to carry this adaptation of an old form to a high pitch of neo-classical elegance and sophistication, in the gilt console-tables with goat's-head capitals that he provided for the gallery at Harewood about 1771 (Fig. 111).

With a remarkable series of drawings, all dated 1765, for 'table frames' at Syon House, Adam showed his complete mastery of the neo-classical formula embodied in James Stuart's Spencer House and Kedleston drawings. A drawing

[1] E. Harris, Fig. 104.   [2] E. Harris, Fig. 18.

of a 'Table frame for the Dining-Room at Sion' (Fig. 15) is followed very closely by the set of three gilt side-tables now in the ante-room there (Fig. 95).

No drawing survives for the finest of all the side-tables at Syon, those in the Red drawing-room (Fig. 93). It was possibly lost or destroyed either by the craftsman, or by the engraver who made the plate from Adam's design for Volume III of *The Works*, which consisted of a number of plates not included in the earlier volumes, and was published in 1822 by Priestley and Weale. These tables, with their satisfying proportions, the ram's-head capitals, and bold yet refined ornament in frieze and legs, are among the most splendid articles devised by Adam in this transitional but richly promising phase of his work.

Another drawing inscribed by Adam 'Table frame for the Drawing-Room at Sion' (Soane, vol. 17, no. 4), 1765, is very similar to the foregoing tables, except in having female masks as capitals to the legs instead of the more fully classical ram's-heads. These tables were eventually executed, not for Syon, but for the gallery at Croome Court, and are now in the Philadelphia Museum of Art.[1]

The influence of Stuart and Kent seems to give place to French inspiration, possibly for the first time in Adam's furniture designs, in the drawing, dated 1765, of a 'Table frame for the two Porphyry Tables' (Fig. 17), made for Sir Charles Farnaby, no doubt for Kippington Park, Kent, for which Adam also designed some chimney-pieces. The Ionic capitals, small in proportion to the bulk of the legs, and the severe square tapering legs with deep triple-fluting surmounted with bolt-heads, and the Vitruvian scroll of the frieze, all have their counterparts in the volumes of Neufforge's *Recueil*.[2]

Adam possessed volumes 4, 5 and 6 at the time of his death, and probably had done since they were first published, in 1761, 1763 and 1768 respectively. It is probably from such a design as this that the well-known library tables at Osterley and Alnwick evolved a few years later (see page 98 and Fig. 39). Indeed, John Linnell, who is believed to have made the tables, has left several drawings embodying the very distinctive features which have been mentioned (Fig. 36).

The chairs made to an early Adam design of about 1767 for the eating-room at Osterley (Fig. 60) show surviving traditional influences in the bow-shaped back-rails in the Chippendale *Director* manner, and the dining-room chairs of almost all the Adam houses — Croome, Kedleston, and Newby, are of this early type, whether designed by Adam or not. Only at Syon are oval-back chairs found in the

[1] E. Harris, Fig. 11.   [2] J.-F. Neufforge, Vol. 5, 1763, Plate 310.

dining-room, but these are presumably of later date, probably about 1775, and may have been introduced from another room.

Although many of Adam's drawings of his transitional period are bold and masculine in style, they never equalled the heaviness of the French *style mâle*, the manner of the early French neo-classical furniture such as that of Prieur and Le Lorrain. The feminine tendencies in Adam's designs first become apparent in the drawing of the 'Table frame for the Earl of Coventry' dated August 1767 (Soane, vol. 17, no. 10).[1] This design shows a form of leg intermediate between the bold square supports of his early neo-classical tables and the slender baluster legs which are to be so distinctive of his later furniture. Adam's 'Design of a Table Frame for the Side Board of the Eating Room at Osterley, for Robert Child, Esq.', which is preserved at the house, is of similar character and date (Fig. 18).

Robert Adam's early ventures in mirror design resulted in the fine series of upright pier-glasses with broad, mitred frames and crestings of scrolled foliage. Those of the drawing-room at Syon House still retain a touch of early Georgian character with their enlarged corners and strings of diminishing husks at the sides (Fig. 155). The type is also represented in the mirrors made to Adam's designs in the dining-room at Syon,[2] at Corsham Court,[3] and an example in the long gallery at Osterley.[4]

The transitional period sees the introduction of Adam's distinctive type of mirror, of tripartite form, based upon the Venetian window, in which the central portion, sometimes rounded, sometimes flat-topped, is flanked by two narrow upright glasses. In one or two early designs the three portions were divided vertically by slender tapering pilasters carrying female busts, as in an undated sketch (Soane, vol. 3, no. 31) for the mirrors at Kenwood.[5]

Later the supports were made in the form of attenuated terms with three-quarter-length figures, drawn with an engaging freedom of pose, as in the design for a mirror at Luton of 1772, which was engraved in *The Works* (Fig. 27). The originals of such elongated terms with three-quarter-length figures that turn with a comparable sideways movement may be found in the decorations of the triclinium walls in the House of the Vettii at Pompeii.[6] These figures in Adam's mirrors were often linked by festoons and supported other decorations such as sphinxes, tablets and medallions. The tripartite type is especially appro-

---

[1] E. Harris, Fig. 14.   [2] E. Harris, Fig. 54.   [3] E. Harris, Fig. 55.   [4] E. Harris, Fig. 56.

[5] E. Harris, Fig. 59 and in a design dated 1770 (Soane, vol. 20, no. 38) of an overmantel mirror for Mr. Child, Berkeley Square, London.

[6] M. Brion, *Pompeii and Herculaneum*, Elek, London, 1960.

priate as an overmantel mirror, where greater width in relation to height is needed than in other forms, or in important centralized compositions, such as that of an alcove with a sofa, which was in fact Adam's first tripartite design, made for the library at Kenwood.[1]

It was published in *The Works*, vol. III, 1772, Plate VIII. Although this conception of a mirror is a highly sophisticated one, characteristic of Adam's maturity, in this original example the members of the framework are still bold in scale. In the designs as drawn and executed for the glass drawing-room at Northumberland House, in 1773 and 1774, the overmantel from which is preserved at the Victoria and Albert Museum,[2] the supports and decoration are beginning to assume an extreme delicacy that removes such articles from the realm of furniture and causes them to become instead part of the wall decoration.[2]

In Adam's later mirror designs, such as one dated 1778 and intended for Apsley House (Fig. 22), and the design of 1777 from which the tripartite mirror in the breakfast-room at Osterley was made (Fig. 158), structural form has almost completely merged into linear decoration, and the terminal figures of the supports have lost their early charm and become attenuated, stiff and stereotyped.

Adam's oval mirrors and girandoles are a class of furniture which had a very great appeal for him, and are the subject of his most varied invention (Figs. 162 and 163). They begin with designs of striking baroque character, as in a mirror in the drawing-room at Kedleston of 1765[3] and proceed to creations showing naturalistic rococo influence with interlacings of foliage, shown in a design of 1770 for the Earl of Shelburne at Lansdowne House (Soane, vol. 20, no. 22),[4] and express the final sophistication of his later development, about 1778, in frames of extreme delicacy supporting neo-classical motifs of sphinxes, festoons, tablets, medallions, urns and paterae of such ultimate refinement that they appear as applied grotesques rather than as solid furniture, as in the girandoles for Apsley House (Soane, vol. 20, nos. 178 and 179).[4]

The period of Adam's mature style, from 1769 to 1777, is the time of his largest output of furniture drawings, and also of the widest range of the articles he designed as well as of the decorative motifs he used. His style became assured and fully-formed, and acquired a suave feminine sophistication that is noticeably different from the masculine boldness of his earlier work. Many of the more satisfying early forms, like the square tapering legs of sideboards, were retained,

---

[1] E. Harris, Fig. 59.   [2] E. Harris, Fig. 67.
[3] E. Harris, Fig. 82.   [4] E. Harris, Fig. 85.

but in a more refined and elegant form. This is the age when he was designing furniture for some of his loveliest interiors — Saltram House in Devonshire; Nostell Priory, Yorkshire; and the later rooms at Osterley. The more assured sense of elegance of this period is found in the delightful pier-tables of the velvet drawing-room at Saltram (Fig. 100) which were made by the craftsman Perfetti (see page 95) to a design by Adam dated 1771. The tables have delightful features of round, tapering reeded legs entwined by festoons, a device which was not so successfully adopted by the same craftsman in the side-tables for the saloon there (Fig. 101).

The famous side-tables at Nostell Priory, Yorkshire, which again correspond almost exactly with existing drawings, of 1775, also possess the sumptuous grace of this period. The pair in the saloon (Fig. 97) are among the most beautiful articles ever designed by Adam, and are only equalled in rich elegance of design by the pier-table in the tapestry room at Osterley (Fig. 99).

During Adam's maturity the scrolled foliage crestings of his broad-framed pier-glasses gave place to compositions of a central urn, medallion or similar feature supported by exquisitely modelled female figures, sphinxes or gryphons. This delightful type is represented in the pier-glasses at Kenwood, *c.* 1767–8 (illustrated in *The Works*, vol. 1, no. II, 1774, Plate VIII) at Saltram (Figs. 100 and 101) made to Adam's designs of 1769 and 1771–2 and, in an especially beautiful form in the drawing-room at Osterley made to a design in the house dated 1773, and also in the Etruscan room there, made to a design of 1775 (Fig. 156).

Robert Adam gave no consideration to beds other than those intended for state bedrooms which served 'the parade of life'. His designs for this type of furniture are thus few in number, but they compensated for their rarity by their spectacular character and remarkable quality. The state bed of Adam design which is now at Hampton Court is often erroneously supposed to be the one referred to by Horace Walpole on 9 September 1762, when he wrote 'Our next monarch was christened last night . . . the Queen's bed, magnificent, and they say in taste, was placed in the great drawing room'. Although Adam had been designing doors and chimney-pieces for the 'Queen's House', or Buckingham House (later rebuilt as Buckingham Palace) a year earlier, the Hampton Court bed[1] has the character of Adam's work of the 1770's, especially in the small scale decoration in the straight cornice with ante-fixae at the corners. The posts are turned, partly plain, and partly fluted, the lower portions bulbous and with carved leaf-decoration. Al-

1 Bolton, Vol. 2, p. 294.

though the feet are tapering and fluted, the posts are similar to those in the Soane Museum design of 1772 of a bed for the Hon. Fred. Thynne (vol. 17, no. 153).[1]

Of Adam's seven designs for beds, only two that were executed are known to exist; one of these is the state bed at Osterley (Fig. 109). The designs for this bed form a group of some of the finest drawings in the whole of the Soane collection, and provide alternative suggestions for the general form, and separate drawings for the counterpane, head board and interior of the domed canopy. The other bed executed to Adam's design is a less elaborate one made for the Taffeta Room (Soane, vol. 17, no. 163, 1779), which is not at present open to the public.[2]

The earliest surviving of Adam's rare designs for commodes appears in 1771, with a drawing intended for Sir George Colebrooke (Fig. 114). It displays a less sophisticated spirit than most of the designs for this period, and it is especially interesting in that it embodies several characteristics found in the furniture being made by Chippendale about this time, especially the monumental library tables he supplied to Nostell and Harewood (Figs. 166 and 167). The terminal-shaped pilaster supports derive from those used earlier by William Kent and William Vile, but now have the neo-classical rams'-heads capitals and square block-feet with narrow necking, all of them features typical of Chippendale's work.

The decoration in the Colebrooke drawing is in the form of grotesques, which Adam is now using in furniture apparently for the first time. It consists of large isolated motifs of an urn and tripods (presumably to be painted). A rough preliminary sketch for this design also survives (Soane, vol. 6, no. 124).

Another commode design, for the Duke of Bolton (Fig. 115) with its corresponding preliminary sketch is basically similar, but with human masks as capitals and lion-paw feet and bow-fronted instead of straight. The decoration, which is clearly intended for painting, has a greater delicacy and elegance more typical of this date, with painted figure subjects in large medallions, and small ones serving as accents to the decorative composition. This drawing is obviously an intermediate design for the superb pair of semi-circular commodes in the drawing-room at Osterley, where the same type of elevation is used, with decorative panels containing figure-subjects. This use of panels painted with figures, or with landscape scenes, may be regarded as corresponding in furniture to the Pompeiian fashion of painted wall-decoration for rooms which Adam had adopted, especially for dining-rooms as at Harewood and Osterley (Fig. 92). The drawing is Adam's first design for a semi-circular commode and, as realized in the commodes at Osterley

[1] E. Harris, Fig. 126.　　　　　[2] Note 9, p. 174.

(see page 97), represents the prototype of all the bow-fronted commodes that are such distinctive examples of the furniture of the Hepplewhite period later.

Adam's designs for baluster legs assume various forms during these years of his mature development. They range from an attenuated vase-form with slender neck shown in the drawing of 1770 for a 'Sopha for Sir Laurence Dundas' (Fig. 16) to the full-formed 'French' type of slender fluted baluster leg with leaf-decoration below the neck. This is seen in the oval-back chairs with sphinx back-supports designed for Mr. Child at Osterley in 1777 and now in the state bedroom there (Fig. 66) (see also 99). The two drawings for these chairs are in rich colour and are among the finest of all Adam's furniture designs. A similar design for oval-back chairs with sphinx supports (Soane, vol. 17, no. 86), 1779, has vase-shaped capitals to the legs. They were intended for Sir Abraham Hume's house in Hill Street.[1] These, and the various sets of chairs in the tapestry rooms of several of the Adam houses, would seem to have derived their oval backs from the Nielson-Boucher tapestries of these rooms, with their figure-subjects in oval borders (Fig. 102, and see page 98). No design by Adam for chairs of this type appears to exist earlier than his drawing of 1776, although the first English examples of the type had appeared in 1769 at Croome Court (see page 65).

From the late seventeenth century stands for candles, lamps, busts, urns and vases had been designed upon classical models of varying degrees of purity. An important and popular type was known as a term, therm or herm, otherwise a terminus or terminal column. These stands, square in section and tapering towards the base, were moulded in the upper part into the shape of a sculptured human figure, originally representing Terminus, the god of boundaries, which they were used to mark. In architecture they were adopted as structural supports. Term pedestals surmounted by an entablature instead of a head or figure appear in the designs of Chippendale and of Ince and Mayhew, and in other pattern books of the eighteenth century. The pedestals or terms that Adam was designing in 1765 (Fig. 19), appear to be based on models produced by William Kent early in the century, such as those at Rousham, Oxfordshire, and it is true that in such pieces, as in many other instances, Kent was displaying a neo-classical feeling much in advance of his time.

A number of Adam's drawings for term pedestals survive at the Soane Museum. One design intended for Sir John Griffin Griffin at Audley End (Fig. 144), was executed in the form of six pedestals, which may be seen there today. This and

[1] E. Harris, Fig. 122.

another design (vol. 17, no. 58) inscribed 'Term for Sir John Astley, Baronet, 1765' (of Patshull, Staffs.), are similar to a term pedestal, painted white, carved and gilt, which is now in the Victoria and Albert Museum.[1] It is one of a set of six originally executed for Sir Laurence Dundas, at 19 Arlington Street, London.

The Roman altar in the form of a tripod supporting a sacrificial basin or incense-burner was an object of antiquity made familiar to collectors, connoisseurs and designers by the engravings of Piranesi and of the comte de Caylus in the early days of the neo-classical movement, and we have already seen that Robert Adam applied it in two-dimensional form as an element of wall-decoration at an early stage in the gallery of Syon House in 1769, and in a later phase as gilt ornaments in the wall-decoration of glass, coloured with metal foil to simulate porphyry, of the drawing-room at Northumberland House, London, of about 1773, which is preserved at the Victoria and Albert Museum.

Possibly the most important early English examples of the adaptation of the ancient tripod form to furniture are the stands probably designed by Stuart himself for Spencer House between 1759 and 1765, which are now at Althorp, Northants. (Fig. 9). As early as 1761 Adam adopted the classical tripod as the model for an ornamental incense-burner to stand on a table for Nathaniel Curzon, later Lord Scarsdale, at Kedleston (Fig. 2). It is almost beyond question that he derived the idea from what are believed to be James Stuart's designs for the hall at Kedleston of *c.* 1757 (Fig. 6), and for the Painted Room at Spencer House of 1759 (Fig. 3), in both of which a small tripod candelabrum of this form appears (see page 41).

One of Adam's earliest designs based on French models was a drawing for which he charged Lord Coventry £1:10:0 in May, 1767, of 'A Tripod altered from a French design for a Water Stand'.[2] This links up with a sketch at the Soane Museum (vol. 6, no. 177) of a 'Water Stand',[3] intended for Lord Coventry. This tripod is similar in form to the type which originated in France in 1763, and which in 1773 became known there as 'athéniennes' (see page 71). Adam's sketch was obviously the basis of two designs for tripods which appear in *The Works in Architecture*, 1773, one of which was executed for Sir Laurence Dundas and also for the Duke of Bolton at his house in Russell Square (Fig. 28). Designs for tripods of similar form, but displaying the greater delicacy and slenderness of Adam's middle period, were also published as engravings in *The Works*, as intended for the drawing-room of the Earl of Bute at Luton (Fig. 27). They are

[1] E. Harris, Fig. 131.   [2] Croome accounts.   [3] E. Harris, Fig. 134.

typical of many stands based on the design of the sacrificial tripods of antiquity that were executed for various Adam houses.

A beautiful example of this type is to be seen in the drawing-room at Osterley (Fig. 144), and another variation of the design was applied in the beautiful gilt-wood tripod stands made for the saloon at Saltram, Devonshire, in or about 1768, and where they are to be seen carrying the splendid candelabra of 'Blue John' Derbyshire feldspar and tortoiseshell, mounted with ormolu, supplied for the house by Matthew Boulton in 1770 (Fig. 145).

The extreme delicacy of Adam's final phase in this type of furniture is conveyed by his drawing of a 'Tripod for the first room at Sir Abraham Hume's in Hill Street' (Soane, vol. 17, no. 65) dated 1779. The form is now excessively delicate and simplified, the slender attenuated legs carrying a bowl on which rest three sphinxes supporting a shallow vase on the tips of their wings. Numerous other examples of this latest period exist, many of them of great beauty and charm, usually with slender tall legs, sometimes decorated with rams'-heads, standing on a triangular base, and supporting a highly simplified drum-shaped top for a candelabrum.

An important and distinctive type of tripod-stand in Adam's mature period consists of a triangular pedestal with slightly tapering, almost parallel concave sides, supported on lion-paw feet on a triangular plinth carried on the heads of sphinxes or gryphons, resting in turn on a similar plinth. Stands of this type are to be seen at Osterley (Fig. 146) and Alnwick Castle,[1] and other examples (Fig. 148) were also made for various houses to Adam's designs, embodying different variations in the disposition of the several classical features of which they are composed. A later Adam type, related in form to the early Stuart pedestals, is that of the tripods once at 20 St. James's Square, which are now at the Victoria and Albert Museum.[2] The upper half is a tripod with its legs resting on the small top of a triangular pedestal with its sides curving strongly outwards to a broad base carried on sphinxes. Adam's drawing for the pieces as executed (Soane, vol. 6, no. 49) is undated, but two other related drawings (Soane, vol. 6, nos. 53 and 54) are dated 1777.

From 1775 onwards a large number of designs exist for the tops of side-tables, or 'slabs' as they were usually called, to be carried out either in scagliola or painted wood. The earliest of these were executed for the side-tables in the saloon at Nostell (Fig. 97) and they all display typical Adam motifs of shell ornament,

[1] E. Harris, Fig. 137.   [2] E. Harris, Fig. 139.

usually as the central feature of a semi-circular design, with medallions containing heads or figures, or paterae, linked by delicate festoons of husks or bell-flowers in an open pattern. Among other interesting 'designs for slabs' is one made for Sir Abraham Hume in 1779 (Fig. 25).

Early in the century William Kent had adopted the theme of caryatid supports for tables. These derived from Italian furniture in which the figures sometimes represented the Four Seasons. The same feature appears in a design by Adam of 1768 of a 'Glass and Table Frame for Shelburne House'. A drawing for a harpsichord (Soane, vol. 6, no. 127) undated, also indicates caryatid supports. This theme, which has found expression in beautiful surviving pieces of the Adam period (Fig. 104) was also the subject of one of two designs for 'Frames for Marble Slabs' in the third edition of Chippendale's *Director* published in 1762 (Plate CLXXVI). This is in fact one of the most completely classical designs in the *Director*, and the contrast between it and a rococo table-frame shown below it is made even more violent by Chippendale's having shown a violently rococo wine cistern beneath the classical piece.

Adam's 'Etruscan' style makes its appearance in 1775 in the furniture for Lord Stanley at Derby House, which is the subject of several designs. One of these (Soane, vol. 17, no. 94) for an armchair with square, tapering legs and block-feet, shows fine leaf-ornament in terracotta on a black ground.[1] The design was repeated by Adam (with very slight alterations) a year later in a drawing of a 'Chair for the Etruscan Room at Osterley', which was eventually followed in the executed pieces for that room (Fig. 67).

Although the French designer Dugourc claimed to have used the Etruscan style in decoration before 1770, it had not become acceptable to the French court much before 1785,[2] and Adam was probably the first to make systematic and extensive use of this scheme of characteristic forms and motifs. The volumes of the comte de Caylus (1752–67) were the first repository of the style, but apart from his own direct observation of so-called 'Etruscan' antiquities at Rome and Pompeii, Adam's own designs must have been richly informed from the pages of the *Antichita di Ercolano* published at Naples in 1757, and by the illustrations of Sir William Hamilton's catalogue of his *Collection of Etruscan, Greek and Roman Antiquities*, published at Naples in 1766–7, a set of which Adam possessed. It was perhaps in his Etruscan style that his use of colour reached its fullest development, especially in such designs as the important series of 1780 for Cumberland House,

---

[1] E. Harris, Fig. 116. [2] F. J. B. Watson, *Wallace Collection: Catalogue of furniture*, p. XLVII.

including a particularly striking drawing of a dining-room sideboard with urns on pedestals and wine-cistern (Soane, vol. 17, no. 57).[1] The urns are shaped as 'Etruscan' vases decorated in terracotta, black and white, with a broad band of figures, and with figures of monsters in panels on the pedestals and wine-cooler. This fine drawing shows Adam's sense of design in a fully assured form, but although the urns themselves display his latest elegance of line, the table itself harks back to early days with its tapering square-section legs and block feet. For the dining-room these masculine elements still seem the most appropriate, but what now distinguishes them from Adam's earlier work is the extreme slenderness of the proportions.

It would seem that the idea of supports of animal form for furniture, in the manner of ancient models, was but rarely pursued by Robert Adam. Among the few drawings of this kind that exist, however, are some of outstanding importance. They are for a magnificent harpsichord, one of them being published in *The Works*, and described there as 'executed in London, in different Coloured Woods, for the Empress of Russia'. It is not known if the instrument survives. The original drawings dated 1774 are unusual as being in perspective, and are among Adam's most remarkable achievements of draughtsmanship (Fig. 24).

Animal supports of a similar sort are found in the engravings of Piranesi's *Diversi Maniere d'adornare i Cammini* of 1769, a work which demonstrates the close identity between Piranesi and Adam in neo-classical design. Although figures of sphinxes were amongst Adam's favourite motifs, there seem to be no precedents in his own drawings for their use as supports for the console-tables which are sometimes seen among the products of his followers. Such instances are more often found in the neo-classical furniture of the early nineteenth century.

The last phase of Adam's career, from 1778 until his death in 1792, opens with considerable activity almost exclusively in connexion with London houses. He is now occupied with Derby House, 23 Grosvenor Square, for Lord Stanley, the 12th Earl; Roxburgh (later Harewood) House, Hanover Square, for the Duke of Roxburgh; No. 31 Hill Street, for Sir Abraham Hume, Bt.; Cumberland House, Pall Mall, for the Duke of Cumberland; and Apsley House, Piccadilly, for Lord Bathurst; as well as several lesser commissions; yet by 1780 Adam's work in furniture designing is virtually at an end, for after this date hardly any activity is recorded apart from one or two designs for mirrors. These last years of Adam's career see no fresh invention, only a continuation of the refining process which

[1] E. Harris, Fig. 34.

was the essential secret of his art, until his characteristic delicacy and elegance developed into a rarefied sophistication that many of Adam's contemporaries regarded as mere prettiness and tawdry effeminacy.

In one design of 1778, however, of two hall-chairs for Sir Abraham Hume (Soane, vol. 17, no. 98), there is a touch of the vigour and bold style of earlier days notably in the sturdy fluted legs and frieze of garlands and rosettes of one chair, and in their circular backs, one of them with a striking honeysuckle ornament. The other has crossed scroll-supports of a type unusual in Adam's day, but which were to become more popular during the Regency.[1]

With the drawings of commodes for Apsley House, also dated 1778 (Fig. 116), Adam carries his style to such a stage of refinement that form is almost lost sight of in decoration. The supporting pilasters have become extremely attenuated and terminate in almost impossibly delicate foliated feet. The decoration of painted medallions and a sparse arrangement of festoons has been simplified to an extreme degree of elegance, and the ornament of the frieze has been scaled down to the kind of fineness that Chambers stigmatized as 'Adam's seaweed'.

Adam's last surviving furniture drawings are one or two designs for mirrors. There are none later than 1783. In the last nine years of his life Robert Adam was engaged upon Edinburgh University and other great public buildings in Scotland, and seems to have made no furniture designs that have come down to us.

[1] E. Harris, Fig. 119.

ADAM AND THE FRENCH

One of the most intriguing problems in the study of neo-classical furniture is the question of whether in his furniture designs Robert Adam anticipated the characteristics of the later Louis Seize style in France. It is a question which has an especial appeal for those who, conscious of the centuries-long dependence of this country upon the countries of Europe for artistic inspiration, would be pleased to believe that in one brief phase of the history of design, Britain played a unique part in the innovation of a fresh style. The suggestion was first made in 1931 by the late Mr. Fiske Kimball,[1] and expanded in his monumental study *The Creation of the Rococo* in 1943.

Fiske Kimball's theory was reinforced in 1947 by the arguments of Mr. Lees-Milne in his invaluable work *The Age of Adam*, in which he writes:

'In furniture of the neo-classical style Adam undoubtedly gave England a priority over France and the rest of Europe, and the style's abrupt revival here was practically coincident with the return of Robert from Italy.

'At Shardeloes he designed a very early pair of looking-glasses and console tables, of geometrical outlines, with fluted legs, rosettes, and festoons of bell-flower husks, the full complement of those devices which were to become the well-known hallmarks of the Adam family firm . . . at Syon Adam's furniture was designed and executed between 1765 and 1769.

'At Nostell are lyre-backed chairs for which Robert's bills were paid in 1768, and which later became the mode in France. Not until 1770, when the first English engraved plates of such designs were available, did straight fluted legs and those other essentially Adam appendages which we still prefer to term Louis Seize begin to make a tardy appearance across the Channel. . . . The oval backs and straight legs to chairs adopted by Adam in his Moor Park suite for Sir Laurence Dundas in 1766 were scarcely followed in France by 1789.'

Such beliefs were possibly not unreasonable at the time that these authors were

---

[1] Fiske Kimball, 'Les influences anglaises dans la formation du style Louis XVI,' in *Gazette des Beaux-Arts*, 6éme sér., Tem: V, Paris, 1931.

writing, considering the scanty evidence to the contrary then available. Although a portrait of La Live de Jully showing early French neo-classical furniture which has been mentioned in Chapter I was known to Fiske Kimball, he did not perceive in it the manifestation of an enthusiastic movement, but regarded it as it were as a 'sport'. Furthermore it is known that the French court was slow to accept the neo-classical fashion,[1] and furniture in the rococo style continued to be favoured and made up to the time of the Revolution. But in England also, although neo-classical furniture of the Adam inspiration was being provided in various houses in the late 1760's and 1770's, so too did the rococo style continue to command favour, and indeed it was during a period of a decade or so from 1775 onwards that this fashion attained the height of refinement and elegance in its English manifestations (Fig. 40).

The belief in English neo-classical priority gained so strong a hold that it came to be accepted even by such a French scholar as M. Hautecoeur,[2] and the most that was said in rebuttal was that 'neo-classicism was a universal style'.

Robert Adam's first fully neo-classical furniture design is for the sideboard at Kedleston of 1762 (Fig. 2). His earliest known design for neo-classical seat furniture is for a stool at Croome Court dated 1764 (Fig. 16 and see Chapter II). The Croome Court Tapestry Room chairs and settee were made in 1769, those for Moor Park in the same year or later. Neither sets were designed by Adam, so far as is known.

It is now realized that the Shardeloes looking-glasses and side-tables[3] must date from about 1775; and the Nostell furniture bills are, of course, not Adam's, but Chippendale's (see Chapter IV).

Recent researches by Mr. F. J. B. Watson and Mr. Svend Eriksen have established beyond question that neo-classical furniture was appearing in France as early as 1754, and Mrs. Harris has made the interesting suggestion that the neo-classical character of the Moor Park suite to which Mr. Lees-Milnes refers, and of the furniture of the tapestry rooms in various Adam houses, was due to the influence of designs provided by the Gobelins manufactory about 1762.[4]

As we have already seen, C.-N. Cochin was making a spirited attack on the rococo, and advocating the adoption of a pure classical style as early as December, 1754, when he published the first of his two famous articles in the *Mercure de*

---

[1] F. J. B. Watson, *Wallace Collection catalogue of furniture*, p. XL.
[2] L. Hautecoeur, *Histoire de l'architecture classique en France*, 7 vols., Paris, 1943–57.
[3] E. Harris, Fig. 146. [4] E. Harris, pp. 9–10.

France. Justification for the belief that a lively neo-classical movement was in being by 1763 had been given by the remarks of the Baron Melchior de Grimm in his *Correspondance littéraire.*[1]

Writing in that year Grimm reported:

'Depuis quelques années on a recherché les ornamens et les formes antiques . . . et la mode en est devenue si générale que tout se fait aujourd'hui à la grecque. La décoration extérieure et intérieure, des bâtimens, les meubles, les étoffes, les bijoux de tout espèce, tout est à Paris à la grecque.'

A year later Horace Walpole was writing to Sir Horace Mann[2] of the current taste in Paris: 'Everything must be *à la grecque*'. A great deal of allowance must always be made for the exaggerations of fashionable gossip. But although in the context of either of these accounts 'everything' probably means little more than a few things in one or two *avant garde* houses, Fiske Kimball could not have realized that in Paris the interest in neo-classicism had reached a pitch of enthusiasm and intensity possibly even surpassing that existing in the circles around Robert Adam, and that the remarks of Grimm and Walpole could be taken at something approaching their face value.

Incidentally, it is significant, but more in relation to English manifestations of neo-classicism in the Palladian era than to French origins, that Walpole went on to quote the Comte de Guerchy as remarking to the Duchess of Bedford, having seen a Doric fret on a fender at Woburn, 'Comment! Madame, vous avez là du grec, sans le savoir'.[3]

Evidence for the existence of French furniture in the neo-classical taste as early as 1761 exists in a portrait by Alexandre Roslin of the Marquis de Marigny. This portrait, painted in 1761, or possibly even begun in 1760, now at Versailles, has been described by Mr. Svend Eriksen,[4] as showing Marigny seated at a table with round, tapering fluted legs and a frieze mounted with fillets of bronze surrounding rosettes. Other French articles in the same style were a number of frames made for Marigny in 1760 by Honoré Guibert, of oval shape and crested with a heavy classical garland of husks. It is in these frames that Mrs. Harris sees the origin of the oval-back chairs with crestings of husks of the Croome Court and other tapestry-room furniture.[5]

In discussing the change of style in France from the rococo to the neo-classical,

---

[1] M. de Grimm, *Correspondance littéraire, philosophique et critique*, Paris, 17 vols., 1812–13.
[2] April 29th, 1764. Vol. IV, p. 219.   [3] April 29th, 1764. Vol. IV, p. 219.
[4] S. Eriksen, ' "Marigny and Le Goût Grec" '. Article in *Burlington Magazine*, March 1962.
[5] E. Harris, 'Robert Adam and the Gobelins'. Article in *Apollo*, April 1962.

Mr. F. J. B. Watson has drawn attention to a portrait of Madame de Pompadour by François-Hubert Drouais begun in 1763 and finished after her death in 1764,[1] which shows a goat's-mask and laurel swags, and an acanthus frieze in a bookcase, again belonging to the neo-classical repertory of decorative motifs. The portrait of La Live de Jully which has already been mentioned (pages 26 and 57) is one of the chief milestones of neo-classical history. It has been described by Mr. Watson[2] and further commented upon by Mr. Eriksen, who has traced some of the furniture shown in the portrait to the Musée Condé at Chantilly.[3]

The picture is a portrait of Ange-Laurent La Live de Jully, the diplomat and collector who was *Chef des Ambassadeurs* at Versailles. It was painted by Greuze, exhibited at the Paris Salon in 1759, and is now in the National Gallery of Art in Washington, D.C., U.S.A. The stool on which La Live sits is classically rectilinear in form, ornamented with swags and pendants of laurel leaves, rosettes, Vitruvian scrolls and pineapple finials. A writing-table which appears in the picture is also mounted in the frieze with Vitruvian scrolls, and with heavy pendants of laurel which are made to appear as though passing through the tops of the table-legs, which are straight, fluted and ornamented with heavy festoons, all in the ponderous manner that later came to be known as the *style mâle*.

La Live de Jully tells us of the room containing this furniture: '*Il est orné de meubles composés dans le style antique ou, pour me servir du mot dont on abuse si fortement actuellement, dans le goût grec*'. Cochin also wrote in his Memoirs[4] of La Live's furniture as being decorated with vases, heavy swags, and '*guirlandes en forme de cords de puits*'.

La Live's neo-classical furniture was designed by Louis-Joseph Le Lorrain, one of the first decorative artists to adopt neo-classical themes, and so far from being in anything approaching general use, it was confined to one room only in La Live's own house, the rest of which was furnished in the still fashionable rococo taste.[5]

Had La Live's neo-classical pieces been the only instances to be considered, there might have been some foundation for Fiske Kimball's belief that they were merely isolated phenomena, and that furniture of the kind known eventually as

---

[1] F. J. B. Watson, 'Painter and furniture-designer: reflections on taste in the decorative arts in France around 1760'. Article in *The Antique Collector*, December, 1960.

[2] F. J. B. Watson, loc. cit. See also Fiske Kimball, 'The beginning of the Style Pompadour, 1751–9', *Gazette des Beaux-Arts*, 6ème sér. XLIV, 1954, pp. 57–64.

[3] S. Eriksen, 'La Live de Jully's furniture à la grecque'. *Burlington Magazine*, August, 1961, pp. 240–7.

[4] Cochin, *Memoirs*, Paris, 1880.   [5] S. Eriksen, 'La Live de Jully's furniture'. loc. cit.

Louis Seize did not come generally into use in France until more than a decade after similar furniture had become well-known in England through the influence of Robert Adam. It is generally accepted that the Louis Seize style was inaugurated, before the accession of that monarch, on the occasion of the fête given by Madame du Barry to Louis XV in her newly-decorated and furnished *Pavillon de Louveciennes* on the night of 2 September, 1771, when furniture in the new style made its first appearance on a grand occasion. A remarkable drawing by J. M. Moreau le Jeune shows the dazzling scene in the supper-room, which was equipped for the occasion with chairs in the new manner, having oval backs and straight, tapering, spirally fluted legs with narrow 'therm' necks.[1] These chairs are no doubt those recorded as having been made for the salon at Louveciennes by Louis Delanois in 1770.[2] Other chairs, but with horseshoe backs, are recorded as having been made by Delanois for Madame du Barry at Louveciennes in 1772.[3]

It seems indeed true that the French court was slow to adopt the new fashion, for some chairs provided for the *Grand Cabinet-interieur* of Marie Antoinette at Versailles by Goudin, Foliot and Babel in 1779[4] mark no advance in style upon those with horseshoe backs made by Delanois for Louveciennes in 1772.[5] In other royal circles however there was greater enthusiasm for novelties of style, as early as 1766.

In an important article entitled 'Early neo-classicism in French furniture'[6] Mr. Svend Eriksen has not only summed up much of the existing knowledge upon the subject, but has called attention, among other hitherto unknown aspects of neo-classicism, to some drawings in the University Library of Warsaw by Jean-Louis Prieur of some chairs intended for the King of Poland. These drawings are dated 1766 and show a 'bergere' that might be considered transitional in style from the baroque to the neo-classical, and another chair that is fully in the new mode, with an oval back and straight legs. Together with some corresponding sofas, they were made for the King of Poland in 1768 by Delanois, and it seems possible that the neo-classical chairs which this craftsman made for Madame du Barry derived their oval backs and straight legs from the same source. Mr. Eriksen also reproduces the well-known engraving entitled 'Le Lever' after a gouache exhibited at

---

[1] F. J. B. Watson, *Louis XVI furniture*, Pl. 1 and note. [2] Salverte, p. 83.
[3] *Grands ébénistes et menuisiers parisiens*. Musée des arts décoratifs, Paris, 1956, Pl. 74. See also Salverte, Pl. XVI and F. J. B. Watson, *Louis XVI furniture*, p. 143.
[4] P. Verlet, *French Royal furniture*, 1963, Fig. 30.
[5] *Grands ébénistes et menuisiers parisiens*, Pl. 74. [6] *Apollo*, November, 1963, p. 344.

the Paris Salon by Pierre-Antoine Baudouin in 1765. It shows a chair with an oval back, straight square fluted legs, heavy swags and pendants of leaves, and a key-pattern frieze. This chair, and those designed by Prieur for the King of Poland, are all in the ponderous style of early French neo-classical furniture.

An English chair exhibiting pronounced neo-classical features as early as 1759, designed by Sir William Chambers, has been brought to the present author's notice by Mr. John Harris. This is the President's chair of the (now Royal) Society of Arts, mentioned in the Minutes of the Society for 7 November, 1759, recording that a 'Drawing of a Chair for the President was produced for the Society by Mr. Chambers'. Apparently he also designed for the Society certain tables and benches, which have been destroyed. The President's chair, still used on formal occasions, is of mahogany, and below the seat is, in Mr. Harris's words, 'uncompromisingly neo-classical', having straight, round, tapering legs with a Vitruvian scroll. The arm-supports, however, are curved, and the back-rail is carved with 'a rococo flourish'. That the source of the design is French is suggested by a drawing in Sir William Chambers's album in the Victoria and Albert Museum, containing various drawings made by him in Italy and France while studying on the Continent. The chair-drawing belongs most probably to the period 1749–50 when he was staying in Paris. Not only there but in Rome, Chambers had become closely acquainted with the leading French architects such as Le Roy and de Wailly, and throughout his later life continued to correspond with them, being given information by them of architectural and academic progress in France, and receiving French books on architecture in return for English books of the same kind which he sent them from London.[1]

Mr. Harris has also noted the appearance of other early English examples of neo-classical furniture in certain paintings by Sir Joshua Reynolds, one as early as 1762, and another in 1765. The former is the chair used by Reynolds for several of his sitters, particularly Emma Gilbert, Countess of Mount Edgecumbe.[2] This chair has straight, square-section, fluted legs and a seat-rail in the form of a Doric frieze. The second example is a stool of similar design shown supporting a portable spinet in Reynolds's painting of the Payne sisters (now in the Lady Lever Art Gallery).[3]

Considering the strong architectural character of this furniture, and the fact of Chambers's close friendship with Reynolds at this time, it seems highly

[1] H. M. Colvin, p. 131.　　[2] E. K. Waterhouse, *Reynolds*, Kegan Paul, London, 1941, Fig. 79.
[3] E. K. Waterhouse, op. cit., Fig. 115.

probable that Chambers was the designer. The chair was bequeathed by Reynolds to the Royal Academy of Arts and it is now preserved by them. Judging by the early date of these instances of neo-classical furniture design in England, occurring in the case of the President's chair as much as five years before Adam's first neo-classical designs, it would appear that Sir William Chambers anticipated his rival in this regard, without being aware of the significance of his priority, and that consequently, to adapt Walpole's quotation from the Comte de Guerchy (see page 58), Chambers had the neo-classical taste 'sans le savoir'!

Although no articles of neo-classical furniture have so far been identified as having existed in France at such an early date as the designs of Chambers, it is quite clear that he obtained his inspiration from a French source, and that the basis of his sketch of 1749–50 was not merely a drawing-board project, but something he had himself observed, for he has included precise dimensions in the drawing.

The articles of furniture which were especially regarded by Fiske Kimball and others as anticipating and influencing the development of the Louis Seize style are the chairs with oval backs and straight legs which are found in the tapestry rooms at Croome Court, Moor Park, Newby Hall, and Osterley, all of them houses in which Adam carried out extensive works. Fiske Kimball went so far as to say 'it was precisely the designs for the Moor Park furniture which were among the very first examples to make known the Adam style in France'. None of this furniture, however, is earlier than the French neo-classical pieces already mentioned. The Croome Court articles were made in 1769, those for Moor Park probably in the same year or later, and those for Osterley about 1776.

In the past it has often been assumed that Adam was the designer of the chairs and sofas found in the tapestry rooms, but Mrs. Harris points out that no designs exist at the Soane Museum or elsewhere for any tapestry furniture for Moor Park, Croome, Newby or Osterley, and concludes that the character of the furniture for the rooms was not suggested by Adam, but was indicated in designs supposed to have been supplied by the Gobelins factory to the purchasers of the tapestries.[1]

Mr. Eriksen has called attention to the close contacts that could have existed between the Gobelins factory and the leaders of neo-classicism through Soufflot, Director of the factory, and the comte de Marigny, Director of the Royal manu-factures[2] (see also page 24). Together with La Live and Caylus, they were members of the *coterie* of modernists led by Madame Geoffrin, who held her *salon* in a house only a few doors away from La Live.

[1] E. Harris, pp. 9–13. [2] S. Eriksen, op. cit.

It will be remembered that the tapestries consisted not only of wall hangings, but also covers for settees and chairs. Mrs. Harris further suggests that the craftsmen who made the furniture were 'responsible for making the final designs and adjusting them to English tastes'.[1]

That Adam did himself produce designs for chairs for Croome Court is known, however, from entries in the Croome accounts for 1765 which refer to payments to Adam for a 'Design for a Chair for Gallery at Croome . . . 2:2:0:' and 'to parts at large of an armchair for Gallery at Croome . . . 3:3:0:'.

Very soon after the tapestry-room was decided upon some chairs were supplied to Croome Court by the firm of John Cobb (Fig. 58). They have straight, fluted classical legs very similar to the type of those in Adam's 'sopha' design of 1765. They are the subject of an entry in a bill of Cobb's (No. 29) for 9 March, 1765, and a pair of them are at present displayed at Cannon Hall, near Barnsley, Yorkshire, on loan from the Croome Trustees. John Cobb mentions in his bill, 'Carving all the arms and front feet, all the rest carved by Mr. Alken'. This craftsman would have been Seferin Alken, who was employed at Croome for especially fine carving on windows and doors. The back-splats of the chairs, which would have been his work, are carved with a highly Adamesque double-anthemion motif. So closely do the legs correspond with those of Adam's 'sopha' design (Fig. 16) that it is difficult to avoid the conclusion that they are the chairs referred to in Adam's bill, and that they are consequently his earliest authenticated chairs of neo-classical design.

In the face of the evidence already presented by the various authorities referred to, and outlined in the foregoing pages, there can be no possible justification for the continued acceptance of the notion that in the furniture designed by Robert Adam he initiated neo-classical features which later became characteristic of the Louis Seize period in France.

The question of the origin and development of other neo-classical English furniture, not of Adam's design, particularly the furniture of the tapestry rooms in the Adam houses, presents, however, a number of complexities.

The tapestries in these houses were among those produced under a new system of design and manufacture that was put into operation shortly before the end of the Seven Years War. With the signing of the Treaty of Paris in February, 1763, a long break in Anglo-French trade that had been occasioned by the War was brought to an end. Under the protection of Marigny and the direction of Soufflot,

[1] E. Harris, p. 92.

and with Jacques Nielson as manager of the *baisse-lisse* atelier, the Royal Gobelins factory had been re-organized. Furthermore, the services of François Boucher had been secured, and in September, 1762, a new composition adopted for the tapestry designs. This, the result of a suggestion by Soufflot,[1] was based on medallions containing scenes from Boucher, appearing as though in oval frames suspended from a sculptured cornice garnish of panels covered with swags and groups of flowers. The new form of design was admirably adapted for multiple production, for the background panels could be extended to fit the dimensions and shape of particular walls, while the Boucher medallions, the mouldings and flower borders remained little changed. A coloured drawing is known to have been prepared in 1762 by Maurice Jacques, the principal decorative artist at the Gobelins, '*représentant un Apartement tel qu'il doit être, avec les tentures de la tapisserie, le lit, le fauteuil et le canapé.*'[2]

This was intended to show the completed effect of the scheme, and to '*faire décider*' the patrons who might be considering the work. The furniture was intended to have tapestry coverings decorated with floral bouquets or, in the case of the furniture at Osterley, with figure designs from Boucher's *Enfants* series, one of a number of special sets which up till then had been reserved strictly for Madame de Pompadour.

It is drawings of this sort which Mrs. Harris assumes were supplied to purchasers of the tapestries and gave the key to the character of the furniture provided. This theory would indeed appear to provide the most plausible and satisfactory solution to the problem of the origin of neo-classical or Louis Seize elements (the two are not necessarily the same) in the furniture of the Adam tapestry rooms, but a vital link between the Gobelins factory and the furniture is at present lacking. There is no evidence that any designs for the tapestry rooms were supplied to the English purchasers, other than perhaps in one instance where a 'French design' is known to have been provided, which was for Croome Court, where Adam had been remodelling the rooms for the sixth Earl of Coventry since 1760. In August, 1763, six months after peace was signed, the Earl had journeyed to Paris to purchase furnishing for Croome Court, and after his return to England summoned Adam to attend him there in October of the same year.

The following month Adam produced various drawings for 'the Tapestry Room'. The fact that he charged in his bills for 'Altering the French designs of the

---

[1] Fenaille, Vol. IV, p. 229.   [2] Fenaille, Vol. IV, p. 246.

Tapestry Room in colour' suggests that he had seen a drawing from the Gobelins factory. This is undoubtedly true. What is by no means certain is whether this particular design did show furniture at all, or if it did, that it was of the Louis Seize character eventually adopted for the tapestry rooms. There is, in fact, as will be seen, evidence to the contrary. For Croome the furniture was not made until 1769, six years later. The tapestries themselves were not installed until June, 1771, by the firm of 'Mayhew and Ince' [sic].[1]

Following Lord Coventry's purchase of medallion tapestries, several other Englishmen had bought sets for their houses, notably William Weddell of Newby Hall, Yorkshire; Sir Henry Bridgeman of Weston Park, Staffordshire; and Sir Laurence Dundas of Moor Park, Hertfordshire; Robert Child for Osterley, Middlesex; the Duke of Northumberland for Syon; Lord Fife; and William Beckford. Those for Moor Park were supplied in 1769, Nielson's bill being dated 15th May of that year.[2]

The oval backs of the chairs which were supplied for the tapestry rooms were obviously supposed to echo the oval frames of the medallions in the tapestries, and were thus of the type which eventually came to be known by the French term 'fauteuil à medaillon'.

As the chairs and settee for the Croome Court tapestry room were made by Ince and Mayhew in 1769, and those for Moor Park in the same year or later, it is of course questionable whether the designs for them could have corresponded at all with anything appearing in a Gobelins drawing of 1762. Neither the 'French design' from which Adam worked nor any other drawings from the Gobelins factory showing medallion tapestry, either with or without furniture, are known to be in existence.

If the French design included furniture at all, which is by no means certain, it cannot at present be established positively that the furniture shown possessed oval backs and straight legs. There is a strong possibility that the design showed cartouche-shaped backs, of the currently fashionable rococo form, to accord with which the legs would have been curved. The back of the Croome Court settee is of this shape, and is essential in order to accommodate some details of the tapestry design, which in this piece is obviously not intended for an oval back. The original designs for chair-backs by Maurice Jacques or Jules Tessier (their style cannot be differentiated) which are preserved at the Musée des Gobelins, Paris, are of cartouche shape, not oval. Two of these designs correspond exactly with the

[1] Croome accounts.   [2] Note 4, p. 173.

tapestry coverings of two of the Croome Court chairbacks.[1] It therefore seems clear that these tapestry chair-backs were not intended for oval-back chairs, and that at the time they were made, about 1762–5, the use of oval-back chairs was not contemplated at the Gobelins. Moreover, the tapestry covers for the backs of the Moor Park chairs and settee, the designs of which have branches reaching into the corners, seem also to have been intended for a cartouche shape rather than for oval backs. A further point is that in none of the sets of Gobelins wall-hangings do the ovals have crestings of neo-classical husks, as in Marigny's oval picture-frames from which they are supposed to derive, but instead have floral crestings. The Croome Court chairs, however, do possess this advanced feature.

A curious feature of Mayhew and Ince's account for the Croome Court tapestry chairs is that the words 'the patterns included' have been added to the entry in another hand. A mention of this sort does not appear in any other of the accounts and it suggests that the provision of 'patterns' may have been an unusual and important matter, possibly involving additional expenditure. Were Ince and Mayhew called upon to obtain patterns specially, in view of the fact that the furniture was to have the Gobelins coverings and to be in harmony with the tapestries, and from what source did they obtain the designs? The very pronounced character of the husk ornament to the backs and around the seats suggests no other inspiration but Marigny's oval frames of 1760, and the Gobelins factory as the channel through which it was transmitted. Whatever the source of the 'patterns' may have been, it does not seem likely, from the evidence we have considered, that they could derive from any Gobelins drawing connected with the tapestries of c. 1762, but that they were provided specifically for the making of the furniture in 1769, the motifs of oval backs and straight legs having by that date become established in the Gobelins repertoire of designs.

If the source of the Croome furniture designs was English, we know from the remarkably advanced neo-classical character of the marquetry commodes made by Ince and Mayhew in 1765[2] (Fig. 119 and see page 118) that the firm could call upon a designer, whoever he may have been, who was fully capable of producing such an original and distinctive design as that of this tapestry room furniture. The Croome chairs of 1769 are extremely rich in character, in a far more mature Louis Seize style than even the Louveciennes chairs of 1770, especially in the

---

[1] *Decorative art from the Samuel H. Kress Collection at the Metropolitan Museum of Art*, London, 1964, p. 54, and Fig. 35–6.

[2] Note 5, p. 173.

carving of the legs. The Moor Park chairs and settee (Figs. 61 and 82), however, have square panelled legs almost of an early Georgian English character, with a grafting of neo-classical coin-moulding, and are far more primitive in spirit. With regard to the chairs of the tapestry room at Osterley made in 1775 (Fig. 65), and those of the state bedroom there, designed by Adam in 1776 (Fig. 66), they represent no fundamental innovations of neo-classical design, but are fairly well in accord with the spirit of the Louis Seize style as it existed in France at that date.

What still remains obscure is the exact nature of the link between the French neo-classical origins and English furniture designers and craftsmen. If the very convincing theory of Mrs. Harris is correct, the solution must depend upon the discovery of original French drawings for the tapestry rooms showing furniture of neo-classical character. However, the discoveries of Mr. John Harris have now opened up the possibilities of English craftsmen and designers deriving inspiration from the French sources through the medium of Sir William Chambers. In conservative circles this architect, with his known contacts with neo-classical enthusiasts in France and Rome, might well have been regarded as a dependable guide to the new style, especially after his having designed the President's chair for the Society of Arts, and the furniture of Sir Joshua Reynolds, all of which would have aroused great interest among designers and craftsmen.

A special problem is presented by the straight chair legs of the type that were most numerously found in the ornate carved and gilt drawing-room and bedroom furniture of the late Louis Seize period; that is, of baluster shape, round in section, tapering and fluted, and with richly-carved leaf-ornament on the swell of the baluster. In the earlier phases of the neo-classical movement in France the straight legs of square section and of more severely architectural character were general, and remained so for the library and other rooms that were devoted predominantly to masculine occupations. The Croome Court tapestry room chairs are of the former, more florid sort. An early form of this baluster-shaped leg appears in France as early as 1765 in the model chair that was the *pièce de maîtrise* of the craftsman Georges Jacob.[1]

Legs of this type appeared in England during the Adam phase in 1768, with the chairs supplied by Thomas Chippendale for the library at Nostell Priory (Fig. 62). A year earlier Robert Adam had produced a drawing showing spirally fluted, round leaf-encrusted legs with his design of a 'Table-frame for the Earl of Coventry'.[2] Adam's design for the sideboard at Osterley (Fig. 18) is similar in

<hr>

[1] H. Lefuel, *Georges Jacob*, Pl. II.   [2] E. Harris, Fig. 14.

character and was made in the same year. A pure example of this type of neo-classical chair-leg, straight, of round-section baluster form, with acanthus-leaf carving on the baluster appears however in England as early as 1735–40, in the settee made for Devonshire House presumably to the design of William Kent.[1] This example must certainly be regarded as part of the picture of William Kent's early neo-classicism, and perhaps also as part of a more or less uninterrupted tradition of classical design in England, developing from features of ancient origin, such as the turned legs of late seventeenth century furniture, but purified by new reference to authentic antique models which Kent must have seen in Italy.

Obviously it cannot be maintained that oval backs and straight legs were 'scarcely followed in France by 1789', for by that year of the Revolution the Louis Seize style was beginning to be discredited, and already Georges Jacob had supplied furniture of a new and more archeologically correct classical character to the designs of the painter J.-L. David for use as pictorial properties in his studio. This furniture was later to provide models for the new Republican style in France.

Although it has been conclusively established that the distinctively Louis Seize feature of oval-back chairs and oval mirror- or picture-frames with husk crestings and other neo-classical features originated with the French, the no less characteristic feature of that period of lyre-back chairs seems unquestionably to have been the invention of Robert Adam. No evidence appears to be known of the existence of the motif in France before Adam's drawing of 1767 (Soane, vol. 19, no. 93) of a lyre-back chair for Osterley.[2] The lyre-back chairs in the eating-room at Osterley (Fig. 60) were executed with a different type of leg from those shown in this design, probably from a final drawing that did not survive. As executed they have straight tapering round-section legs with narrow 'therm' necking, in fact of the shape used three years later in the chairs made by Delanois for Louveciennes.

Another distinctive feature of the Louis XVI style seems almost certainly to have originated in England, in the early endeavours of Thomas Chippendale to evolve a classical style to accord with the new character of the houses that were being remodelled by Robert Adam, and which he was furnishing between 1767 and 1773.

One of the earliest pieces provided by Chippendale for Harewood, about 1767, is a dining-chair made in the established English tradition, in which classical

[1] R. Edwards, *The shorter dictionary*, p. 463, Fig. 2.
[2] R. W. Symonds, *Adam and Chippendale: a myth exploded*, p. 54.

elements have been introduced, especially in the straight top-rail back-supports and with its fluted moulding (Fig. 59). For the tapestry room at Nostell Priory, Chippendale supplied, about six years later, some gilt chairs of more advanced neo-classical character, still with a straight top-rail, but with the back-supports formed as fluted columns, and enclosing a carved musical trophy with a lyre, trumpets and a wreath (Fig. 69). The chair is at this early date completely in the manner of the chairs with columnar supports and straight top rails enclosing lyres and other carved emblems, trophies and monograms that were not seen in France until about 1785, in chairs made by Georges Jacob, P. Bernard, and N. S. Courtois,[1] and especially in the chairs made by the latter two for Marie Antoinette's boudoir in that year.

There were no doubt numerous opportunities for the interchange of ideas of design in both directions, through the contacts that Thomas Chippendale must have had with France in connexion with the importation by him of chairs and other furniture for the Continent, in which he is known to have been engaged (see page 83).

It is evident from the Croome Court accounts that the Earl of Coventry bought not only tapestries but also quantities of French furniture while he was on the Continent from the *marchand-mercier* Simon-Philippe Poirier of the Rue St. Honoré, who was noted as a '*connaisseur averté et d'un savant expert*'.[2]

As the supplier of considerable quantities of furniture for the *Pavillon de Louveciennes*, Poirier may be presumed to have been in the forefront of fashion, but the records at Croome give no indication of the character of the furniture bought from him by Lord Coventry. The commode which the Earl bought from the London cabinet-maker Peter de Langlois in 1765 for the tapestry room and which is also now at the Metropolitan Museum, is fully rococo in style. It is somewhat remarkable that while detailed accounts for furnishings and upholstery at Croome Court exist from 1757 onwards, no bills or accounts seem to survive for the purchase either of the Gobelins tapestries, or indeed for any other of Lord Coventry's purchases in Paris, other than for those from Poirier, and for numerous embroidered waistcoats!

There can, of course, be no question of Adam's consciousness in his mature years of his debt to the French spirit in the designing of interiors. In *The Works* he wrote 'The French style . . . is best calculated for the convenience and elegance of life', and again 'To understand thoroughly the art of living, it is necessary

[1] J. Nicolay, p. 19.   [2] Salverte, p. 257.

perhaps, to have passed some time amongst the French'. Adam himself possessed copies of a number of the pioneer French neo-classical treatises by which he seems to have been influenced, including Bernard de Montfaucon's *Antiquité expliquée* of 1719–24, but especially the *Recueil d'Antiquités* of the comte de Caylus, the first five volumes of which, published between 1752 and were in his library. Clearly he was indebted also to the *Recueil d'Architecture* of the French architect J.-F. Neufforge, which was the first general collection of purely neo-classical designs applied to domestic architecture, decoration and furnishing. It was published in nine volumes between 1757 and 1768, with a Supplement of thirty between 1772 and 1777. The sale catalogue of Adam's library[1] shows that Adam did possess at the time of his death the 4th (1761), 5th (1763) and 6th parts of Neufforge's work, and it is these volumes that contain the designs upon which Adam seems chiefly to have drawn. They undoubtedly provided him with motifs for the design of the delightful iron balustrades for staircase railings which are among his most distinctive work, and they might possibly also have inspired the type of square tapering table leg with scroll-shaped upper part seen in his design of 1765 of the table for the vestibule at Syon (Neufforge, vol. V, no. 297), though it is just as likely that he derived this theme from Kentian models. Adam adopted also the favourite Neufforge motif of a medallion, and used it as early as 1762 in his first sketches for the Kedleston sofa (Plate 24) and for other early sofas (Plate 16. Neufforge, vol. I, 1757, Plates 64, 65, 66). Adam may even have taken his famous 'flowing *rainceau*' from Neufforge, for this type of ornament is certainly mentioned there.

The typical French composition for a wall-bay, consisting of a tall mirror grouped with a side-table or commode in an architectural framework, was also adopted by him from Neufforge. The French architect's furniture-designs are extremely ponderous, however, and seem to relate more to the seventeenth century classicism that derived from Italian Renaissance sources. Such designers as Neufforge were consciously turning back to the traditions of the French Academy under Louis XIV rather than trying to find a new approach to classical design, whereas Adam was reacting against the clumsiness of Renaissance classicism, and even though he had inherited as a birthright the stylistic repertoire of Kent, was discarding the ponderous forms of the Palladians, and endeavouring to recreate in an entirely fresh manner 'the beautiful spirit of antiquity'.

The design for the tapestry room at Croome Court was not the only French

[1] Bolton, Vol. II, p. 30.

drawing of which Adam had made use. As we have seen (page 51), Adam's drawing of a 'Water Stand' for which he charged Lord Coventry £1:10:0 in May 1767, was for 'A Tripod altered from a French design for a Water Stand'. Tripods of this type had become established in the popular imagination in France as familiar accessories of the antique scene in 1763, when at the Paris Salon was exhibited J.-B. Vien's painting entitled '*La Vertueuse Athénienne*', which showed a young priestess burning incense at such a tripod. Such articles did not become popular in France, however, as adornments of rooms until 1773, when candelabra of this form were first given the name of 'athénienne' by J. H. Eberts,[1] a furnisher who adapted the design for an article that could be used in a number of different ways; as an occasional table, a stand for a plant, lamp or candelabrum, as an incense-burner, chafing-dish or brazier, or as a goldfish bowl, as described in his catalogue.

It appears that Sir William Chambers anticipated Robert Adam's neo-classicism in this type of article, as well as in respect of other furniture. In the painting by Sir Joshua Reynolds of 'Lady Sarah Bunbury sacrificing to the Graces',[2] she is shown burning incense at a metal tripod and bowl of pure antique form. The picture was exhibited at the Society of Artists in 1765, two years before Adam's 'Water Stand' design. Again we may suppose that Reynolds derived this feature in his painting through Sir William Chambers from the French sources to which the latter had access.

The inspiration for various other types of furniture, especially such preponderantly feminine types as the 'confidante', the 'duchesse', the 'bonheur-du-jour' and many other articles associated with the boudoir, also undoubtedly came from France, but not apparently until the late 1770's.

Although Adam cannot be credited with the first application of Etruscan motifs to decoration and furnishing, he was undoubtedly early in applying it on an extensive scale. Many of his important designs in this manner were made in 1775 for Derby House and Osterley, whereas, although introduced in France in the 1770's, the style did not come into general favour at the French court until after 1780.[3]

Adam himself wrote in *The Works* that it 'differs from anything hitherto practised in Europe' and 'we have not been able to discover . . . in the works

[1] F. J. B. Watson, *Wallace Collection, Catalogue of furniture*, 1956, p. 92, and S. Eriksen and F. J. B. Watson, 'The "Athénienne" and the revival of the classical tripod', Article in *The Burlington Magazine*, March 1963.

[2] E. K. Waterhouse, Fig. 101.   [3] F. J. B. Watson, op. cit., p. XLVII.

of modern artists any idea of applying this taste to the decoration of apartments'.

French influence was the chief factor also in the development of designs not only for tapestry, but also for carving, ormolu, and especially for marquetry.

During the Louis XV period in France, marquetry designs were mostly of geometrical patterns, or trailing sprays of flowers more or less formally drawn. From about 1765 onwards in both France and England a new spirit found expression in marquetry, as it were a neo-pastoral movement accompanying the neo-classical. This new enthusiasm for rural life emanated partly from Jean Jacques Rousseau, whose purpose was social reform, and from Dr. Theodore Trochin, whose teaching that outdoor life was beneficial to the complexion and conducive to a youthful appearance had a special appeal for the strongly feminine element in the French court. This new enthusiasm, which eventually found expression in the delightful pastoral fantasy of Marie Antoinette's model farm, *Le Hameau*, at Versailles, was quickly reflected in the addition to the repertory of motifs for ornament and decoration of various kinds, of groups of gardening implements, baskets or bunches of flowers naturalistically treated (Figs. 63, 72 and 165), and figures of ladies and children gardening (Fig. 65). The neo-classical taste mingled with the neo-pastoral mood in the marquetry and painted decorations representing the nymphs and shepherds of the classical *Arcadia* of Virgil's *Eclogues*, or the swains and shepherdesses of the English equivalent, James Thomson's poem *The Seasons*, published in 1730 (Fig. 88).

As well as the motif of the classical lyre, an important decorative feature in certain articles by Weisweiler seems also to owe its origin to Robert Adam. This is the device of the pendent border or fringe in ormolu of the semi-circular commodes at Osterley based on a drawing by Adam. The ormolu borders to the lower part of the pier-tables believed to have been made by the French *ébéniste* and supplied to the Prince of Wales at Carlton House,[1] do not seem to appear in French furniture until quite ten years after the Osterley commodes were designed in 1773. In this respect Adam undoubtedly must be conceded the primacy.

The fact that Georges Jacob seems to have borrowed the English idea of bamboo-pattern furniture from chairs made by John Linnell for Shardeloes when he made almost identical ones for the *Folie St. James* in Paris,[2] having possibly seen examples brought from England by a French collector, is a clear demonstra-

[1] C. Musgrave, *Regency furniture*, 1961, see also Note 7, p. 173.
[2] Note 6, p. 173.

tion that inspiration could at times flow from this country across the Channel, and Robert Adam himself must have been keenly alive to the prestige to be gained from the prevalent Anglo-mania when he published *The Works in Architecture* with a French version in parallel columns with the English text.

ADAM AND CHIPPENDALE

One of the remarkable aspects of the Adam movement is the collaboration that took place between the architect and such distinguished artists as Joseph Rose the stuccoist, Antonio Zucchi and his wife Angelica Kauffmann the decorative painters, the engravers Bartolozzi and Cipriani, the landscape painter William Hamilton, Josiah Wedgwood the potter, Matthew Boulton the creator of English ormolu, and many others who were leaders in their particular spheres. It was long believed that a similar association must have existed between the architect and Thomas Chippendale, so magnificent are the collections of furniture from this craftsman's workshop that are to be found in some of the greatest Adam houses.

Our knowledge of the world of furniture-making in the eighteenth century was transformed several years ago by Ralph Edwards and the late Margaret Jourdain in their definitive work, *Georgian Cabinet Makers*. Revealing that the legendary triad, Chippendale, Hepplewhite and Sheraton were not wholly responsible for the entire output of Georgian furniture, they called attention to a host of other important designers and craftsmen like William Vile, John Linnell and Thomas Cobb. They also expressed the conviction that the finest work produced by Chippendale did not so much consist of articles made in accordance with the designs of mid-eighteenth century character given in the various editions of his *Gentleman and Cabinet Maker's Director*, but in the works carried out by him during the 1770's which are found in the glorious interiors designed by Robert Adam at Harewood and Nostell. In these articles the flowing, serpentine forms of the rococo gave place to the simpler, rectilinear lines inspired by neo-classical thought, and in their decoration, inlaid and painted designs of classical vases, urns, trophies, figures, festoons of bell-flowers, paterae, fluting, honeysuckle and other motifs deriving from the Adam repertory of ornament took the place of marquetry designs of naturalistic flowers, leaves and shells of the mid-century rococo taste, or of the dark, richly carved mahogany furniture of the earlier Georgian style.

It has been widely supposed that the larger part of the furniture in these houses was actually designed by Adam himself, and that Chippendale must rank amongst the other famous collaborators of the architect. Over fifty years ago Percy MacQuoid declared that three great houses, Nostell Priory, Harewood and Osterley, possessed 'specimens that are unquestionably designed by Adam and executed by Chippendale'. It can, however, no longer be assumed that all furniture in neo-classic style found in the Adam houses was necessarily designed by the architect himself. No bills or correspondence relating to furniture designed by Adam and made by Chippendale have so far come to light in any of the houses where both these men carried out work.

The late Mr. R. W. Symonds[1] showed that in houses such as Nostell and Harewood, which were designed by Adam, the furniture made by Chippendale was not designed by the former architect, but by the craftsman himself, and was ordered by the owner from him direct. On the other hand, if in any instance the furniture were executed to a design by Adam, it would have been ordered by him from a different craftsman, as in the case of the furniture at Moor Park, made by Samuel Norman, and that at Kenwood, made by the firm of France and Beckwith.

One finds that in the latter circumstances the work was carried out by smaller enterprises than Chippendale's. When the latter craftsman was employed he was of course perfectly capable of providing his own designs. There is ample evidence that he did so.

On 19 July 1767, Chippendale wrote to Sir Rowland Winn at Nostell apologizing for not having been to see him, and giving the reason that 'as soon as I had got to Mr. Lascelles and looked over the whole of ye house I found that I should want many designs. I knowing that I had time enough went to York to do them, but before I could get all adone I was taken very ill with the quinzy.'

That Chippendale himself was the author of furniture designs in the Adam manner is also confirmed by the fact that a drawing of an oval mirror in neo-classical style appears on the back of a letter from him to Sir Rowland Winn dated 1 October 1767.

Mr. Symonds went so far as to assert that Adam despised Chippendale as a mere tradesman and a social inferior, unlike the professional artists who were Adam's collaborators, but such a view can hardly be supported in the light of important

[1] R. W. Symonds, *Adam and Chippendale: a myth exploded.*

evidence discovered by the late Miss Jourdain,[1] attention to which has been freshly drawn by Mr. John Fleming.[2]

This evidence makes it clear that Robert Adam must have been acquainted with Thomas Chippendale soon after his return from Italy, in 1758, or even before, in connexion with the furnishing of Dumfries House, the interior decoration of which was the first large and important commission given to the Adam brothers. While Robert was still in Rome, in 1756, 'superfine silks and damasks' were ordered from the firm of Chippendale and Rannie in London. While touring the London shops in 1754, Robert had reported to Lord Dumfries that he had seen 'a thousand things every day that would answer charmingly for your habitation, and that would tempt a Saint', and it is quite conceivable that Chippendale's workshops were among the places he visited. Apart from the fact that Chippendale's firm was already one of the most fashionable of the London purveyors of furnishings, it is possible that the introduction to Lord Dumfries and to Adam had been through the partner James Rannie, if, as seems likely from his Scottish-sounding name, he was a fellow-countryman. The furniture ordered from Chippendale was delivered to Dumfries in 1759. There is no evidence that Adam provided the designs, and indeed the Dumfries furniture is of rococo and traditional character of the type illustrated in the first (1754) edition of the *Director*. Robert was by this date himself settled in London.

At this time Chippendale was aged about forty-one and well-established as one of the most distinguished cabinet-makers in London. He had been born at Otley in Yorkshire in 1718, the son of a joiner and grandson of a carpenter. He was settled in London and married by the age of thirty, and by 1753 he had taken premises in the cabinet-making centre of St. Martin's Lane. About a year later, at the age of thirty-six, he published the most remarkable volume of designs in the whole history of furniture, *The Gentleman and Cabinet-Maker's Director*. The work consisted very largely of rococo designs in the French, Gothic and Chinese tastes, together with a number of designs, especially those for bedroom and dressing-room furniture, of plainer, traditional character, although many of them embodied to a greater or lesser extent details in the new fashions.

Chippendale possessed a strong sense of style, design and quality, by which he was enabled to recognize these instincts in others. Thus he included in the *Director* designs not only from his own pencil, but others by some of the most original and advanced designers of the day — Matthias Lock, a pioneer of the

[1] M. Jourdain, 'Furniture supplied to Dumfries House', pp. 76–9.   [2] J. Fleming, p. 97.

rococo in England, and H. Copland. So popular was the work that a second edition followed a year later.

A third edition of the *Director* appeared in 1760, and now a number of designs of pronounced classical character were included, no doubt under the pressure of the growing enthusiasm. Many of these designs embody such typical details as straight, square-section, tapering and fluted legs, block-feet, lion-feet, and strings of husks, especially in such engravings as the hall chairs, No. XVII and No. XXV (Fig. 36), a sofa, No. XXX, a writing-table, No. LXXIV, various designs for term-pedestals, No. CXLVII, for tripod-pedestals, No. CL, and a chair, No. XXV.

One of the Chippendale designs for a sideboard-table (Plate LXI), in particular displays this primitive classical character in the straight legs of very pronounced taper, with narrow 'therm' necking and disproportionately small Ionic capitals, of a kind later found in several of Adam's designs (Fig. 14). This straight, sharply tapering leg used both by Kent and Chippendale, with Ionic or foliate capitals, sometimes without, and the block-feet, clearly derive from the classical therm or terminal column that is such a prevalent theme in seventeenth century interior design (Plate 38). The tradition runs in English furniture of the time of Charles II, and in such articles as the side-tables with straight, square, tapering legs, made by James Moore about 1715, as well as in French furniture of the Louis XIV period and earlier. Some of these designs were published as early as 1753, and thus owed nothing to Adam's influence.

Chippendale's classical designs with their vigorous quality seem to derive from traditional seventeenth and early eighteenth century models, themselves based on Renaissance classical designs that were not always of the purest and most scholarly order. Adam, no less than Chippendale, may have sought inspiration in these sources, the former transforming the character of his models by his refining process.

From 1766 onwards, under the influence of the new approach to classicism as it was now being exploited by Adam, Chippendale was producing furniture of an increasingly advanced classical character. In 1767–8 Chippendale was supplying furniture to Sir Edward Knatchbull at Mersham-le-Hatch, which Adam had built between 1762 and 1765. Most of this furniture seems to have been of conventional character, but some pieces supplied in 1767,[1] a set of four mahogany stools, are of primitive classical type, having square, tapering legs

[1] R. Edwards, *The shorter dictionary*, p. 507, Fig. 47.

with block-feet, block-capitals ornamented with paterae, and strings of husks in the leg-panels.

Great weight was attached by Mr. Symonds to the fact that in the only document known to be in existence directly connecting Adam and Chippendale, the former embodied a penalty clause in the event of late delivery of goods ordered. This document[1] is an agreement for the supply by Chippendale of glass for the great mirrors in the library at Kenwood, which Adam was designing for Lord Mansfield in 1766. The agreement provided that Chippendale should 'deliver in about Two Months to Mr. Adam, Architect, the Following French Plate Glass in London Silver'd and ready to put up'. In this work Chippendale was acting only as a glass merchant, not as a maker of mirror-frames. The frames themselves were made, as was much of the best furniture at Kenwood, between 1768 and 1771 by the firm of France and Beckwith. Apparently Chippendale had asked for part payment in advance, for a receipt was made out by France as follows, dated 25 August 1769:

'Received from Lord Mansfield by a Draft Upon Messrs. Hoare and Co. the sum of £170:0:0 to be paid to Thos. Chippendale on account of an agreement entered into by him with Robert Adam, Esq., & in Case the said Mr. Chippendale shall not within three months deliver all ye Glass pursuant to his agreement in good condition: I do engage that the said Mr. Chippendale shall upon Demand repay ye said sum of £170:0:0 or in Case of any Neglect on his part, I hereby promise to pay ye same to His Lordship. Wm. France.'

The fact that Robert Adam gave the commission for carving and gilding the mirror-frame to William France, instead of to Chippendale, who could have executed the work with equal if not greater skill, and also that he made France responsible for exacting the penalty in the event of late delivery of the glasses, was regarded by Mr. Symonds as highly insulting to a firm of Chippendale's standing and as suggesting that the architect viewed the craftsman not merely with mistrust, but with dislike and contempt; a view said to have been borne out by the absence of any reference to Chippendale in Adam's letters.

In two instances where Chippendale was supplying furniture to houses designed by Adam, the owners, Sir Edward Knatchbull at Mersham and Sir Rowland Winn at Nostell, had occasion to complain to Chippendale over the tardy delivery of furniture ordered. They did not in either case make their complaints to Adam, as it is suggested they would have done in respect of craftsmen who were

1 Kenwood archives.

under his control and supervision as architect, but wrote direct to Chippendale.

The significance of the differences in tone between the letters of Robert Adam and those of Chippendale to their mutual patron, Sir Rowland Winn, has been greatly exaggerated. The assumption of a tone of equality and indeed familiarity was natural to such a snob as Adam, who cultivated the art of 'living amongst the great'. Indeed, the Rev. W. Mason of Aston, writing to Horace Walpole referred to Robert Adam and his brother James as two 'Scotch coxcombs'.[1] Chippendale's reticent and dignified rejoinders to Winn's complaints contain a discreet reminder that he had been over-much preoccupied with executing commissions 'for His Majesty'.

If Adam did not deal with Chippendale direct over the supply of furniture it was undoubtedly because the architect had the greatest admiration for his ability, and respected his independence and his high status as the premier craftsman of the day. To impose a penalty clause was, and still is, a customary routine procedure, and one need not therefore read anything out of the ordinary into this circumstance.

There are many reasons why a different firm from Chippendale's should have been selected to make the Kenwood mirror-frames. The personal preferences of Lord Mansfield might easily have been involved, and in any event Adam might have wished to spread his custom over more than one firm. It might have been well known that Chippendale was too fully occupied with other commissions at the time to have been able to supply Kenwood within the time desired, and he may have been employed to supply the 'French glass', then a new product, because he had special experience of, and facilities for, importing such material from the Continent. Moreover, it was needed in large sizes, the handling of which might have presented problems for a small firm like France and Beckwith, and indeed to any but the largest enterprises like Chippendale's.

The creation by Chippendale of a great masterpiece of design and craftsmanship such as the magnificent writing-table at Harewood (Fig. 167), or of the monumental group of sideboard, urns and pedestals there (Fig. 136), must have been a matter of the greatest interest and concern to Adam, and it is clear from such examples that there must have been a greater measure of interdependence between Chippendale and Adam than between the latter and any other craftsman who supplied furniture to the Adam houses, and this must have become progressively stronger during their long association.

[1] H. Walpole, *Letters*, Vol. 5, p. 501.

The idea that Robert Adam despised and held in contempt a craftsman who had been known to him at the very outset of his career, and who continued to be associated with the supply of the principal furniture to so many of the houses where Adam carried out important works — Harewood, Nostell, Newby, Mersham-le-Hatch, Lansdowne House, David Garrick's house, and 20 St. James's Square — cannot possibly be maintained. It would have been remarkable that Adam, who was extremely outspoken and jealous of his status as adviser to a client on every problem of decoration and furnishing, and who had pretensions to being a social equal of his patrons, should have tolerated his clients patronizing a person of whom he did not approve, in the vital question of the furnishing of the interiors in which so much depended upon their perfect harmony and unity with the setting that he himself devised. The architect must in fact have had the greatest respect for the craftsman's skill and remarkable facility in practising the new mode of neo-classical design.

Moreover, it is inconceivable that Chippendale's rapid mastery of the new style could have been attained without close co-operation with Adam, in fact without an intimate acquaintance and ample opportunity to study Adam's neo-classical designs, which could hardly have come about except through an association going back through the years to 1754, the days of the work at Dumfries, the architect's first independent country house commission. They were both members of the Society of Arts, which Chippendale joined in 1760, two years after Adam became a member upon his return from Rome.

We know that Chippendale was quick to grasp and exploit fresh developments of style, as he did in the case of the rococo fashion in the *Director*, and it would seem very likely that Chippendale must have been allowed access to Adam's drawing office at the Adelphi, at times when the two men were engaged upon some identical major project.

The pressure of work upon Robert Adam made it impossible for him to concern himself with designing the whole of the movables required for his houses, and recognizing, as he must have done, the masterly excellence of the work of Chippendale and his firm, he must have been well content to be able to leave Chippendale, with complete confidence, to provide furniture worthy of the interiors that he himself was creating. Furthermore, it is hardly conceivable that Adam, knowing Chippendale was commissioned to provide furniture for his own houses, would have denied the craftsman the means of creating a perfect unity in the new style which was the architect's overmastering ideal.

Evidence in support of some such close co-operation appears to exist in the case of several works that are believed to come from Chippendale's workshop. Among them are the sideboard (Fig. 137) together with the accompanying urns and pedestals (Fig. 140), at Newby Hall, Yorkshire, where he is known to have been working in 1776.[1]

The legs of the sideboard are of an unusual reeded form, corresponding with an Adam design dated 1772 (Fig. 27), reproduced in *The Works*,[2] of a sideboard for the Earl of Bute at Luton. A pair made to this design are today at Mount Stuart, Isle of Bute, among other Adam furniture. The date of the design is a likely one for the sideboard. Adam was producing a number of designs for Newby between 1770 and 1775. An interesting point is that the frieze of the sideboard, inlaid with a meandering vine-leaf design, very closely resembles the frieze decoration in a drawing by Adam for a sideboard in the house he designed for W. G. Hamilton in 1787 (Fig. 26). The drawing itself is undated. Was it one of an early date that he adopted for this purpose, or did Adam even copy from Chippendale?

The handsome bow-fronted commode of black and gold lacquer at Osterley (Fig. 123) is also believed to be a Chippendale piece, on the grounds of the characteristic ram's-head capitals and the tapering, fluted short legs with block feet. The fine ormolu ornament in the pilasters is identical with that shown in Adam's design of a commode for the Countess of Derby, illustrated in *The Works*.[3]

A number of features appearing in attested pieces by Chippendale may serve towards establishing a canon for the identification of other articles thought possibly to come from his workshop, for instance in the library table supplied by Chippendale to Nostell in 1767 (Fig. 166) there appear small carved scrolls at the heads of the supports. Scrolls of this shape, somewhat resembling the complete volute of an Ionic capital, are found also in the beautiful dressing-commode supplied by Chippendale to Harewood in 1773 (Fig. 121), and may be taken as a distinctive Chippendale feature. The individual character of the legs of the dressing-commode may also assist in establishing a code of Chippendale design. Tapering with a concave curve, they are finished with a square tapering block unlike any feature found in the designs of Adam, although it was later adopted by Sheraton. The half-domed knee-recess in this commode is another characteristic Chippendale feature, appearing in the design for an earlier model of a dressing-

---

[1] Harewood archives. Steward's letter-book, 1763–92, p. 289.
[2] *The Works*, Vol. 3, 1822, Pl. 8.   [3] Harris, Fig. 47.

commode in the third edition of Chippendale's *Director*, of 1762, plate CXVIII. It appears also in several designs by Linnell for similar pieces (P. Ward-Jackson, Fig. 239).

These distinctive features of legs and scroll ornament, this time combined with the gilt bronze leaf-decoration exactly as seen in the Harewood dressing-commode, are also found in the pair of tall china cabinets (Fig. 172), at Firle Place, Sussex, the seat of the Viscount Gage. They came to Lady Gage from Panshanger.[1] The inlay upon the satinwood of these cabinets has the same liveliness of scrolling foliage that is shown in all those neo-classical pieces that can be ascribed to Chippendale.[2] There is a refined yet at the same time spirited elegance of design in this ornament that seems to be lacking in the stiffly formal ornament of Adam (cf. Figs. 114, 116).

In its superb furniture collections, the Lady Lever Art Gallery at Port Sunlight, Cheshire, possesses a number of important neo-classical pieces of great beauty, at least one of which can confidently be ascribed to Chippendale (Fig. 125). This is a commode of satinwood with two doors, each inlaid with an oval containing a vase of flowers. The term-shaped supports, ornamented with overlapping coin moulding, have ram's-head capitals, and familiar scroll-ornament where the supports meet the top of the piece, are again found, exactly in the manner of Chippendale's attested works. The short legs, however, are of a different form, being of square section and swept outwards, the feet being formed as blocks with a gilt key-pattern ornament on the fronts. Again the feeling is of robust elegance, which is so characteristic of Chippendale's work at this period.

A number of magnificent writing-desks are in existence, in which the side-pedestals are oval in plan. Some of the finest of these were made in the late Hepplewhite and Sheraton periods, and are often believed to owe their splendid form to the genius of the latter designer,[3] who published a number of charming designs embodying oval shapes. The form originates, however, in Chippendale's *Director* in a design (third edition, 1762, LXXX) for a 'Library table' with oval pedestals, in which details are shown alternatively in a traditional classical manner and also in rococo fashion.

The development of certain classical features which eventually became distinctive marks of the late Louis Seize style, years after they had appeared in England, may also be due to Chippendale, particularly in his design for square-

[1] Note 8, p. 174.
[2] See Edwards and Jourdain, p. 44. [3] C. Musgrave, *Regency furniture*, Fig. 7.

back chairs with columnar back-supports. We see the genesis of the form in the chairs he designed for the Harewood dining-room about 1767 (Fig. 59); this he developed into the more markedly classical spirit of the chairs which he supplied for the tapestry room at Nostell about 1771 (Fig. 69). Chairs of this kind, having open backs with column supports and a straight back-rail, containing a lyre, a trophy of musical instruments, or of a bow with a quiver and arrows, or a monogram, were later greatly favoured by French patrons and craftsmen, especially by Georges Jacob and by P. Bernard and N. S. Courtois, notably in the chairs made by the latter two for Marie Antoinette's boudoir in 1785.[1]

It also appears that Chippendale provided an early example of the fully formed leaf-ornamented baluster leg that became one of the outstanding features of the late Louis Seize style, as well as of the Adam movement. This had first appeared in France, in a simpler form, in the *pièce de maîtrise* executed by Georges Jacob in 1765 (see page 67), but an even earlier example exists in the hall-seat designed, presumably by William Kent, for Devonshire House, about 1735–40 (see page 68). Chippendale's version of this feature may be seen in the chairs supplied by him for the library at Nostell in 1768 (Fig. 62), having probably been inspired from some such source as Adam's side-table design for Osterley in 1767 (Fig. 18).

Chippendale's firm must in fact have served as one of this country's principal links with French style and taste, for it is known that he imported French chairs from the Continent, most of them presumably of the rococo type illustrated in the *Director*, and in 1769 he was actually penalized by the Customs authorities for undervaluing a consignment.[2]

Chippendale presumably had agents in Paris, and it is not at all improbable that he or his son made visits there. It seems extremely likely that considerable traffic in both furniture and ideas went on in both directions between London and Paris.

One of the most celebrated and most delightful suites of furniture designed by Chippendale is the bedroom furniture supplied by him to his friend David Garrick the actor, possibly for his villa at Hampton, Middlesex, where Adam carried out various works, including a 'Shakespeare temple' about 1775. The suite which is now preserved at the Victoria and Albert Museum, is especially interesting in embodying the Chinese taste, in a similar manner to the bedroom furniture at Nostell, and was similarly used in a chamber hung with a Chinese wallpaper. The furniture is japanned in cream, gold and green, and includes a bed having a coved canopy supported on reeded columns with square bases. There

---

[1] Nicolay, Fig. H.   [2] E. T. Joy, *Chippendale in trouble*, p. 569.

are a pair of wardrobes japanned with Chinese landscapes, and a set of chairs with trellis-pattern backs and rush seats.

A delightful canopy bed, japanned in cream, red and green in naturalistic leaf designs, is to be seen at Claydon, Bucks. This piece also is believed to have been provided by Chippendale for David Garrick, at his apartment in the Adelphi, where the craftsman was employed in decoration and furnishing in 1771–2.

The magnificence of Chippendale's later furniture made for the principal Adam houses, and the rapidity of the craftsman's response to the demands of the new school of design is one of the most remarkable aspects of the neo-classical movement. Chippendale's library table at Nostell (Fig. 166) stands in the logical line of development between the writing-desks of Kent and Vile, and his own library table from Harewood[1] (Fig. 167). The smooth dignity of form of the latter showed the way for the noble writing-tables of the Sheraton period. Chippendale's significance is that he may have provided Adam with inspiration for some of his neo-classical developments, and certainly that he absorbed Adam's innovations into his own interpretations of classicism, and thus assured them of a place in the main stream of the English furniture tradition.

Thomas Chippendale died in 1777 at the age of about sixty-one, and his business was carried on by his son, Thomas Chippendale the younger, who must have been active in the design and execution of furniture for some time before this date. The younger Chippendale's work seems to be distinguished by a suave elegance of form, by the greater use of light-toned woods, and by a fondness for strongly contrasting inlays such as of ebony in ivory, mahogany in sycamore, and similar combinations (Figs. 121, 126 and 174). His authenticated work belongs to the period c. 1791 to 1794, including the sturdily elegant furniture he supplied to the banker Sir Richard Colt-Hoare at Stourhead. The lion-headed pier-tables in the gallery at Harewood (Fig. D), were also supplied by him, in 1796,[2] and it can be presumed that a great deal of fine furniture must have been provided by his firm during the late Adam and Hepplewhite periods.

[1] Note 1, p. 173.   [2] Harewood accounts.

FURNITURE IN THE ADAM HOUSES

It is fortunate for the student that almost all the drawings of Robert Adam may be studied in one place, the Soane Museum. Happily also a great deal of furniture which was designed or inspired by him is preserved in a number of the great houses for which it was made, many of them being open to the public. These collections of furniture are described in the following pages, house by house.

KEDLESTON

At several houses where he was engaged in the course of his career, at Harewood and at Nostell Priory, Adam superseded an architect of a more old-fashioned school. At Kedleston in Derbyshire he was called upon in 1760 by Nathaniel Curzon, later Lord Scarsdale, to complete a scheme of rebuilding begun by the Palladian architect James Paine. Although at Kedleston Adam created one of the greatest monuments of neo-classical interior planning, a completeness and unity of furnishing in the new style was not achieved to the extent that it was at Harewood and Osterley, probably for the same financial reasons that caused Lord Scarsdale to curtail the original elaborate scheme for the exterior. Furthermore, he may have been reluctant entirely to replace the splendid gilt furniture of the William and Mary period, and some in the William Kent style, which had furnished the earlier Wren house on the site, and which is still to be seen in some of the rooms. Nevertheless, the furniture provided during the early days of Adam's activities there, consisting of the famous palm-tree furniture (Figs. 37 and 38) of the state bedroom and boudoir, and the 'mer-folk' sofas of the state drawing-room (Fig. 34) are possibly the most sensational pieces to be seen in any of his houses. Few articles in the whole realm of English furniture can compare in grandiloquence with these sofas, which in boldness of form and richness of gilding fitly equip the state drawing-room, one of Adam's most beautiful rooms, with its Venetian window and columns of pink Derbyshire alabaster. Each sofa is some twelve feet long, having ends carved with figures of 'mer-folk' or tritons and sirens, blowing their 'wreathèd horns' of conch shells (Fig. 33), the whole being designed in an elaborate Venetian manner exceeding in their baroque floridity almost anything ever created by William Kent. As executed, their design is probably more due to the exuberant imagination of John Linnell, their maker, than to the timid and hesitant drawing by Adam upon which they are supposed to have been based. This is inscribed 'Design for the sopha for Lord Scarsdale and also executed for Mrs. Montagu in Hill Street', and dated 1762 (Fig. 29, see also page 39). Linnell's executed pieces are obviously more suitable in scale for the saloon at Kedleston than Adam's original suggestion would have been. Drawings by Linnell which are preserved at Kedleston and in a collection at the Victoria and Albert Museum, show clearly the transition from Adam's conceptions to the sofas as finally executed (Figs. 30, 31 and 32). Linnell was almost certainly inspired also by the great tritons which had appeared only a year earlier on the State Coach[1] that was designed for the Coronation of King George III by Sir William Chambers.

Linnell may also have been encouraged in the use of palm-trees as supports for the fantastic bed he made for Kedleston, and for the columns of the bedroom torchères and the supports of the mirror in the boudoir, by Chambers's use of them for the door-columns of the State Coach.

However, Adam himself may have provided the inspiration for the palm-tree columns at Kedleston, for he used this motif in a drawing preserved at the house for a State Barge of which the mast and the supports of the canopy took this form (Fig. 35). These motifs were by no means new, and certainly not neo-classical. They had appeared in France as early as 1707.[2]

Athenian Stuart and John Vardy had used them at Spencer House in London in 1759. John Webb had already exploited the same theme in a design of a bed-alcove for King Charles II in 1669. They were a favourite baroque and rococo theme, until the French designer Cochin, attacking the rococo taste in the *Mercure de France*, scorned them as the 'dearest resource of contemporary decorators'.[3]

Flanking the pink alabaster columns of the glorious Venetian window in the

---

[1] E. Croft-Murray, *Three famous state coaches.*   [2] Fiske Kimball, *Le style Louis XVI*, p. 92.
[3] *Mercure de France*, December 1754. Supplication aux orfèvres, ciseleurs, sculpteurs en bois pour les appartements et autres.

state drawing-room are a pair of large oval mirrors made closely in accordance with a design by Adam of 1765.[1] The exuberant scrolling of leaves accords well with Linnell's baroque sofas although making no progress towards the neo-classical ideal later achieved in the dining-room.

Adam's comprehensive scheme for equipping the serving apse in the dining-room at Kedleston is shown in his drawing there, dated 1762 (Fig. 2). The side-tables in the alcove (Fig. 1) closely follow this drawing and are his first strictly neo-classical furniture, deriving from drawings made apparently by James Stuart for Kedleston about 1757 and for Spencer House in 1759 (see page 40). The side-tables between the windows of the room must also be to Adam's design, and are rather more handsome, being entirely gilt and having the leaf ornaments to the feet which are omitted in the other tables (Fig. 4). The chairs in the dining-room, however, are of Chippendale 'Director' type with cabriole legs in the old tradition.

Beautiful armchairs with oval-backs and round, tapering fluted legs with leaf-capitals in the mature Adam manner of the 1770's are to be seen in the saloon and the drawing-room, those in the former finished in green and gold, those in the latter wholly gilt. Some remarkable armchairs in golden satinwood have delicate rococo cabriole legs, and oval backs carved with a neo-classical honeysuckle design of astonishing boldness and vigour. They are probably of the 1780's, made by a craftsman combining the rococo French taste still current in the Hepplewhite period with fresh neo-classical features.

SYON HOUSE

Syon House, which was the first and one of the most palatial of Adam's unified neo-classical interiors, provides important examples of furniture inspired by some of the architect's earliest designs (Fig. 15) as well as articles in the later Adam manner.

Outstanding amongst the furniture of his early phase is the series of large side-tables with tapering legs of square section, which are found in the immense Palladian entrance hall, in the gorgeously palatial ante-room, in the dining-room and the red drawing-room. The finest of these are the pair of side-tables in the drawing-room (Fig. 93) which are comparable in richness with those of the

[1] E. Harris, Fig. 82.

music-room at Harewood (Fig. 94). The former pieces combine the strictness of Adam's early style with the delicacy that distinguishes all his work, in the bold form of the square-section legs, the fine decoration of the legs and frieze, and the pendent, fan-shaped ornaments below the frieze. The table-tops are of scagliola mosaic, in geometrical patterns. These are said to have been found 'in the ruins of the Baths of Titus' in Rome, but this is probably as much due to inventive Italian salesmanship as the legend that the beautiful columns of the ante-room were dredged from the Tiber. At least one of the columns is scagliola; and others may be also. A pair of columns at Newby are also said to have been recovered from the same source! Some smaller side-tables in the same room have baluster-shaped legs that indicate a later development in Adam's style, and these tables have scagliola tops of a finer design, having a representation in the centre of the Temple of Vesta in Rome, for long one of the classical monuments most favoured by the English lovers of antiquity.[1]

Like the side-tables, the tall upright 'picture-frame' mirrors of the dining-room and drawing-room possess the satisfying form of this transitional phase of Adam's work (see page 46). The pier-glasses in the former room (Fig. 155) have terminal figures in profile at the sides which are repeated in the frame of Michael Spang's sculptured marble plaque of the Three Graces in the chimney-piece.[2] The pier-glasses of the drawing-room have plainer frame-mouldings, but these are overlaid with scrolling of foliage at crest and foot of a scale as bold and fully modelled as the ceiling-ornament of the dining-room.[3]

The famous Long Gallery, which looks out over the broad, slowly-flowing reaches of the Thames, must surely be one of the most enchanting rooms in England, with its delicate feminine ornament in softly recessive pinks and pale green that are so appropriate to its purpose as the ladies' withdrawing room. The main furnishings are two splendid side-tables that complete the magnificent range of these articles at Syon, all with inlaid marble tops of striking neo-classical design. One pair, dating from about 1765, are of early neo-classical form (Fig. 8) with straight fluted inwardly-canted legs and lion-paw feet deriving apparently from the form of ancient tripods.

Others, a set of four, are of a slightly later date, about 1770, and are of more sophisticated character with round, baluster shaped legs with leaf-ornament, and

---

[1] Bolton, Vol. 1, p. 266, as then in the Gallery.
[2] The 'Three Graces' may be seen reflected in the mirror, E. Harris, Fig. 54.
[3] E. Harris, Fig. 53.

B   A commode-chest by Thomas Chippendale, about 1775

having stretchers carrying urns, in the manner of earlier English and French side-tables (Fig. 96). Although of greater elegance than the earlier tables they possess the satisfying robustness of proportion that is absent in Adam's later works.

The feminine atmosphere of the gallery is heightened by a quantity of satinwood furniture of a later period as well as of earlier date, and among the most beautiful and important of these are a pair of satinwood chests with flat inlaid tops, tall square, tapering legs, fitted with long drawers, and ornamented with marquetry of various woods in neo-classical designs.[1] Comparison with articles known to have come from Chippendale's workshop suggests that they were supplied from the same source about 1775. A similar chest, but with a coved top is illustrated in Fig. B.

Some small card-tables with round fluted legs, and inlaid tops of remarkable quality, possess the solidity combined with elegance that is the mark of Adam's mature style of the 1770's. They may have been designed by Peter Langlois who is recorded in the Syon accounts as having supplied a card-table to the house. Elsewhere in the gallery the sofas, stools and window seats express the characteristic beauty of the Adam manner, while the set of arm-chairs, with cartouche-shaped backs and curved legs represent the extreme delicacy of the rococo spirit that was still cultivated in the Hepplewhite period (Fig. 40).

HAREWOOD

Robert Adam began his work at Harewood in 1759. As well as designing the interiors, Adam's plans and elevations of the exterior which are at the Soane Museum suggest that John Carr of York (1723–1807), the Palladian architect earlier engaged by Mr. Edwin Lascelles, was not entirely responsible for the building as it was finally carried out.

Of all the Adam houses, Harewood must rank as possessing the richest and most extensive surviving collection of furniture in the Adam style, including some of the greatest masterpieces of the neo-classical movement. Although Chippendale's accounts at Harewood at present seem far from complete, there is little doubt from such evidence as they provide, and from his letters at Nostell, that his firm supplied the whole of the new furniture in the house.

Among the most important early specimens are the pair of splendid gilt side-

---

[1] R. Edwards, *The shorter dictionary*, p. 210, Fig. 40.

tables in the music-room (Fig. 94). With their sturdy square-section tapering legs, solid swags of husks and satyr-mask in the centre of the frieze, they are in the robust manner of Adam's early furniture, similar in character to his great side-tables of the 1760's in the red drawing-room at Syon (Fig. 93). A smaller and easily overlooked gilt side-table in the old library is extremely unusual in the elegant shaping of the square section tapering legs with their delicate curve and the surface-carving of leaf-form (Fig. 107), the curling leaf-top forming a graceful capital. In the state bedroom a small commode japanned in green and gold is in the manner of the green furniture of the state bedroom at Nostell, for which a list of Chippendale's attests to authorship. This elegant little piece is a survivor of a much larger group of japanned furniture once at Harewood and probably supplied by Chippendale, now in a private collection.[1] The bed itself, decorated in ivory and gold, has fluted bed-posts, vase-shaped towards the base in the manner later to be popularized in the designs of Hepplewhite (Fig. 177).

The gilt console-tables in the gallery, their curved supports given goat's-heads and hooves (Fig. III) are among the very earliest pieces of furniture inspired by Adam. They have affinities with his drawing in the Soane Museum (Fig. 21) dated 1765 of a console-table actually made for Sir Laurence Dundas at Moor Park, and later moved to 19 Arlington Street,[2] but display a more extreme degree of streamlined refinement. The gilt console-tables in the rose drawing-room (Fig. 112) seem to represent a development from French *Régence* examples (see page 203) with their slender curved supports surmounted by women's-heads *en espagnolette*, and with the stretchers of each carrying figures of *putti*. Between the windows opposite, an oval girandole, designed almost certainly by Chippendale, is one of the loveliest examples of a type of mirror of which Adam was extremely fond.[3] It has a lively cresting of delicate scrolling with fantastic half-figures of *putti* emerging from the stalks. Above the fireplace in the same room the mirror is of the distinctive tripartite form that Adam evolved, but here given highly individual character (no doubt by Chippendale) in the extreme narrowness of the side-glasses, the supports of which are shaped as terminal figures surmounted by sphinxes, above which is a crest belonging to the same class as Adam's mirror-crestings of the 1770's, in which human or animal figures support an urn or medallion. Here two widely spaced *putti* hang festoons to a central vase, as in the crestings of the great pier-glasses in the gallery (colour plate D).

[1] L. G. G. Ramsey, 'Chinoiserie in the Western Isles'. Article in *The Connoisseur*, September 1963.
[2] E. Harris, Fig. 8.   [3] The Harewood Guide, p. 14.

Despite the importance attached by Adam to the dining-room as a social arena where major political decisions were often made, even though it was 'over the bottle', it was only at Saltram and Kenwood and Kedleston that his distinctive composition of dining equipment approached the splendour it was given at Harewood, with the mahogany sideboard, flanking urns on pedestals and wine-cooler, supplied by Chippendale. These exhibit the excellence of English ormolu in the fine modelling and chasing of the gilt mounts, in a design of ram's-heads and *guilloche* bands. Here even the mastery of the French in this field was equalled (Fig. 136).

An outstanding feature of the Harewood furniture is the great variety of chairs, also presumably made by Chippendale. They fall into three or four main classes. Those in the library, with their cabriole legs, show little Adam influence beyond some small neo-classic ornament of a wreath and swags. Those of the dining-room, with their plume-like back-splats and straight, fluted back-rail with a cresting, and their square tapering legs, take a form that is transitional between the Chippendale, or 'Director', types and the neo-classical (Fig. 59). The chairs with cartouche-backs and tapering, fluted legs in the green drawing-room, and the richly carved oval-back chairs of the music-room (Fig. 70) combine strong French influence with Chippendale's robust classicism. The chairs of the gallery are severely neo-classical with their square backs (Fig. 71).

Also unsurpassed elsewhere is the remarkable group of inlaid marquetry neo-classic furniture at Harewood. Some of these pieces stand in the private apart-ments, and are not usually seen by the public. Among them are a large dressing-commode and an upright secretaire which are described with the rest of the collection in another chapter (see page 81) (Fig. 174). The strong French influence may again be noted, for the upright secretaire was a type then gaining much favour in Paris. Bearing in mind Chippendale's close commercial contacts with France (see page 83), it seems likely that the French influence in the Harewood furniture was more directly due to the craftsman than to Adam's use of French motifs.

The small mahogany commode in the green drawing-room represents the transition from the rococo to the neo-classical in the use of the newer motifs of ram's-heads in the ormolu corner-mounts and of circles and ovals of husks in the inlay, although the form of the piece, with its serpentine lines, is still of early character (Fig. 118).

The magnificent library table formerly in the gallery (see Note 1, p. 173) is one of the supreme masterpieces of Chippendale's work, and indeed one of the greatest in the entire realm of furniture. Of rosewood, with marquetry in various contrasting woods, the severity of its plain surfaces is set off by the richness of the English ormolu mounts (Fig. 167).

The crowning *tour-de-force* of the Harewood furnishings is the set of remarkable carved gilt curtain pelmets in the gallery, which have 'drapery' astonishingly carved in wood and painted to simulate festooned curtains. These features are saved from being mere curiosities of craftsmanship by the spirited style of the carving, the marks of gouge and chisel imparting a satisfying sculptural quality to the illusion of cloth (Fig. D).

NOSTELL PRIORY

At Nostell Priory, near Wakefield in Yorkshire, Robert Adam was commissioned in 1766 by Sir Rowland Winn, Baronet, to complete an elaborate scheme of rebuilding begun in 1745 by the Palladian architect James Paine. As at Kedleston in Derbyshire, where Adam supplanted the same architect, the projected layout was for a central block connected by quadrant corridors to four outlying pavilions. Two of these were built, but one only survives.

Nostell shares with Harewood the distinction not only of housing a remarkable collection of furniture from the workshops of Thomas Chippendale, but of preserving in the house the craftsman's bills, and in this case a great deal of correspondence also between him and his patron, Sir Rowland Winn. The collection of furniture has the special interest of belonging chiefly to Chippendale's middle period, when in forming his new classical style, he was continuing a direct line of evolution from the classical manner practised earlier in the century by William Kent and William Vile, and also at times still retaining motifs of the naturalistic rococo manner. The most important articles of furniture at Nostell represent not only this particular episode of nascent neo-classical design, but also illustrate significant turning points in the evolution of the various classes of furniture to which they belong. These latter points are more fully discussed in another chapter (see page 193).

The earliest piece supplied for the new interior is the magnificent writing-table in the library, the first room to be transformed by Adam. Chippendale charged £72:10:0 for this piece in 1767. It has massive and deeply carved terminal supports with lion-paw feet in the bold manner of William Kent which Chippendale adopted until he had attained his complete realization of the neo-classical spirit with the flat decoration of wood-inlay in the library table at Harewood about four years later (Fig. 166, and cf. 167).

The library chairs also take an important place in the evolution of neo-classical style in England (see page 67) in showing Chippendale's robust interpretation of new forms, notably in the round leaf-ornamented leg with a block capital (Fig. 62).

Elegant features of the saloon are the pair of pier-tables and glasses (Fig. 97). These are remarkable in being among the few articles known to have been executed almost exactly as shown in surviving drawings, which are dated 1775. With the oval medallion ornaments heading the square tapering legs, the graceful festoons and the figures of cupids carrying urns on the stretchers, these tables express the continuation of delicacy and refinement with satisfying form which is apparent in Adam's mature work of the 1770's (see page 48). In the upper hall are another pair of side-tables, made also by Richter and Bartholi almost exactly to a design appearing on the same drawing as the saloon pier-tables. These have supports shaped as slender terminal figures (Fig. 98) (see page 200).

The chairs in both of these rooms bear a family resemblance to those at Harewood, also supplied by Chippendale, and are typical of his style in the vigorous carving of frieze and legs. Particularly noteworthy, however, the hall chairs in the upper hall are unusual for this type in having arms. They are remarkable also for the early appearance of a circular-back, and even more for the impertinent vitality of the design (Fig. 68).

The dining-room provides an interesting comparison between the Palladian spirit of the interior architecture of James Paine and the stucco panels which Robert Adam later introduced. The large sideboard, of sombre San Domingo mahogany, although probably supplied by Chippendale about 1765, has the massive scrolled supports and deep carving characteristic of the earlier Georgian age, and offers another example of the ponderous furniture that was superseded elsewhere by Adam's more elegant conceptions.

In the tapestry room are two commodes, both representing the transition from the rococo to the neo-classical style (see page 91). The form of each is in the French mode of the mid-eighteenth century, serpentine in form and with asymmetrical panels, but the decoration is in the new fashion with classical vases inlaid upon doors and sides, one showing a greater degree of advance than the other, in that the inlaid decoration is entirely classical, consisting of a vase in an oval with festoons of husks. The other commode exhibits the new taste only in the inclusion of a classical urn among festoons of realistic flowers, in the true rococo manner.

Two of the most charming rooms at Nostell are the state bedroom and dressing-room, where the deeply coved ceilings date from about 1745 and are in the older style of Thomas Paine. The walls were hung with seventeen sheets of green imported Chinese paper (called indiscriminately 'India' paper) supplied by Chippendale at a cost of £12:15:0.

The clothes-press or wardrobe-cupboard (usually found in the dressing-room) is almost identical in form with a design for a commode clothes press in the *Director* (3rd ed., no. CXXX). It has the same serpentine front, canted angles and similar bracket feet. The Nostell piece, however, is japanned in green and gold to match the other pieces. Instead of the ovals of rococo carving on the door-fronts, a Chinese palace garden spreads itself in gold, and in place of the carved fretwork upon the angles shown in the *Director* drawing, there are strings of husks. These, and the fluted frieze, are the passport for the admittance of this piece into the neo-classical scheme.[1]

No account has been traced for that most important item, the green and gold dressing-commode, which is *en suite* with the other furniture; but various details of design indicate that it must unquestionably have come from Chippendale's workshop (see page 81) and it is mentioned in a list of articles in the room drawn up by Chippendale and dated 1771. It is not only the handsomest piece in these rooms, but one of the most delightful amongst all Chippendale's furniture (Fig. 120). These, the japanned wardrobe and commode, represent a continuation into the neo-classical world of the Chinese influences that were so fully exploited in the rococo designs of *The Director*, and it is noteworthy that the small 'dressing-table and bason-stand', in the same room, and also in green and gold, present no features aspiring to the new classical taste, but have slender cabriole legs in the earlier French manner.[2]

The 'green and gold chintz bed' mentioned in Chippendale's account is no doubt the state bed, with its circular canopy.[3] The bed in the dressing-room is hardly less elaborate, with its scroll pediment and richly carved posts.[4]

---

[1] R. Edwards and M. Jourdain, Fig. 132.
[2] A. Coleridge, 'Chippendale: interior decorator and house furnisher'. Article in *Apollo*, April 1963.
[3] C. Hussey, in *Country Life*, May 23, 1952.   [4] Op. cit., May 30, 1952, p. 1654, Fig. 8.

SALTRAM HOUSE

The interest of Saltram House, near Plymouth, Devonshire, lies not in any perfection of its interior unity, as at Syon or Harewood, but in the contrast between the decorative style of the age of George II and that of Robert Adam, in the two rooms that were remodelled by him, and in the extreme beauty of these additions, which were carried out for John Parker (later the First Lord Borington) between 1770 and 1788.

The furniture in the two rooms is of special interest as being among the comparatively few articles which have been executed exactly as dictated by Adam's surviving drawings for the pieces, and further that the maker, Joseph Perfetti, was a craftsman or purveyor unrecorded in connexion with any other house.

Calling attention in his *Works in Architecture* to the innovations he had introduced, Adam poured scorn on the decorative motifs of the earlier age, but at Saltram there is no inequality of excellence. Now a natural succession from the best of one age to the finest of another prevails, and the lively rococo plasterwork of the earlier ceilings gives place to the serenely formal stucco ornaments of Adam in the later apartments.

Adam softened the transition between the George II velvet drawing-room and the new saloon by means of a pair of carved and gilt wood pier-glasses, and tables with black marble tops, which he placed against the background of the original Genoa red silk velvet, on either side of the double-doors leading into the later room. The tables are delightfully ornamented with festoons spiralling down the fluted legs. The mirrors have the cresting of modelled figures, in this case of female sphinxes, characteristic of the 1770's (Fig. 100).

In the saloon itself are found a set of four larger wall-mirrors, with a cresting of charmingly posed seated female figures. Beneath the mirrors stand a pair of large rectangular carved and gilt wood side-tables with inlaid marble tops. These are again adorned with spiral festoons, and there are pendant pieces and a central ram's-head decoration below the frieze (Fig. 101).

Four carved and gilt wood stands for candelabra form an interesting variation on the theme of the classical tripod, the legs having ram's-heads and feet. The candelabra themselves were delivered in 1770. Of Blue John Derbyshire fluorspar and tortoiseshell, mounted in ormolu, they are almost identical with a single candelabrum supplied by Boulton in 1772 at a cost of £31:14:0, and can be presumed with a fair degree of certainty to have been made by this famous manufacturer (Fig. 145).

Saltram provides a distinguished example of the work of Chippendale in the suite of two settees and eighteen chairs in the saloon.[1] Detailed invoices for these articles do not survive, but the chairs closely resemble those in the green drawing-room at Harewood, which are known to have been supplied by Chippendale. Furthermore, John Parker's account book records for 20 May 1771, payment of 'Chippendale's bill £120'. With the combination of the cartouche-shaped backs of the chairs, the serpentine front of the settee and the sinuous arms of all the pieces, together with the straight legs and fluted friezes, this furniture combines both the rococo and the neo-classical influences in a manner not uncommon at the time.

The dining-room ranks with those of Syon and Harewood as one of Adam's grandest theatres for the formal ritual of dining, and it is of especial interest in that the sideboard-table is made in three sections fitting exactly into the serving bay (Fig. 142).

This bay was not originally built for the purpose by Adam as were the semi-circular dining-room apses at Kedleston, but was arranged in the angular window-bay of the mid-Georgian house, the alcoves having been formed from two of the windows which Adam had blocked up. The flanking urns are on separate pedestals, which are of the rather low proportions of Adam's earlier examples. They, and especially the urns, are among the most beautiful ever devised by Adam, and are distinctively Grecian in outline, or, as he would have called them, 'Etruscan'.

OSTERLEY PARK HOUSE

Osterley, which offers a vista in its successive rooms of the changing styles of Robert Adam in the course of his creation of palatial interiors, provides also a series of furnishings covering an unusually wide range of years, from 1763 to 1780, and matching in their richness the splendour and beauty of the house that Horace Walpole called 'the palace of palaces'.

As at Syon, Adam was confronted with an earlier house, this time an Eliza-bethan mansion built in 1577 for Sir Thomas Gresham. The form of this red-brick

---

[1] Geoffrey Wills, *Robert Adam at Saltram.*

courtyard house remains, with its four angle towers each capped with ogival cupolas of Tudor type. For his client, the banker Robert Child, Adam closed in the courtyard with an impressive Ionic portico, with a double colonnade and a flight of steps between the projecting side-wings. He also raised the courtyard floor so as to create a *piano nobile* of state apartments on the first floor.

In the great hall the seats are in Adam's early Kentian manner, with high scrolled ends and almost fiercely naturalistic lion-paw legs.[1]

One of the earliest rooms is the eating-room, and here there are lyre-back mahogany chairs of a similar date to the bow-shaped back-rail of Chippendale's *Director* period. The gilt side-table with slender baluster legs and pendent under-frieze ornament is one of Adam's handsomest pieces, displaying the beginnings of his characteristic mature elegance in the very narrow necking of the legs, and the lotus capitals beneath the blocks. His drawing for it, dated 1767, 'for Robert Child, Esqr.', hangs in the corridor (Fig. 18). The pair of white painted and gilded urns on pedestals are believed to have been provided by John Linnell, on the evidence that he is known to have made similar urns for Shardeloes (Fig. 139). The library table, although not as immense as the one at Harewood, rivals it in beauty and richness. Its light mahogany is veneered with harewood (green stained sycamore) inlaid with emblems of the arts of architecture, sculpture, music and painting, and again a Vitruvian scroll frieze. A pair of writing tables are in a similar style (Fig. 39).

In the library, completed in 1773 (Fig. 39), the furniture is similar in character to the superb group of inlaid neo-classic furniture supplied by Chippendale for Harewood about 1770 (Fig. 167). Here are the notable chairs, of which the splats, as Walpole wrote in 1773, 'are taken from antique lyres and make charming harmony' (Fig. 64). The backs are arched, and the square legs are ornamented with drooping ormolu swags in the manner of early French neo-classical furniture. The seat-rail is inlaid with a distinctive Vitruvian scroll, reminiscent of the Kentian phase of Adam's work, and of exactly the same pattern as in the latter's drawing of tables for Sir Charles Farnaby (Fig. 17). It is believed that these chairs must have come from the workshop of John Linnell, for there are several drawings in the collection of that craftsman's designs in the Victoria and Albert Museum for lyre-back chairs of very similar character, including one with the distinctive and unusual trefoil-shaped back. The Vitruvian scroll is also of the same type as that appearing in Linnell's drawings. Similarities such as these,

---

[1] A. T. Bolton, Vol. 1, p. 285.

and the evidence of the urns and pedestals at Osterley, have led to the belief that Linnell was chiefly responsible for much of the furniture at Osterley (see page 208).

Adam's rooms, particularly his dining-rooms, sometimes tend to repeat themselves in various features, but the glorious drawing-room at Osterley is unmatched in any other of his houses, with its astonishing coffered ceiling and central ornament of ostrich feathers radiating from a golden sunflower. The carpet repeats the hexagonal compartments of the ceiling, each with a sunflower ornament, and to give restful relief to the whole design the walls are covered with a dark green silk damask. The pair of large commodes between the windows fittingly complete the room, which Walpole described as 'worthy of Eve before the Fall'. These remarkable pieces are the only commodes known to be in existence which are authenticated by Adam's own designs (Figs. 115 and 122). They are not only some of the finest creations in the whole realm of Adam furniture, but are also the forerunners of the large class of bow-fronted commodes that are among the most favoured articles of the Hepplewhite period. The gilded gryphons supporting a medallion in the frieze of each commode are repeated in the frieze of the doorways of the room, and are inspired by similar motifs in the Villa Madama designed by Raphael's pupil Giovanni da Udine. Above the commodes the pier-glasses have the narrow, mitred frames of Adam's maturity, and the typical cresting of this period with modelled female figures and sphinxes supporting an urn with scrolls of foliage. The design for these glasses, dated 1773, is also preserved at Osterley.

The tapestry room houses one of the famous sets of tapestry produced by the Gobelins factory under its workshop manager, Jacques Nielson, which are more fully discussed in another chapter (page 62). These tapestries are dated 1775 and represent 'The loves of the Gods' after paintings by Boucher. The figure subjects are woven in a manner to represent framed paintings hanging against a red damask wall covering suspended by ribbons, and even the nails from which they are supposed to hang are represented in the tapestry (Fig. C). The armchairs, sofa and firescreens are upholstered in tapestry designed *en suite* (Fig. 64).

The gilt side-table between the windows corresponds to a design in the Soane Museum dated 1775 and is one of the handsomest of Adam's mature phase, the exquisite detail of the ornament never obscuring the satisfying form of the piece. Its top is of the inlaid marble work carried out by the Italian craftsman Bossi, who practised this secret technique in Dublin (see page 170) (Fig. 99). Adam's drawing for the pair of painted and gilt tripod-stands also survives and they are among the most beautiful articles of the kind ever devised by him (Fig. 146). The ormolu perfume-burners upon them are almost certainly the work of Matthew Boulton, the famous metal-worker of Soho, near Birmingham, whose productions rivalled those of the French in excellence.

Next door the gigantic state bed almost fills the small square state bedroom (Fig. 109). It is the most magnificent of all Adam's beds, with its elaborate cornice projecting at the angles, providing supports again for Adam's favourite sphinxes. The dome of the canopy provoked one of Walpole's most wittily malicious outbursts. It was 'too theatric', he wrote, and 'too like a modern head-dress, for round the outside of the dome are festoons of artificial flowers. What would Vitruvius think of a dome decorated by a milliner?'. The chairs of the room, made also to Adam's design, are exquisitely graceful, and their oval backs give another opportunity for the use of figures of insouciant female sphinxes (Fig. 66). Between the window stands a magnificent commode of black and gold Chinese lacquer (Fig. 123).

The pilaster supports have ram's-head capital and festoons in a style suggesting that they might have come from the firm of Chippendale. The short fluted legs and tapering block-feet are also characteristic of his work. The pier-glass[1] above the commode, executed to a design dated 1775, has a cresting of sphinxes, and *putti* with an urn, repeating details of the headpiece of the bed. It is executed in the smoothly simplified manner, with little use of foliage scrolls, that marks the later development of this type of mirror. The last room to be seen is one of five rooms designed by Adam during the 1770's in what he erroneously called the 'Etruscan' style. The so-called 'Etruscan' vases, from which this kind of decoration derived its name, were not the work of the true Etruscans, the predecessors of the Romans, but late Greek red-figured pottery of the fifth century A.D. In fact Adam used these characteristic black and red decorations in a manner more appropriate to the Roman and Renaissance grotesques that appeared so often in his interiors, and which William Kent had used earlier at Rousham in Oxfordshire and in the presence chamber at Kensington Palace.

Walpole observed, in one of his most indignant outbursts, that after the other splendid rooms it was 'like going out from a palace into a potter's field'. This little room, however, was never intended as the culmination of the range of state apartments, but as a dressing-room or ante-room to the bedroom. Adam's

[1] E. Harris, Fig. 70.

designs for the chairs were followed closely, with splats appropriately shaped as vases (Fig. 67).

The black and gold japanned commode between the windows in this room, one of a pair of which the other is at present in the Victoria and Albert Museum, very closely resembles the green and gold japanned commode which Chippendale supplied to Nostell, with its four term-shaped supports, front bowed in the centre, and short tapering fluted feet. It is also very similar to the commode in the state bedroom. If, as the character of these three lacquer commodes suggests, they were made by Chippendale, it is conceivable that he may have supplied other furniture to Osterley.

HEPPLEWHITE AND THE
ADAM DISSEMINATION

Changes as revolutionary as those introduced by Robert Adam in decoration and furnishing, especially when attended by fashionable success, are likely not only to inspire admiration and imitation, but to provoke criticism, jealousy, rivalry and even outright antagonism. We have already seen that Sir William Chambers, Adam's close contemporary, was in the realm of official architecture at least, his most prominent rival. Chambers was also his most outspoken critic. He described Adam's delicate decoration as 'filigraine toy-work', and referred to his painted compartment ceiling in the red drawing-room at Syon as 'like a supper-table dished out with indifferent copies of bad antiques'.[1]

An even more formidable competitor than Chambers, on account of the enormous extent of the practice that he developed, was James Wyatt, who in 1770 at the age of twenty-four, leaped into the first rank of British designers when he was selected by competition as architect of the Pantheon, the 'Winter Ranelagh' in Oxford Street, opened in 1772, and which Horace Walpole pronounced 'the most beautiful edifice in England'. It has been suggested by Antony Dale[2] that the publication by the Adam brothers of the first folio of *The Works in Architecture* in 1773, so soon after the opening of the Pantheon, was to a great extent stimulated by their desire 'to counteract the new force working against the Adam influence'.

It is a curious fact that Wyatt was associated with Adam in the building of Shardeloes, indeed, in the decoration of a single room, the library, about 1775. By 1784 Wyatt had finished one of his earliest important commissions, the completion of Heveningham Hall, Suffolk, for the banker Sir Gerald Vanneck, the rebuilding of which had first been in the hands of Sir Robert Taylor. Again the pattern was repeated of a conventional Palladian architect being supplanted by a practitioner of the newly fashionable neo-classical mode, as had been the case in so many houses with which Adam was associated. In the splendid great hall, the

---

[1] Chambers, *Civil Architecture*.   [2] A. Dale, *James Wyatt*.

dining-room, library and ballroom, Wyatt closely followed Adam's manner. Many of the details of stucco arabesques and other features are almost indistinguishable from those at Syon and other works of Adam. The library at Goodwood House, Sussex, also seems to show some Adam influence.

The *Farington Diary*[1] quotes a report of Benjamin West that Wyatt had told King George III that 'there had been no regular architecture since Sir William Chambers in that when he came from Italy he found the public taste corrupted by the Adams and he was obliged to comply with it'. With growing success Wyatt quickly consolidated his own personal style, which is expressed in the private rooms at Heveningham. These were presumably the last to be finished.

For these rooms Wyatt designed a quantity of furniture in an individual interpretation of the neo-classical manner. The oval-back dining chairs were of mahogany (Fig. 73), but most of the other objects — tripods and pedestals for lights (Figs. 151 and 152), and a curved side-table for the dining-room apse — are painted. The furniture of Wyatt's charming Etruscan room is painted in pale green, white and Etruscan red. The chairs here, with a branching palm-tree design in the oval backs, are especially delightful.[2]

All these pieces form such a closely integrated part of the decorative scheme of the rooms that it seems beyond question that they were designed by Wyatt himself. They display a strong sense of three-dimensional form and sculptural quality and great inventiveness in detail, all of which qualities were absent from the works of Adam at this date.

There seems to be a possibility that some gilt side-tables with goat-head ornaments (Fig. 113) were also designed by James Wyatt. They were made for the neo-classical drawing-room at Stanmer Park near Brighton, Sussex, the seat of the Earls of Chichester, probably about 1777, when some English chairs in the rococo French taste, bearing this date, were also made for the house. The ornament of linked wreaths in the frieze of the tables is repeated in the cornice of the room and in the overdoors, and is of the same character as the ornament in the frieze of the fireplace in the library at Goodwood, Sussex, which is believed to have been designed by James Wyatt. It is recorded in the Goodwood archives that a craftsman named Riley painted the library ceiling. One of the Stanmer chairs is signed 'John Riley' and this circumstance may also provide a link between the two houses and with Wyatt.

A number of articles of furniture now in private collections are associated with

[1] *Farington Diary*, 1923, Vol. II, p. 180.   [2] *Country Life*, September 19 and 26, 1925.

houses designed by Wyatt, but without fuller evidence than is known, at present, it is difficult to establish the extent to which they owe their design to Wyatt himself or to the craftsmen by whom they were supplied.

Horace Walpole had given much generous praise to Adam's early work at Syon, at Kedleston, and in the chief rooms at Osterley, but after 1773, when Adam's style itself began to alter from a plastic, three dimensional conception to a linear, superficial one, his admiration changed to ridicule. Adam's design for the gateway at Syon he wrote of as '*croquant* as his frames for tables. . . . From Kent's mahogany we are dwindled to Adam's filigree'.[1]

It seems to have been due to his influence, moreover, that Mrs. Elizabeth Montague, who had written enthusiastically to her friends of Adam's work in her Hill Street house in 1767, dismissed Adam and engaged James Stuart instead to decorate her new house in Portman Square, only a few doors away from Home House. After visiting the former house in 1782, Walpole made his famous crushing pronouncement 'It is grand, not tawdry, nor larded and embroidered and pomponned with shreds and remnants and *clinquant* like all the harlequinades of Adam, which never let the eye repose a moment.' Three years later Walpole saw the work which Henry Holland was carrying out at Carlton House for the Prince of Wales and remarked 'How sick one shall be, after this chaste palace, of Mr. Adam's gingerbread and snippets of embroidery!'

Although Adam's creations were intended to minister to 'the parade, the convenience and social pleasures of life', principally in large palatial establishments, he had also shown how his principles of variety and 'movement' in the planning of rooms, and of charm in their decoration could be applied to small houses such as Marlborough House, Brighton, which he designed for Mr. W. G. Hamilton in 1787.

Thomas Leverton (1743–1824) was a follower of Adam rather than a rival, and his success in practising the new style may have been due largely to his employing Adam's pupil Joseph Bonomi as an assistant, and to engaging the services of John Flaxman. Several of the houses in Bedford Square, including his own residence, No. 13, were designed by him, and Woodhall Park, Herts., which he built for Sir Thomas Rumbold from 1777–82, was one of several country houses he designed. In recent years a number of fine articles of furniture once at Woodhall Park[2] have appeared upon the market, but they vary very strongly in character,

---

[1] Walpole, Letter to the Rev. William Mason, 1773.
[2] M. Jourdain, 'The furniture of Woodhall Park'. Article in *Country Life*, April 26, 1930.

and there is no evidence known that they were designed by Leverton himself, and not by the craftsmen concerned (Figs. 103 and 134).

Despite the strictures upon Adam's decorative style, the ideals of grace and elegance, of delicacy and refinement that he had introduced into furniture design had by now become deeply implanted in the English furniture tradition, and a multitude of designers, cabinet-makers and tradesmen popularized the Adam style in the realm of furniture, modifying its character to meet the tastes of the general public, especially the middle classes, to give furniture sufficient robustness for family use, and to fit in with the increasing development of large-scale workshop production.

The neo-classical style was now to pass from the aristocratic into the democratic sphere with the publication of the designs of George Hepplewhite in his *Cabinet-Maker and Upholsterer's Guide* in 1788, which demonstrated, for all to see, that the style of Robert Adam could be adapted for general consumption.

In the whole history of the arts, George Hepplewhite is one of the most shadowy of the figures whose name has become a household word. Very little is known of his life except that he was an apprentice with the firm of Gillow of Lancaster, and moved to London where, by 1760, he was established in Redcross Street, St. Giles's, Cripplegate. He died in 1786, when his widow, Alice, carried on the business as 'A. Hepplewhite and Co.'. It seems likely that the firm existed by supplying designs for cabinet-makers rather than by the manufacture of furniture, for, as in the case of Sheraton, not a single piece of furniture is authenticated by a bill or other document as having come from his workshop. Two years after his death his widow published *The Cabinet-Maker and Upholsterer's Guide*, a large volume of three hundred designs which was the largest book of its sort to appear since the publication of Chippendale's *Director*. The immediate success of the work caused a second edition to be issued in the following year, and a third edition was published in 1794.

The first two editions of the *Guide* summed up and crystallized, even in a sense petrified, the Adam manner at a time when the reaction against the excessive feminine delicacy and tendency to over-ornamentation in Adam's work was becoming more and more widespread. Yet in one sense the Adam spirit found its chief fulfilment in the furniture of the Hepplewhite era, for many of the loveliest articles made under its influence were created during the years of the architectural decline of the Adam school; indeed, many of the oval-back, wheel-back and shield-back chairs (Figs. 41–4), the bookcases with vase-shaped door-glazing and urn-capped pediments (Figs. 53 and 55), the beds with delicately carved or painted cornices and posts, the bow-fronted commodes of this period (Figs. 117, 126 and 127) may well be regarded as amongst the most beautiful productions in the whole history of furniture.

Hepplewhite's designs compare most closely, in their general character of refinement and elegance with Adam's later drawings of the 1780's; and many parallels may be found in the use of the neo-classical motifs of urns, medallions, paterae, swags and festoons, although it is rarely that any particular features exactly correspond. In the design of chairs, of which so few by Adam survive, Hepplewhite displayed limitless invention especially in the variety of his designs for the backs. The legs were usually tapering and of square section. They are often gently outswept in a manner not seen in Adam's designs. In one or two instances he uses a plain tapering leg of a round section, with a lotus-leaf capital, and occasionally a fluted leg entwined with a ribbon in the French manner. Hepplewhite never illustrated Adam's charming urn-shaped capital for chair or sofa legs. His sofas (Fig. 47) are more streamlined than Adam's, in which richly carved detailing tends to obscure the pure line of the form, as in the latter's *confidante* for Sir Abraham Hume.[1]

Hepplewhite used simple vertical fluting in friezes, but never Adam's highly characteristic and much more complex frieze decoration of linked wreaths and rosettes, or his palmette or anthemion friezes. He did make use, however, of large rosettes in a frieze, sometimes alternating with vases. Hepplewhite probably absorbed almost as much influence from Chippendale as from Adam, especially in his sideboard-tables with their accompanying urns and pedestals (Fig. 45). These articles in Hepplewhite have a robustness of form and boldness of ornament more characteristic of Chippendale's work. In his decorated table-tops, the ornament is usually planned in a centrally-focused composition, with loops of festoons or continuous strings of foliage round a central motif which could be a small rosette or star, or a larger shell-pattern ornament (Fig. 52), whereas in Adam's designs secondary focal-points of interest are disposed around the centre in the shape of medallions or tablets suspending the festoons (Fig. 25). In some of Hepplewhite's designs for the tops of card-tables and pier-tables there are strongly radiating patterns (Fig. 51), which are unknown in Adam's designs.

An interesting aspect of Hepplewhite's style is that he never used human or animal figures, as Adam did so extensively in his designs, nor any plaques, tablets,

[1] E. Harris, Fig. 124.

panels or medallions painted with figures and landscapes of the legendary classical world. Hepplewhite shows no examples of Adam's type of pier-glass with delightfully posed female figures, or sphinxes supporting urns or medallions. Neither does he even adopt Adam's characteristic invention of the tripartite 'Venetian window' mirror with its vertical divisions in the form of female terminal figures (e.g. Fig. 27). Hepplewhite's sadly severe, fastidious spirit seems to have shrunk from contemplating a classical world, even as chastely depicted by Angelica Kauffmann and Zucchi, a world where it was 'always afternoon', but seems instead to have indulged his consummate genius for grace and elegance of design among the abstractions of stylized foliage, urns and vases. There are no military trophies in Hepplewhite, no swords, spears, shields or helmets. There is no Venus, no Diana and no Mars. In many of the plates, such as some of the square-backed chair designs, or in the sofa designs (especially the confidante with separate seats at the ends), there are signs of the Louis Seize influence which infused English furniture more and more during the late 1780's and the 1790's.

On the other hand, some of the furniture types illustrated by Hepplewhite showed little of the influence of the fashionable movement. These consisted of such articles as bookcases, secretaires, bureaux, with tallboys, wardrobes, dressing-chests and other bedroom and dressing-room furniture — in short the articles belonging to the realm of intimate domesticity rather than to the 'parade of life' with which Adam chiefly concerned himself.

The comparatively few articles of this character that were produced in fashionable style owed their origin to the taste of the individual cabinet-maker rather than to Adam and in the designing of articles in the domestic category Hepplewhite sought his precedents in the body of traditional design, then represented by Chippendale's *Director*. The principal ingredients in this tradition, established towards the end of the seventeenth century, were a notable simplicity of form and line, and great restraint in the use of ornament. His plates for a wardrobe and a double chest-of-drawers, in particular, closely resemble some which had appeared in the *Director* more than thirty years earlier. With these, and in those designs that appeared in the first and second editions of the *Guide* for chairs which still retained the curved cabriole leg of the mid-century taste, the publishers probably did no more than represent the continued currency in the furnishing trade of the old style.

Although the *Guide* shows only three chair-designs, and several for stools in the

French rococo taste, it would appear that this style enjoyed continued popularity, or even a revival of interest from about 1770 until 1790, to judge from the large number of chairs of this type, as well as rococo commodes and other articles of furniture of this period that survive. Indeed, in many painted and gilt armchairs (Fig. 40), marquetry commodes and small tables (Fig. 165), an extreme degree of refined elegance and of simplicity of line was achieved by British craftsmen often equalling in grace any productions of the French. This style, sometimes referred to by collectors and connoisseurs by the phrase 'Hepplewhite in the French taste' was probably favoured in the Adam-Hepplewhite era by more conservative patrons, who were distrustful of the new-fangled classical philosophy in decoration and furnishing.

Even before the publication of Hepplewhite's collected designs, they must individually have played an important part in the dissemination of the Adam style throughout the furniture trade in general. Although the author in his preface stated that 'our drawings are all new' they were probably not very different from many which had been executed before his death. The writer went on to say he had 'designedly followed the latest or most prevailing fashion only, purposely omitting those articles, whose recommendation was mere novelty'. Thomas Sheraton, who was extremely sensitive to new trends of fashion, called attention to the outmoded character of some of the Hepplewhite designs in the preface to his *Cabinet-Maker's and Upholsterer's Drawing Book*, the first part of which appeared in 1791.[1] 'If we compare some of the designs, particularly the chairs, with the newest taste,' he wrote, 'we shall find that this work has already caught the decline, and perhaps in a little time, will suddenly die in the disorder.'

Sheraton's criticisms were obviously taken to heart, for when Hepplewhite's successors produced the third edition in 1794, possibly in an attempt to maintain the pre-eminence of the *Guide* over Sheraton's *Drawing-book*, many of the old designs were replaced with new. The cabriole leg was retained only for two drawings of stools. Moreover, Sheraton's development of the square-backed formula for chairs was now followed with about twenty designs of this character in the Hepplewhite *Guide*, but these were far less felicitous than the exquisitely graceful oval- and shield-shaped Hepplewhite designs of the earlier editions, which represent the loveliest aspects of the simplified Adam style. The rectangular backs of sofas, also, which Sheraton had favoured, were repeated in the latest Hepplewhite volume, and some of the oval mirror designs of the earlier *Guide*,

[1] See R. Fastnedge, *Sheraton Furniture*, p. 195.

which had been rather fancifully adorned with profuse neo-classical ornament, were now dropped in favour of plainer rectangular shapes.

The uneasiness of the new rectilinear designs in the later *Guide*, contrasting so strongly with the sensibility of Hepplewhite's earlier curvilinear patterns, demonstrate the profound difference in spirit between the style of the 1780's and that of the 1790's, in which the influence of Sheraton was to become increasingly apparent.

How is the dividing line between the world of Adam and Hepplewhite on the one hand and that of Sheraton on the other to be drawn? Their beauties are distracting to the surveyors of boundaries. The painted medallions after Angelica Kauffmann belong to both worlds; so too does inlaid ornament of Adamesque neo-classical character embodying the ubiquitous husks, paterae, swags and grotesques. The inlay in the form of shells or resembling fans, so often regarded as typically Sheraton, does not in fact appear in any of his books but *is* shown in Hepplewhite's *Guide*. Floral inlay or painted decoration is illustrated by Hepplewhite, but is increasingly favoured by Sheraton in his successive volumes from 1791 to 1794; where neo-classical decoration is concerned the reverse is the case.

In his *Drawing Book*, Sheraton shares almost completely Hepplewhite's avoidance of human and animal figures and of painted groups and landscapes. The occasional landscapes which appear on pole-screens, and the rare *putto* on a frieze are exceptional in Sheraton's work. Panels and medallions painted with figures and scenes from the classical world, even on furniture distinctively of Sheraton character, must therefore be due directly to the influence of Adam. Floral decoration painted in rich colours and with extreme naturalism on satinwood is not a Sheraton innovation, but was developed from the kind of surface decoration favoured by Adam and Hepplewhite, having originated in France. Yet it is seen frequently on cabinets or bookcases which have the swan-neck broken pediment, a survival of the Chippendale *Director* period which Hepplewhite did not continue to favour but which is seen restored in Sheraton. This decoration is also found on cabinets or bookcases with semi-elliptical or segmental pediments which Hepplewhite flirted with but which Sheraton developed more fully, notably by combining them with corresponding apron-pieces of semi-elliptical form in the base of a piece.

Sheraton continued to use traditional bracket-feet for commodes, chests and cabinets just as predecessors like Chippendale had done, and as his contemporaries Hepplewhite, Shearer, and Seddon continued to do, but Sheraton's form may be distinguished by the cusped point he gave to the inner curve of the feet. Wholly of Sheraton's invention are the domed hoods to the upper parts of ladies' writing-tables, dressing-tables and small cupboards and desks. Allied to them are half-domed features, and the concave-curved tops of the side-cupboards in such articles.

The semi-circular shaped commode was established by Adam in his pieces at Osterley, and by Hepplewhite in a distinctive design (Fig. 117) while the latter originated the kidney-shaped table-top, although Sheraton developed it for many types of furniture. The shield-back and oval-back formulae for chairs and settees belong indisputably to Adam and Hepplewhite. The square-back was extensively developed by Sheraton, but had appeared earlier in several examples of Hepple-white's, and was, as we have shown, taken up again in the third edition of the *Guide*. In highly decorated articles, especially in cornices, pediments, and elaborate furniture, the unmistakable mark of Sheraton is the acute nervousness and complexity of design, intense sometimes to the point of neurosis. That Sheraton, living in the most abject poverty, should have attained such heights of pure design, of draughtsmanship and sophisticated elegance is one of the great miracles of genius. It seems as though his fastidious, inventive spirit, cramped by privation, found release in the conception of works of art of a richness, fantasy and beauty he was never to experience in the realities of his own life.

Perhaps the chief importance of Sheraton in the last decade of the eighteenth century is that he gave to English furniture an effective transfusion of the peculiar elegance and delicacy of the Louis Seize period. This is expressed especially in the shaping of break-front table-tops with serpentine or straight fronts and quadrant-shaped ends, and in the delicate scrolling of flower- and leaf-patterns combined with ribbon decoration that he suggested for the 'borders of pier-tables'. It is seen also, perhaps most beautifully of all, in his adaptation from the French of slender turned colonnettes with feet of 'spinning-top' design, as the supports of cabinets and commodes and of pier- and side-tables.

THOMAS SHEARER AND
THE CABINET-MAKER'S LONDON BOOK OF PRICES

Some attention must here be devoted to the designer Thomas Shearer, whose influence was considerable in extending the influence of Adam and Hepplewhite throughout the furniture trade, and consequently throughout the world of domestic furniture at the end of the eighteenth century and even well into the nineteenth century. This influence was exercised by the publication of many designs by Shearer in *The Cabinet-Maker's London Book of Prices* in 1788. Thomas Shearer's designs and this work itself have been fully described by Mr. Ralph Fastnedge in his *Sheraton Furniture* and *Shearer Furniture Designs*.

The Cabinet-Maker's London Book of Prices was produced for the London Society of Cabinet-Makers and was intended, not so much as a repository of designs, but as a guide to the pricing of cabinet-makers' work. The cost of labour involved in every operation was set out precisely, together with detailed tables showing how the cost of various extras or omissions should be calculated. The designs and prices related only to cabinet-work, such as bureaux, bookcases, library and writing-tables, sideboards and bedroom furniture. Chairs, beds, mirror-frames and upholstery-work were not considered. The book was first published in 1788, and a revised edition with greatly enlarged text and additional plates followed in 1793. It was subsequently re-issued in five other editions until 1866, and the work continued to convey something of the spirit of Adam and Hepplewhite design as long as the book remained in circulation. In the later years their influence was felt less among the fashionable cabinet-makers of the towns than among the more conservative craftsmen of the provinces and country districts.

Seventeen of the twenty furniture designs in the first edition of the *Book of Prices* were by Thomas Shearer, about whose life even less is known than of his contemporary, Hepplewhite. It is clear, however, from his having been chosen by the Society to provide most of the plates that his reputation must have been sound. Shearer's designs possessed the elegance which had become absorbed into the English tradition of furniture design through the influence of Robert Adam, without a trace of pretentiousness. In some instances they derived more directly, as indeed did many of Hepplewhite's designs, from the simpler pieces inspired by Chippendale's *Director*. In many respects Shearer seems to have anticipated the character and details of much furniture that goes by the name of Sheraton. The latter, who probably knew them both, regarded Shearer's designs as superior to Hepplewhite's. In the introduction to his *Cabinet-Maker's and Upholsterer's Drawing Book* of 1791, Sheraton wrote:

'In the same year [1788] I was given a quarto book of different pieces of furniture, with *The Cabinet-Maker's London Book of Prices*; and, considering that it did not make its appearance under the title of *A Book of Designs*, but only to illustrate the prices, it certainly lays claim to merit, and does honour to the publishers. Whether they had the advantage of seeing Hepplewhite's book before theirs was published I know not; but it may be observed, with justice, that their designs are more fashionable and useful than his, in proportion to their number.'

So successfully did Shearer express the unique spirit of simplicity and elegance which had evolved by the 1780's in English furniture-making that a great deal of furniture that is now loosely regarded as 'Hepplewhite' might more justly be ascribed to Shearer.

In the second and third editions of the *Book of Prices*, published in 1793 and 1803 respectively, six of the nine additional plates that were included were stated to have been drawn by Hepplewhite. These might have been plates which Shearer acquired from the designer during the latter's lifetime, but otherwise must have been supplied by an unknown draughtsman working for the firm of Hepplewhite and Co.

Shearer was probably responsible for perpetuating through the 1780's and '90's the swan-neck pediment on bookcases, bureaux and cabinets. This was a characteristic Chippendale *Director* device which was not adopted by Hepplewhite; it was however, retained by Sheraton. At the same time he used the more fashionable shell-like angle ornaments, urns, and curved pediments. He did not favour to the same extent the more delicate features that Hepplewhite indicated, such as festoons of husks between the urns. Shearer also continued to use the solid bracket feet of the Chippendale mode, though he also shows one or two examples of Hepplewhite's newer slender, swept bracket-foot, and even carried the idea further with the tall curved legs of his 'Lady's Dressing-Table'. Shearer was particularly fond of ingeniously-fitted dressing- and writing-tables, incorporating elaborate mechanical movements. He also shows a greater variety of these types than does Hepplewhite, including several for tambour writing-tables, cylinder-fall desks, and for portable desks, tambour ink-stands and dressing-cases, most of them with ingenious and complicated interior fitments. One of his most distinctive characteristics is that he carried the serpentine form of cabinets and tables, which had been a development of the rococo period, to fresh degrees of elegance. Hepplewhite had shown a few charming designs for serpentine chests, but Shearer may have been the means by which the French spirit was expressed in many serpentine-fronted chests commodes and library tables of the period. Almost all Shearer's designs show neo-classical features such as tapering legs and classical decoration, and his minor articles of furniture, such as corner 'bason-stands' and shaving-stands, and other bedroom and dressing-room accessories, embody the modern spirit more completely than did similar articles in Hepplewhite's book, where they retain much more of the flavour of the *Director* period.

One of Shearer's most important contributions to the development of furniture design was the semi-circular cellaret-sideboard. This admirable form, which became so characteristic of the late eighteenth century dining-room, survives in many articles which closely follow Shearer's designs.

The *Book of Prices* was practical to an even greater extent than was Hepplewhite's book, and many details are shown of the interior fittings of dressing-tables and chests, washing-stands, library desks and writing-tables. Important features which are commonly regarded as especially typical of the Sheraton period such as the spade-foot, or tapering block of square section for legs of tables and cabinets, etc., and also the foot which consists of a small, square block above a slightly shaped foot, are shown in this work.

The continued popularity of Shearer's designs over a great many years is remarkable, especially during the early Regency period, when new fashions and influences, often of a most outlandish kind, were being more and more eagerly sought. However, the drawings in the *Book of Prices* had the great advantage of being so essentially practical that they greatly facilitated the execution of the designs. They were moreover free of those extravagances of ornament that might put off the average customer of a more democratic age, or cause a piece of furniture to appear dated in a short time. For such reasons the designs retained for a long time their appeal for the more conservative public, even if they were no longer 'in the newest taste'.

THE ADAM CRAFTSMEN

The period of sixty or seventy years after 1760 represented not only the zenith of English cabinet-making, in the achievement of a perfect harmony between the quality of the materials, the excellence of the design, and the standard of craftsmanship, but also in the position of cabinet-making and the furniture trade which had become one of the largest and most prosperous sections of British industry. In relation to the population of the principal cities — the inhabitants of London numbered less than a million during the Adam period — the volume of work in the furniture trade was immense. This is evident from the size of such firms as those of Chippendale, of Gates and of Seddon, which last employed over four hundred workmen, although many of them would have been employed in ancillary trades like decorative or upholstery work. In these circumstances it is surprising that so little is known concerning the making of the furniture for the Adam houses. In only a few instances do any considerable number of accounts or other documents exist, as at Harewood, Croome Court and Nostell Priory, but mostly such records are sparse and inconclusive.

Adam's relations with his craftsmen varied considerably. Samuel Norman seems to have executed his designs faithfully, so far as we can tell from the furniture for Arlington Street which corresponds closely to Adam's drawings and which is usually supposed to have been made by this craftsman (see page 123).

William France prefaced his accounts for the furniture he made for Kenwood with the statement that 'the undermentioned articles are what I perform'd from Mr. Adam's designs'. On the other hand, in some instances Adam seems to have stood in a state of some detachment from the craftsmen who supplied furniture to his houses, as in the case of Thomas Chippendale, whose work has been discussed fully in chapter four.

Yet it was by means of the furniture-makers and purveyors that the Adam ideals attained their widest realization, for through them the new spirit of grace and refinement entered into thousands of homes where no interior decorative work of Adam character was ever executed. In his *Lectures on Architecture* (1809–36) Sir John Soane wrote:

'The light and elegant ornaments . . . were soon applied in designs for Chairs, Tables, Carpets, and every other species of Furniture. To Mr. Adam's taste in the Ornaments of his Buildings and Furniture we stand indebted, inasmuch as Manufacturers of every kind felt, as it were, the electric power of this Revolution in Art.'

Much work remains to be done in identifying the craftsmen responsible for the familiar masterpieces of Adam-style furniture in Adam's great houses, such as the principal pieces at Syon, and the splendid works in neo-classical style that, appearing as it were out of some limbo of lost treasures, come to light in the salerooms from time to time. The following brief accounts of the principal cabinet-makers and firms associated with furniture of the Adam and Hepplewhite period may serve to aid those who are endeavouring to connect more closely the craftsmen and individual pieces of the period. They are arranged in alphabetical order.

SAMUEL BECKWITH

The partner of Edward France (q.v.), his name is included among the Royal cabinet-makers from 1784 to 1810. He was a subscriber to Sheraton's *Cabinet-Maker's Drawing Book* (1791–4), and supplied furniture to the Earl of Verulam at Gorhambury Park in 1795, at which date his address was given as 101 Great St. Martin's Lane.

CHIPCHASE AND LAMBERT

Information regarding this hitherto unknown firm has been brought to light by Mr. Anthony Coleridge,[1] in the course of identifying certain furniture supplied to the Duke of Atholl at Blair Castle, Fifeshire. In bills which are preserved at the Castle the firm is described as 'Upholsterers, Cabinet-makers, etc., Warwick Street, Golden Square,' London. Furniture referred to in the bills includes a set of painted chairs and a settee, and a set of gilt chairs and a settee.

[1] A. Coleridge, op. cit.

JOHN COBB

John Cobb was in partnership at 72 St. Martin's Lane, London, until 1765 with William Vile, the celebrated cabinet-maker to King George III, whose finely carved mahogany furniture in a vigorous form of the rococo style is unsurpassed even by the productions of the firm of Chippendale. From 1766 onwards Cobb was in business alone, and appears to have enjoyed considerable repute. J. T. Smith records[1] that King George III 'frequently employed him for cabinet work of the most elaborate and expressive sort' while at the same time he 'smiled at his pomposity'. Smith called him 'one of the proudest men in England', and of 'singularly haughty character'. The fact that he left a fairly considerable fortune speaks of the success and scope of his business. Only a few articles may be ascribed to him with certainty, principally the remarkable commode and pair of vase-stands at Corsham Court, for which the maker's bill exists.[2] This commode is of *bombé* rococo form, the panels inlaid with vases of flowers with oval medallions surrounded by strings of husks. The doors have classical borders of a bold key pattern, containing an inverted honeysuckle device which may be taken as a distinguishing Cobb feature, and which suggests that a similar commode in the Victoria and Albert Museum is from Cobb's firm.[3] Another similar commode is in the Hart Collection at the Villa Millbrook, Jersey.[4] The possibility of other articles of classical form by Cobb coming to light must not be discounted.

A number of articles are recorded as having been supplied to Croome Court by the firm of Vile and Cobb up to 5 July 1760, and by John Cobb from 1764 to 1765 and from 1768 to 1773, but, whether the items are of neo-classical character does not emerge from the accounts, except in the case of the remarkable chairs supplied for the gallery at Croome Court in 1765. The arms and front feet were carved by Cobb while the rest was executed by Seferin Alken, who was responsible for much carving in the house (Fig. 58 and see page 63).

RICHARD COLLINS

This craftsman is known only through his having supplied to Sir Watkin Williams Wynne at 20 St. James's Square 'Two Bookcases Extraordinary, to a

[1] J. T. Smith, *Nollekens and his Times*, 1829, Vol. II, p. 243.   [2] Edwards and Jourdain, Fig. 58.
[3] Edwards and Jourdain, Fig. 57 and J. Hayward, *Commodes*.
[4] Clifford Musgrave, *The Connoisseur*, June 1965.

design of Messrs. Robt and James Adam. £15:18:7¼d.'. They were of 'rich mahogany' with '12 Ovall Patterae let into the Legs' and '130 Small [Paterae] let into the Pannells of the Doors'.

The account is among those preserved at the National Museum of Wales, and the relevant designs are at the Soane Museum (vol. 17, no. 220–2, and vol. 23, no. 239).

WILLIAM FRANCE

This cabinet-maker is notable for having supplied most of the furniture to Lord Mansfield for one of Adam's most important houses, Kenwood, where his accounts are preserved. He is also significant in being one of the few craftsmen to state that his work was 'performed from Mr. Adam's designs', but he does not seem to have been associated with any work of strikingly neo-classical character. The sofas supplied by him to Kenwood in 1768[1] have the Kentian shell back-rail ornament and outward-scrolling arms with coin-moulding, of Adam's early semi-baroque style, while the legs are very stumpy, and in a rather florid neo-classical style more suggestive of late Regency furniture than of the Adam style in its purest and most elegant form. France was one of the important makers of furniture to the Royal Family, from 1763 onwards. By 1770 he was described as 'the late William France', but the firm of France and Beckwith, with his son Edward as partner, of St. Martin's Lane, was still supplying furniture 'by Order of the Lord Chamberlain for His Majesty's Service' in 1791. They were included in the list of master cabinet-makers at the end of Sheraton's *Drawing Book* which was published in that year.

WILLIAM GATES

Although so few pieces by this cabinet-maker have been authenticated, they are of such outstanding excellence and so distinctive in character that it would be surprising if no other examples survive to be identified. His speciality was marquetry furniture inlaid with neo-classical designs, and his principal known works are the pair of commodes[2] made for the Prince of Wales's apartment in

[1] R. Edwards, *The shorter dictionary*, Fig. 48.   [2] R. Edwards and M. Jourdain, Fig. 143.

the Queen's House, St. James's Park, in 1781. Gates's bill describes them as 'two very fine Sattenwood inlaid commode tables to stand under piers . . . the doors, drawers and tops richly engraved with urns, vases, flowers and other ornaments in wood of different colours.' The Prince of Wales had a pair of somewhat similar inlaid commodes[1] made for Carlton House and later placed them in the oriental surroundings of the Brighton Pavilion, despite the classical vases within laurel wreaths with which the doors are decorated. These, too, are almost certainly by Gates. He also supplied a pair of 'superb tripods or therms' to the Prince, who is mentioned by Gates in a note on his bill.

JOHN GILBERT

This craftsman was a carver of some importance during the 1750's, when he supplied considerable quantities of furniture for the Mansion House, including carved mirror-frames and brackets. During the Adam period he supplied furniture to Lord Shelburne at Shelburne (later Lansdowne) House. The Shelburne accounts record that between March 1767 and December 1768 he charged for 'carving a table frame enriched for hall' and 'making carving and gilding in burnished gold a large glass frame with ornaments at top and bottom'.

GILLOW AND SON

The firm of Gillow, of Lancaster and London, was one of the largest and most famous of the furnishing firms of the late eighteenth and early nineteenth centuries. The founder, Robert Gillow, established the firm at Lancaster, and in 1757 took his son Richard into partnership. The London premises in Oxford Street were taken in 1760. In 1772 the firm was known as Gillow and Taylor, in 1776 as Gillow, and in 1790 as Robert Gillow and Company. In 1811, on the death of Richard, the title became G. and R. Gillow and Company. The business continued to be carried on for many years later under that name, although no members of the family were connected with it. Their records for several years, in the form of a series of cost-books, which are still preserved by the firm, provide an invaluable source of information on the furniture of the late eighteenth century.

[1] R. Edwards and M. Jourdain, Fig. 142.

Gillows specialized in furniture for export to the West Indies and other colonies, and in articles of sound and unpretentious domestic type, and few articles of pronounced neo-classical style are known. The significance of the firm for our present study is that they were an important factor in disseminating throughout the domestic market the ideas of refinement and delicacy in furniture expressed in the designs of Hepplewhite and, to a greater extent, of Sheraton.

WILLIAM INCE AND JOHN MAYHEW

This firm is chiefly famous for the large folio volume of designs which they published in parts between 1759 and 1763 entitled *The Universal System of Household Furniture*. These designs are all rococo in character, and are very similar to those in Chippendale's *Director*, a work which it follows very closely in scope. As the firm was active, however, from 1758 to as late as 1810, not a little of the furniture they produced must have been in neo-classical style. Documentary records of the firm are scarce, and very little furniture can definitely be assigned to the firm. A set of twenty-four chairs were supplied by them in 1793 to the Westminster Fire Office, where they remain today.[1] The backs are carved with Prince of Wales's feathers (a common Hepplewhite motif) above the portcullis badge of the Office.

Numerous items are recorded in the accounts of Croome Court as having been supplied to the house by the firm between 1757 and 1792, but again the character of the pieces is evident from the descriptions only in a few instances. A pair of commodes mentioned in a bill for 21 September 1765 have their doors inlaid with classical vases (Fig. 119). They were displayed in the momentous exhibition 'The Adam Style in furniture' at the Iveagh Bequest, Kenwood House, London, in 1764 (Catalogue no. 6). These articles are very remarkable in displaying neo-classical marquetry and plain rectangular form at a date when Adam's neo-classical designs were confined to the straight-legged side-tables at Syon. Marquetry of comparable character does not appear in other furniture, even in the work of Chippendale, until 1770. That articles of such strongly individual character should have been produced as early as 1765 suggests the existence of a designer of unusual talent connected with the firm. He would most probably have been one of the partners, since they had produced one of the most celebrated furniture

[1] R. Edwards, preface to *The Universal System*, reprinted 1960. Edwards and Jourdain, p. 158.

design books of the period. Such a designer would have been fully equal to producing the revolutionary design of the tapestry-covered furniture for Croome Court (Fig. 102) in 1769, for which they made special note in their account that they had supplied 'the patterns' (see page 66). It is evident that the firm was of considerable standing and size, and it would be remarkable if a fair amount of furniture of Adam or Hepplewhite character by them had not survived.

PETER LANGLOIS

It seems highly probable that this craftsman was the Pierre Eloi Langlois (1738–1805) whose work is described by Salverte,[1] although this authority makes no mention of his working in England. His trade card, issued from Tottenham Court Road, is printed in French and English, and states 'all sorts of fine cabinets and commodes made and inlaid in the politest manner with brass and tortoise-shell, and likewise all rich ornamental clock cases and inlaid work mended with great care'.

It was stated in Mortimer's *Universal Director*, 1763, that he 'performs all sorts of curious inlaid work, particularly commodes in the foreign taste inlaid with tortoiseshell, brass, etc.'. Metal inlay of the kind associated with Boulle (1642–1732) never entirely went out of fashion in France throughout the eighteenth century, and was revived during the Regency period in England, but any of the work of Langlois in England during the Adam period is more likely to be of wood inlay.

Langlois is the only cabinet-maker who is specifically mentioned in documents as being connected with Syon. The first Duchess of Northumberland noted the purchase of 'a table inlaid woods by Langlois', which is probably one of the inlaid card-tables in the gallery at Syon (see page 88), and he may conceivably have made several of the other articles of delicate character there: he must not, however, be supposed to have executed all the furniture at Syon, particularly such sturdily magnificent pieces as the gilt side-tables in the drawing-room (Fig. 93). Chippendale, Vile and Linnell are all known to have supplied furniture to the Duke of Northumberland, and are more likely to have been responsible for such monumental pieces as these. A bill amongst the Croome Court papers (no. 18) dated 20 June 1764, records that the Earl of Coventry bought from the London

[1] Salverte, *Les ébénistes du dixhuitième siècle*, p. 181.

workshop of Langlois a commode having 'floral marquetry with gilt bronze mounts'. This commode, which stood in the tapestry room at Croome, was also transferred to the Metropolitan Museum, New York. It is of pure rococo character, with the richly ornate type of floral inlay associated with this craftsman.[1]

A pair of handsome and unusual commodes, inlaid in the neo-classical manner, and with ram's-head mounts, which are in the state bedroom at Woburn Abbey, may also be ascribed to Langlois (Fig. 124). He is known from a bill at Woburn to have supplied a commode to the Duke of Bedford in 1762, but this is most probably the splendid rococo piece now in the private apartments there.

The neo-classical commodes are mentioned in an inventory of 1771, and they are eminently of the class of furniture described on Langlois' trade-card, which was printed in French and English, 'Inserulez des fleurs en Bois et Marqueteries garnies de Bronzes doreez'[2] (see also Note 11, p. 174).

A pair of inlaid pier-tables and a set of painted and gilt furniture of about 1770 at Audley End are attributed to Langlois by Ralph Edwards.[3]

JOHN LINNELL

John Linnell is the craftsman who, next to Thomas Chippendale and Samuel Norman, is believed to have been concerned most considerably in the supply of furniture for the Adam houses. He is also notable in that a greater quantity of his original drawings for furniture survives than is the case with any other craftsman. These are preserved at the Victoria and Albert Museum, in many large folio boxes, and in a volume containing a selection made in 1800 by the architect Charles Heathcote Tatham, who referred on the title page to Linnell as 'in the first line of his profession'.[4] The names of the clients which are marked on each drawing are evidence of the repute in which he was held. They include Lord Scarsdale, Mr. Lascelles, the Duke of Cumberland, Mr. Thrale, Lord Donegal, Lord Poulett and Peter Beckford.

Linnell's 'House and Ware Rooms' were at 28 Berkeley Square, and his predecessor there was William Linnell, presumably his father or uncle. He died in 1796.

1 *Decorative art from the Samuel H. Kress Collection*, Fig. 1.
2 See also E. H. Pinto, The furniture . . . at Woburn Abbey. Article in *Apollo*, March 1956.
3 R. Edwards and M. Jourdain, 'Georgian cabinet makers', p. 103.
4 P. Ward-Jackson, p. 54.

Comparatively few of the drawings are neo-classical in character; the majority are rococo designs for mirror-frames (Figs. 25–8). Linnell's draughtsmanship is vigorous and fluid in character, unlike Adam's rather hesitant, spotty manner. It possesses a lively engaging quality especially well suited to his more baroque designs.

The principal Adam houses with which Linnell was connected are Kedleston, Shardeloes, Croome and Osterley. The Kedleston furniture has already been fully discussed (see page 85). At Shardeloes, Linnell provided furniture between 1763 and 1768, by the end of which time his bills amounted to £1,056. An undated drawing of pier-glasses and tables for Shardeloes (no. E241) in the Victoria and Albert collection shows, by means of a flap, alternative treatments for the cresting, one with an urn between sphinxes, the other showing a vase between foliate scrolls. The drawing is not known to have been executed. One of the pair of splendid mirrors and gilt wood side-tables once in the drawing-room at Shardeloes is now in the collection of the Rijksmuseum, Amsterdam,[1] but no design of Adam's or bill of Linnell's for these pieces is known.

The assumption that Linnell supplied the furniture for Osterley is based on a reference in one of Linnell's Shardeloes accounts, for 2 October 1767, in which he refers to the making of urns and pedestals for the dining-room at Shardeloes 'like Mr. Child's' (at Osterley) (Fig. 139). Among Linnell's drawings are several for chairs with lyre-shaped splats, and inserts of portrait medallions, similar to those seen in furniture at Osterley, and one design in the Tatham volume shows a trefoil-shaped back closely resembling the library chairs there (Fig. 64). Many instances occur in the drawings also of Linnell's characteristic Vitruvian scroll ornament, which is seen in the frieze of the library tables at Osterley (Fig. 39), and in writing-tables there and at Syon and Alnwick. This ornament is distinctive in the flattening given to the curves of the scroll where the two directions of the wave-pattern join in the centre. This type of ornament, and also the motif of ormolu swags on the legs of tables, is represented in Linnell's drawing no. 303 in Tatham's volume (Fig. 36), and has its prototype in Adam's drawing of a table for Sir Charles Farnaby of 1765 (Fig. 17).

Linnell's ornament is often similar to that in Adam's own drawings, especially in the case of mouldings composed of rosettes in a *guilloche* or in an interlace. As Adam must have been acquainted with Linnell from 1759, when the former began his work at Shardeloes, until the late years of the 1780's when Osterley

[1] E. Harris, Fig. 146.

was being completed and furnished, their association was undoubtedly extremely close, and it is hardly surprising that similar features are to be found in their compositions. A drawing (V. & A.M. Box W3, 369, 4 Sept. 1773), intended for Lady Abdy, is for a typical Adam semi-circular side-table, with bulbous baluster-type legs and block capitals. Another design (V. & A.M. Box W3, 375) is for a palm-tree vase-stand, similar to those made for Kedleston, but intended for the Duke of Cumberland.

Documentary evidence exists that Linnell supplied furniture to the Earl of Harrowby to the value of £400 up to 1 August 1777,[1] and to the Duke of Northumberland in 1765 and 1766.

At Ammerdown, in Somerset, Linnell was employed by Thomas Samuel Joliffe in 1795, together with the firm of Thomas Andrewes, in the furnishing of the house, which had been built by James Wyatt seven years earlier. Linnell seems to have provided the more important furniture, including the side-tables in the dining-room described in his account as 'gilt in burnished gold in the best manner for your slabs', at a cost of £15:15:0, and an especially beautiful set of satinwood furniture in the drawing-room. Linnell charged £44:0:0 for '8 Satinwood tablet-backed elbow chairs' and £28:0:0 for '2 large sophas to match'. An attractive feature of the furniture is the unusual design of the arms. The termination of these is carved with a ball enclosed by a cluster of four bay leaves. Several of the pieces retain their original green tabaret covering.[2]

WILLIAM MOORE

This craftsman is known to have been in business in Dublin from about 1782, after having worked with the firm of Ince and Mayhew in London.[3]

In an advertisement in the *Dublin Evening Post* (May 1782) he speaks of having brought the manufacture of inlaid work 'to such perfection to be able to sell for almost one half his original prices; as the greatest demand is for Pier-tables, he has just finished in the newest taste a great variety of patterns, sizes and prices, from three guineas to twenty; Card tables on a new construction (both orna-mented and plain) which appear like small Pier Tables . . .'. It would appear from this that many small pier-tables and folding card-tables now existing came from

---

[1] Harrowby Accounts, Vol. 337, Card 3.   [2] *Country Life*, 1929.
[3] R. Edwards and M. Jourdain, p. 112.

the workshop of William Moore. He flourished until about 1815. A bow-fronted marquetry commode in the Victoria and Albert Museum is attributed to him[1] on stylistic grounds. An oval medallion on the front is inlaid with a spray of flowers, and there is other delicate neo-classical marquetry of scrolling, vases, tripods, festoons and ribbons. In the later years of his career Moore described himself as a 'Cabinet and Pianoforte maker', and one of his instruments is illustrated in Fig. 170.

SAMUEL NORMAN

This craftsman was probably the one responsible for the execution of much of Adam's most important early furniture, that supplied to Sir Laurence Dundas, Bt., for his country seat, Moor Park, and for his London residence, 19 Arlington Street (see page 43).

He was in business in King Street, Covent Garden, together with James Whittle and John Mayhew in 1758, but a year later the premises were destroyed by fire and the partnership seems then to have broken up, for in 1759 Mayhew announced that he had joined forces with William Ince (see page 118). In 1763 Norman was described in Mortimer's *Universal Director* as 'Sculptor and carver to their Majesties, and Surveyor of the curious carvings in Windsor Castle' — a title reminiscent of a similar functionary in the legendary castle of Gormenghast.[2]

His address was then given as Soho Square. In that year it was stated he had supplied Sir Laurence Dundas with furniture 'to the amount of ten thousand'. This sum probably included the furniture for both of Sir Laurence's houses. Writing to the first Earl of Malmesbury, his mother mentions[3] that she had spent the whole morning with Norman 'partly at Whitehall and partly at his warehouse, and had given what are, for us, I think, large orders, though not as great as those of Sir Laurence Dundas'. It is almost beyond question that Norman made the gilt settees (Fig. 51), and chairs (Fig. 57), which were at Moor Park, and later at Arlington Street, and which correspond to Robert Adam's drawing in the Soane Museum (see page 43).

The amounts paid to Norman by Dundas must have represented an enormous amount of furniture, and since we know that Adam designed a number of pieces of furniture for that gentleman, it is likely that much of Norman's work for these

[1] R. Edwards and M. Jourdain, *Georgian cabinet-makers*, p. 113 and Fig. 232.
[2] Mervyn Peake, *Titus Groan*, 1946.
[3] *Letters of the First Earl of Malmesbury*, 1745–1820, Vol. 1, p. 94, August 20, 1763 (1870).

two houses was made under Adam's personal supervision. Much of the furniture from these, and possibly other houses where the two men collaborated remains to be identified.

The possible inspiration of the decoration and furnishings of Woburn Abbey in Robert Adam's designs has been touched upon (see page 43). It is known that Samuel Norman supplied much of the furniture at Woburn, including gilt sofas, chairs, mirrors and the state bed, in 1759 and 1760.[1] It is possible that the link with Adam and the house existed through his association with the craftsman.

R. PARKER

A craftsman of this name is recorded[2] as having made in 1782 a neo-classical commode which stood in the print room at Woodhall House, Hertfordshire, a house built for Sir Thomas Rumbold between 1777 and 1782 by the architect Thomas Leverton (see page 103).

JOSEPH PERFETTI

Joseph Perfetti is known to have executed gilded and painted stucco work at Lansdowne House, one of Adam's early town houses, begun in 1762 for the Earl of Bute and completed about 1769 for Lord Lansdowne.[3] The name Perfetti occurs also in the account books kept from 1770 to 1788 by John Parker, who employed Robert Adam in the decoration of Saltram House near Plymouth, Devonshire, between these years. In one instance, for 5 February 1778, the entry reads 'To Mrs. Perfetti for frames . . . £8:17:0'. Imagining a family of Italian stuccoists and gilders working in London, is it not possible that Mrs. Perfetti was the business manager, sending out accounts and receiving payments? There was a long and close friendship between Lord Lansdowne and John Parker, who were both Whigs and stayed for long periods at each other's houses and gambled together. It is likely that it was through this friendship that Adam was induced to carry out work for Parker at Saltram, so far from his usual field of activity (Figs. 100 and 101, see also page 95).

[1] G. S. Thomson, *Family background*, Cape, 1949.
[2] Article by C. Hussey in *Country Life*, February 7, 1925.   [3] Bolton, Vol II, p. 12.

WILLIAM RHODES

This craftsman is known to have supplied a pair of painted side-tables with marble tops for £72:0:0, to Lord George Sackville at Drayton House, Northamptonshire, in 1771. This was part of the scheme of decorating and furnishing undertaken by Rhodes in that year.[1] The side-tables are in the robust Adam manner with square legs tapering sharply to small leaf-and-ball feet. There are pendent ornaments and swags at the frieze, and a central oval under-cresting. A craftsman of the same name was established as an Upholder and Cabinet-maker at 127 Lower Holborn, opposite Fetter Lane, London, between 1779 and 1793.

GEORGE SEDDON AND SONS

Hepplewhite and Shearer disseminated the Adam influence throughout the furniture trade by means of their published designs, and one of the principal channels through which the spirit of these designs reached the public was in the form of furniture by the important firm of George Seddon and Sons.

More of this firm and its famous founder is known than of any other of the late eighteenth century, excepting perhaps Gillows of Lancaster. George Seddon was born in 1727, presumably of wealthy parents, because immediately after completing his apprenticeship at the age of twenty-three, he was established in the business of a master cabinet-maker on a grand scale at London House, Aldersgate. This house, built round a courtyard, had once been the Palace of the Bishops of London. Its pine-panelled state rooms now became the showrooms for the display of furniture and upholstery materials in a manner of great opulence.

Seddon was one of the subscribers to Chippendale's *Director*. In 1768, when the house was burned down, he was employing eighty cabinet-makers. After this and a second fire the premises were rebuilt, but a third disaster followed in which Seddon's younger daughter was burned to death. His twenty-one year old son George was taken into partnership in 1786, and four years later they were joined by the elder son Thomas, and by the son-in-law Thomas Shackleton. At this time the firm's stock was valued at £118,926. We are indebted to the curiosity and interest of a German novelist, Sophie von La Roche for the most complete description of a Georgian furniture establishment that exists.

[1] *The Antique Collector*, Nov.-Dec. 1949.

This lady recorded in her diary a visit to London House which she made on 16 September 1786. The diary, translated by Clare Williams, was published in 1933 under the title of *Sophie in London*. Sophie noted that four hundred men and women were employed in Seddon's workshops, which were established in a building of six wings, and in addition a 'saw-house where as many logs of fine foreign wood be piled, as firs and oaks are seen at our saw-mills. The entire story of the wood, as used for both inexpensive and costly furniture, and the method of treating it, can be traced in this establishment'. Sophie referred also to the 'gilders', or more properly brass-founders, who 'moulded the bronze into graceful patterns'. It is thus clear that Seddon carried out foundry work and gilding for the ormolu mounts and other metalwork for his furniture.

Many of the still numerous surviving articles of Hepplewhite furniture, and indeed also of furniture in the still popular simpler phases of the Chippendale style, must have come from the Seddon showrooms. One of these rooms, as Sophie observed, 'contained nothing but chairs, sofas and stools of every description, some quite simple, others exquisitely carved and made of all varieties of wood'. In other showrooms were arranged 'writing-tables, cupboards, chests-of-drawers, charmingly-fashioned desks, both large and small, work and toilet-tables in all manner of woods and patterns, from the simplest and cheapest to the most elegant and expensive'. One of the largest rooms was devoted to bedroom furniture, including four-posters complete with hangings and counterpanes. Sophie was most of all intrigued by 'the scheme of a dining-room'. 'It contained a mahogany table (obviously a cellaret-sideboard) some feet in breadth, of which a third on either side is reserved for drawers, with an opening in the middle like most writing-tables have . . . by pressing a spring where the drawers are indicated by attractive fittings, a lead-lined compartment flies open with shelves, where the wine-bottles are kept in water with the monteith fixed on either side. There were two pedestals of the same wood and made to match, and fine dark marble vases with lids to them on the side (top). In these pedestals are two tiny cupboards, one lined with sheet iron and meat-grillers on which plates can be heated by the red-hot iron beneath them; the other is meant to keep salt-cellars and other table utensils. The vases up above hold spoons, knives and forks.'

Although Seddon furniture must survive in large numbers, few pieces can be authenticated because the bills have rarely been preserved. A graceful shield-back chair in the Victoria and Albert Museum is associated with a bill made out in 1790 to Mr. D. Tupper, Guernsey. It belonged to a set of '18 Satinwood Elbow Chairs, round fronts and hollow can'd seats neatly Japanned-ornamented with roses in black and peacock feather binder', each costing 73/6. Other furniture of this set is still in existence.

An admirable account of the firm of Seddon and Sons has been given by Mr. G. Bernard Hughes.[1]

He describes at length Seddon's plate-glass manufacturing activities, and how Seddon, who must have been one of the first to apply large-scale factory production to furniture making, was keenly interested in new technical developments, especially improvements in the quality of steel, which brought about a lowering of running costs by reducing the time taken up by the re-sharpening of tools, and by the slow working caused by inefficient tools. Mr. Hughes has described in detail[2] a consignment of the furniture exported in 1793 by the firm of Seddon to the wealthy Norwegian timber-merchant Niels Aalls, Ulefoss Manor House, near Porsgrunn, where some pieces still remain with their priced record of each piece and date of payment. This furniture is mostly of mahogany, but one piece, a three-drawer chest, is japanned in white with a delicate ornament of lines in blue. This, and several other chests-of-drawers, are of the graceful form shown in Hepplewhite's *Guide* with the elegant outward-curving bracket-feet united by a curved apron-piece. One mahogany chest-of-drawers has the top drawer-front of secretaire form opening to form a desk, and the interior drawers and cupboard are fronted with satinwood.[2] Like several other pieces, this is called 'modern' in the bill, which may reflect the fact that the piece is in the new Hepplewhite style, and not in the domestic Chippendale manner of a few years earlier.

After the death of George Seddon, senior, in 1801, the sons George and Thomas succeeded as sole proprietors, Shackleton having died a little earlier, and members of the family continued in business, with various changes of partnership, until well into the reigns of King George IV and William IV.

ROBERT TUSON

This craftsman is known only by his having supplied furniture to Charles Rogers, a distinguished connoisseur and collector, some of whose furniture is now in the possession of the Plymouth Art Gallery and Museum.

[1] G. Bernard Hughes, 'George Seddon of London House'.   [2] Hughes, *loc. cit.*

Rogers, born in 1711, was Clerk of the Certificates at the London Customs House, and died in 1784. Robert Tuson's name first appears in the accounts of the Rogers Collection in 1759, and several times later. He is worthy of remark for having supplied to Rogers on 23 December 1772, 'a Sarcophagus-like Cabinet, etc. 17: 15: o:'. This was the mahogany cabinet which is now at Plymouth. The doors and sides are carved with serpentine fluting in the manner of certain Roman sarcophagi, and incidentally of the dado-panels in the library at Syon. The cabinet, like a low chest in shape, stands on four very ponderous but well-carved paw-feet; another central support in the form of a lion's tail was added to the front, three years later at a cost of 17/-, possibly because the cabinet was used to contain articles of considerable weight. Before the publication of the articles by Mr. James Melton,[1] this cabinet was mistakenly believed to be of Dutch origin.

VICKERS AND RUTLEDGE

This firm is described on their engraved trade card as 'Upholders and Cabinet-makers successors to Thomas Bailey, Conduit Street, Hanover Square'. The card shows a representation of a chair with straight legs, and an oval-back containing a bold carved anthemion device, similar to the satinwood chairs at Kedleston. The firm flourished c. 1775–80.

WALLE AND REILLY

This firm is recorded as having supplied a considerable amount of furniture to the Duke of Northumberland for Alnwick and for Northumberland House, London, in 1768 and 1769. It included 'A Bed a la Polonaise . . . carved and gilt . . .', a 'Compleat Bedsted with its Imperial Dome carved and painted in natural flowers . . . £60:16:0:' and '8 Cabrioles, carved and painted to match the Bedsted at £3:10:0:, £28:0:0:'. The 'Compleat Bedsted' is probably the one at present exhibited in the state apartments at Alnwick. One member of the firm may have been Henry Walle, Upholder, Carver and Gilder, whose address in 1786 was *The Royal Pavilion*, No. 109 St. Martin's Lane, London.

---

[1] *Charles Rogers and his furniture, Apollo*, December 1960 and January 1961.   [2] Heal, p. 182.

TYPES OF FURNITURE

CHAIRS, STOOLS AND WINDOW-SEATS

Hardly any designs by Adam for chairs survive, beyond those for
Osterley and Hill Street, and a few drawings of hall chairs. On the
other hand, these articles are among the most beautiful and characteristic articles in the whole range of furniture in the Adam style — at
Harewood alone there are at least ten variations of design among the chairs
supplied by Chippendale — and it seems scarcely credible that the enormous
output of chairs in a virtually limitless range of neo-classical designs from all the
great craftsmen of the day should have been stimulated without many more
designs having been produced by the master-hand than have come down to us. It
is of course conceivable that he was not in practice able often to concern himself
with designing moveable furniture, but only the more permanent decorative
features of a room such as pier-tables and mirrors.

If Hepplewhite summed up and fixed the Adam style with his *Guide*, he also
immortalized it in the domestic sphere. With his interpretation of the Adam
spirit in his oval- and shield-back patterns, Hepplewhite's chairs have become a
synonym for grace and beauty, even in their most simplified forms (Figs. 41 to 44).
It was probably through Hepplewhite's chair designs that the neo-classical vogue
reached its widest dissemination, and because of their adaptability to every degree
of quality, the spirit of elegance could be and usually was expressed even in the
robust productions of the country furniture maker, who continued to use this
source of inspiration until the end of the century and even beyond. In the extensive range of designs for the backs of chairs, embodying oval, shield, heart and
cartouche shapes, Hepplewhite exhibited remarkable fruitfulness of invention.
The shield-back pattern was not, however, invented by him, as is commonly
believed. A design by Adam for a shield-back hall chair exists (Soane, vol. 17, no.
104), and was executed for Byram, Yorkshire.[1]

[1] Bolton, Vol. II, p. 307.

Hepplewhite's ingenuity is none the less evident in the variety of designs for the ornamentation of the back within whatever enclosing form was chosen. These features included many of the familiar classical motifs; urns and festoons of drapery, ears of wheat, strings of bell-flower husks, rosettes and flowers. The Prince of Wales's feathers as a device for chair-backs is a famous Hepplewhite feature (Figs. 74 and 76) but though the firm claimed that one of their shield-back designs had 'been made with good effect for the Prince of Wales' this is not to say that the firm of Hepplewhite made it, nor is there any record in the Royal accounts of their name. In this respect, however, they are in good company with Chippendale and others. The use of the three ostrich plumes in furniture dates back to the time of George I, when it appeared as the cresting of looking-glasses, possibly indicating support for the Prince of Wales (who eventually became George II) in preference to his Teutonic father. The device appears also on mirrors made for Prince Frederick of Wales, son of George II, who did not survive to succeed his father. These, which were made in 1732 by Benjamin Goodison, are now at Hampton Court.[1] The greatest popularity of this decoration existed, however, in the time of George, Prince of Wales, the son of King George III. It was adopted widely in chairs, pediments of bookcases and cabinets, on bed testers and on mirrors, by adherents of the Whig party, with which the Prince had allied himself in opposition to his father. The device was thus for nearly a century an emblem of the Whig reversion.

Apart from these political implications, the plume of three feathers is a beautiful decorative feature in its own right, and there are many instances of the use of a single ostrich feather in furniture and in glass candelabra (see Note 10, p. 174).

In two of the Hepplewhite shield-back chair designs the back is placed low, instead of being set several inches above the seat, as is more usual. This brought about somewhat of an improvement in the harmony of the proportions (Fig. 44). Another variant of the shield-back in the first edition was the type in which the lower part was angular instead of rounded. The *Guide* recommended having a shield-back upholstered, and these stuffed chairs, of which many survive, were customary for drawing-room use (Fig. 44). Stuffed chairs were referred to in the *Guide* and in other works as 'Cabriole' chairs, the type originating from the chair-like single seat of the cabriolet, the light two-wheeled carriage similar to a modern trotting sulky that was invented by Joseph Child in 1755, and was the

---

[1] R. Edwards and M. Jourdain, *Georgian cabinet-makers*, Fig. 40.

rage in Paris during the Hepplewhite period. The word, whether applied to a chair-leg, a carriage, or a dance, originally derives from 'capriole' meaning a leaping step. Sheraton later made one of his numerous unfounded assertions when he spoke of the cabriole form deriving from a 'French easy chair' named after the person 'who invented or introduced them'.

In the first edition of the *Guide* there were several designs for oval-back chairs, but by the time the third edition was published in 1794 the type seems to have become sufficiently unmodish to have been illustrated only in the form of a hall-chair. Chairs with heart-shaped backs, often with splats of stylized wheat-sheaf form, are typical of the period, but were only represented by one design in the 1788 edition, and none at all in that of 1794. Wheel-back chairs, good examples of which are highly prized by connoisseurs, do not appear in Hepplewhite at all. Chairs with cartouche backs, of a broad inverted pear-shape, derive from the rococo taste (Fig. 44 left). They appear in Chippendale's *Director* (1754–62), and in the *Universal System* (1759–63) of Ince and Mayhew, where they are called 'French chairs'. Chairs with backs of this kind, but with legs and decoration of neo-classical character, are found at Syon and were also made by Chippendale for Harewood, but they are not represented in Hepplewhite. Horseshoe-backs were also popular, but only appear in a rather elaborate rococo form in one design of the first edition of the *Guide*. As we have already noted the square-backed chair that is usually regarded as being so distinctive of the Sheraton style was already represented in the first edition of Hepplewhite's *Guide*, which appeared three years before Sheraton's first work.

It was a more effective design than some of those which the Hepplewhite firm added to the work in the third edition in order to keep in line with the trend towards the more rectilinear style that was soon to prevail in English furniture.

Although Hepplewhite displayed so much originality in his proposals for carved decoration in his designs for chair-backs, he was less enterprising in the form of the legs. They were usually shown as square and tapering, though of great delicacy, and sometimes with a graceful outward curve (Fig. 41), in a manner unknown in Adam chairs but which was to become increasingly popular after the first publication of the *Guide* in 1788, from which date the cabriole leg passed more and more out of favour. The few suggestions that Hepplewhite makes for legs of round section are not elaborate, and consist mostly of a plain tapering shaft with a simple lotus-leaf capital. The fluting of chair-legs, which was one of the hallmarks of the neo-classical vogue, is almost non-existent in his designs (Fig. 42), and there are only two designs for reeding, one of them entwined with a ribbon, in a manner deriving from French Louis Seize models rather than from Adam.

Hepplewhite often provided his square-section chair-legs with a recessed panel on each face. This could be moulded, or left plain, or could have a plain line of beading, but was frequently decorated with a string of husks (Fig. 42). An ornament of overlapping acanthus leaves occurs very occasionally.

In the first edition of the *Guide* not only was the cabriole leg shown, which had remained generally popular since the 1750's and the days of the *Director*, but also the French scroll-foot (Fig. 44). The curved leg was retained in the third edition only for stools, and the scroll-foot had disappeared entirely. The spade-foot was favoured as a finish to a square reeded or fluted leg (Fig. 42), or one with recessed panels on the faces, and in one design, for a leg with leaf-capitals in the Adam manner, Adam's favourite leaf-carved knob-shaped foot was used, although this too was a popular feature of contemporary French chairs. In one design only, for an easy chair with wings, do stretcher-bars appear, although they were frequently added to chairs of Hepplewhite pattern, especially by country craftsmen who could not refrain from imparting a generous measure of provincial strength and robustness to urban delicacy.

Chairs were generally made of mahogany, unless intended for painting, when beech was more often used. The seats could be straight-fronted, bowed, or serpentine in form. In a design in the first edition the front seat-rail was indented, as in a cupid's bow, but with the third edition the straight lines of the neo-classical taste had triumphed over the curves of the rococo in this feature as well.

The seats of chairs were usually stuffed, and covered with red or blue morocco leather, with horsehair, or with silk, plain, striped, or chequered 'at pleasure' (Figs. 41 to 44). A favourite design for silk coverings was in the form of a painted classical medallion. The fashion for this type of decoration had existed for some years, at least since 1768, when in a letter from Woburn Abbey, Arthur Young remarked on the fact that the chairs and sofas 'in the Duchess's dressing room' were covered in 'painted taffeta'.[1]

The proportions recommended in the *Guide* for chairs were 'width in front 20 inches, depth of seat 17 inches, height of the seat frame 17 inches; total length about 3 feet 1 inch'. Different dimensions were 'frequently adopted according

[1] See R. Fastnedge, *English furniture styles*, 1955.

to the size of the room'. Most of the armchairs closely associated with Adam, such as those at Osterley, are of larger proportion than is suggested above, with seats twenty-five inches wide. French chairs of the Louis Seize period were also usually wider than this.

Hall-chairs, with their hard plain wooden seats and heavily carved backs, often embodying the arms of the owner, were intended for the servants, if for any practical use at all, and their designs tended to be uninviting to repose, perhaps intentionally so. Some of the few surviving chairs designed by Robert Adam are for hall-seats. His design for a shield-back chair (Soane: vol. 17, no. 104, c. 1780) may be the earliest of this type. Two others (vol. 17, no. 98) intended for Sir Abraham Hume, and dated 1778, are for circular backs, each with a variant of a honeysuckle design.[1] One of these had cross-framed supports. Another (vol. 17, no. 92), executed for Lord Coventry at Croome Court and dated 1767, is for a back of console design[2] anticipating the scrolled supports of Regency tables and seats based on designs for the antique published by C. H. Tatham in 1799.[3] The hall-chairs at Nostell, which Chippendale supplied, have circular backs carved with a shell design, and are made unusually comfortable by the addition of arms (Fig. 68).

Hepplewhite gave an elegant design for an oval-back and a shield-back type of hall-chair, and one with a back in the form of a large vase with festoons of drapery. This last pattern was frequently copied, but is among his less attractive compositions.

In what manner does the Adam chair differ from the French neo-classical chair of the Louis Seize period? As the latter type was not established before 1770 (see page 60), even if its origins are indeed earlier, no comparison can be made in articles before that date. Technically, the French chair is usually constructed from a greater number of separate pieces than an English chair. On the other hand the French joints were made with remarkable skill, the mortise and tenon joints often being strengthened with wooden plugs which prevented them from loosening with wear and time. French chairs were usually not so highly finished in the unseen parts as the English ones, and common woods including soft fruit-woods were used whereas English chair-makers more frequently used mahogany, or in the unseen parts, beech cased in a thick covering of mahogany. French chairs were usually painted whereas gilding was more general in England. Yet it is in the style and decoration that the differences are most apparent.

[1] E. Harris, Fig. 119.   [2] E. Harris, Fig. 110.
[3] See C. Musgrave, *Regency furniture*, Figs. 1 and 776.

The carving of a French chair is generally more florid and deeply executed than its English counterpart. In the latter the carving is permitted to interfere less with the fine flow of line. French chairs and other carved furniture often possess a 'shaggy' quality absent in English specimens. In general form French chairs tend to appear more ponderous than English examples, the seats wider and lower, the legs shorter and more stumpy. In the finest Hepplewhite chairs of the rococo French taste, the slender attenuation of line, which is so often characteristic of the English adaptation of French forms, surpasses in grace almost anything achieved by French chair makers.

The rear legs of French neo-classical chairs were usually set vertically, whereas those in English chairs were often splayed backwards, but there were many exceptions in both countries. The splaying of a straight neo-classical leg seems to have been an unsatisfactory solution of a difficult problem, that was sometimes settled by the use of a round-section plain leg curving backwards. Circular seats were frequently found in French chairs, whereas the English tended to favour an almost flat curved front rail, or one of serpentine form, but again there is no invariable rule.

STOOLS AND WINDOW-SEATS

The window-seats made for Croome Court to Adam's design in the mid 1760's (Fig. 18), and which he called 'sophas', had high outward curving ends.[1] The window-seats at Syon probably of the 1770's, have low scrolled ends, heavily upholstered on top as well as on the inner side. Also they have tapering, fluted legs of round instead of square section.

The Hepplewhite designs for this kind of furniture follow those of the Adam style in general character, varying only in the motifs of the carving, the shape of the legs, and in the degree of curvature in the high ends, two of the designs having the ends vertical, but with an outward curving roll-end (Fig. 49). The *Guide* specified that window-seats, of which six charming designs were given, should be made of a size to fit the space they were intended to occupy, and that the height should not exceed that of the accompanying chairs.

Stools were upholstered in similar materials to the chairs with which they were *en suite*, but the cabriole leg, in one instance with the French scroll-foot, continued to be shown for a stool in the third edition of the *Guide* although it had

[1] The stool itself is illustrated in E. Harris, Fig. 104.

been dropped for the chairs themselves. A concession to the neo-classical was made in the carving of the knees of the cabriole legs in a simplified shell-motif, or in the form of a string of husks instead of rococo leaf-carving. The seat-rails of rectangular stools were straight, serpentine or bowed like the corresponding chairs, but there were also designs for circular stools. Unlike the chairs, the seat-rails were completely covered with material fastened by a decorative double-row of brass-headed nails.

SOFAS AND SETTEES

Some confusion exists over the proper use of these terms, but they were used with considerable lack of precision by late eighteenth century designers and furniture-makers. We have already noted that Adam called his rather stiff stools or window-seats 'sophas', and Hepplewhite referred to sofas as settees. In the present section the modern practice will be adopted in speaking of sofas as completely upholstered articles, and settees as those consisting of an open frame with cushions. During the Adam period the shapes of sofas were affected by the same significant developments which occurred in the form of chairs.

With these developments, the design of sofas came to be influenced less by traditional English classicism, and more by the French spirit. Adam's adoption of French forms is also represented by his inclusion of the 'confidante' sofa in his repertory. This was an article of great elegance, having an additional separate seat at each end (Fig. 84).

The characteristic Hepplewhite sofas of the 1780's appear to have derived more directly from the rococo influence as expressed in Chippendale's *Director*, with only a slight infusion of neo-classical influence, but modified by that characteristic English attenuation of form that we noted when discussing Hepplewhite's designs for chairs (Fig. 40).

Hepplewhite specified that sofas should correspond with the chairs with which they were associated, both in the material of the frames and the covering. The proportions were to be based on a 'length between 6 and 7 feet, depth about 30 inches, height of the seat-frame 14 inches; total height in the back 3 feet 1 inch'. One of the most beautiful and characteristic of the Hepplewhite designs is the settee with the back made up as three, four or even five united shield-pattern chair-backs (Figs. 48 and 89).

A 'French sofa' with cabriole legs and scroll-foot in the first edition of the *Guide* was supplanted in the third edition of 1794 by a design in the new square-backed mode,[1] with square legs and angular arms. On the other hand a design not thus superseded was for a sofa of French character with a high serpentine back and arms sweeping forward in a continuous deep curve and fitted with straight legs. Many variations of this theme were practised by different craftsmen, who used the general form with varying types of leg-section — round, square, or like a clustered column in the Gothic fashion. Basically rococo in its graceful curvilinear form, this type of sofa remained a popular one almost until the end of the century (Fig. 47).

The French type of 'confidante' sofa which Adam had adopted was also featured by Hepplewhite, who remarked upon them as being 'in pretty general request' for large and spacious suites of apartments, and that 'an elegant drawing-room with modern furniture' was considered 'scarce complete' without one (Fig. 84). Another adaptable device of French origin, intended for the boudoir, was the *Duchesse* (Fig. 86). This consisted of two 'Barjier' (bergère) chairs and a large rectangular stool which could be assembled to form a chaise-longue or sofa for reclining upon, as in the photograph.

In France, long before the Revolution, the habit of reclining on sofas had become part of the increasing relaxation of social manners, and in this country similar tendencies followed, though with the disapproval of the older members of society. Mrs. Delaney tells how when the Princess Amelia paid a visit in 1772 'all the comfortable sophas and great chairs were banished for that day, and the blew damask chairs set in prim form around the room' in the formal manner upon which Humphrey Repton was to pour ridicule not many years later.[2]

CONSOLE-TABLES

PIER-TABLES AND SIDE-TABLES

Console-tables are strictly side-tables which are not entirely self-supporting, but are partly supported by, or at least ostensibly supported by, the wall. The main support is from consoles, or curved or scrolled bracket supports, which could be two, four or more in number, and may be carved in the form of figures. In later Georgian times the term console-table was often given indiscriminately to almost any kind of side-table or pier-table.

[1] R. Edwards, *Hepplewhite furniture designs*, Fig. 20.   [2] H. Repton, *Fragments*, 1816.

Although only one or two designs by Adam for console-tables exist, side-tables and pier-tables form the largest class of furniture for which his drawings survive, apart from mirrors and torchères. Adam no doubt devoted special attention to these articles because they were important adjuncts to 'the parade of life' and were usually the foremost necessities in the equipment of state rooms. Also, unlike chairs, which posed difficult problems of three-dimensional form, the designing of side-tables would be approached as a matter of drawing an elevation, which was more congenial to Adam.

Pier-tables were increasingly recognized as articles in a class distinct from side-tables in the Hepplewhite period. They were said by Hepplewhite to have 'become an article of much fashion, and not being applied to such general use as other tables, admit, with great propriety, of much elegance and ornament'. Indeed, they are often regarded as representative of the beauty of the Hepplewhite school at its best (see also page 109).

The *Guide* gave only two designs for these articles, one break-fronted, the other serpentine, both with deep and highly ornamented friezes (Fig. 51). It showed however eight designs for the tops of pier-tables or card-tables, which could be either inlaid or painted and varnished (Fig. 52). Legs were slender and tapering, either round or square in section, as was now universal. In general, Hepplewhite pier-tables displayed more influence from French Louis Seize models than did the designs of Robert Adam. Their proportions were intended to conform to the size of the pier walls between the windows of a room, and we are told in the *Guide* that the usual height of twenty-eight inches for a table could be exceeded so as 'to rise level with or above the dado of the room, nearly touching the ornaments of the glass'. Frequently they were very long in proportion to their depth, and with a bowed front.

CARD-TABLES

Card-tables, folding in the centre, with two of the legs extending on a gate to support the folding leaf when open, were of circular or serpentine form or rectangular with rounded corners. When not in use for card games, they served as side-tables or pier-tables, when their decorated tops were seen instead of their baize-lined inner surfaces (Figs. 128 and 129).

PEMBROKE TABLES

This type of table was said by Sheraton to have derived its name from that of 'the lady who first gave orders for one of them and who probably gave the first idea of such a table to the workmen . . .' presumably having in mind the Countess of Pembroke of his own day. But the type was in existence already by the middle of the century, and appears in Chippendale's *Director* of 1754, though under the name of a 'Breakfast Table', which has always been their primary purpose. The theory put forward by Mr. John Gloag that the Pembroke table was named after the 9th Earl, an amateur architect who died in 1750, is much more likely to be correct.[1]

They are at once among the most engaging and at the same time most useful types of furniture, expressive of the elegance and simplicity of the Adam and Hepplewhite school, and providing good opportunity for the display of marquetry or painted decoration, which often took the form of husks and shell-patterns. The Pembroke table that was probably designed by Adam himself for the Etruscan room at Osterley is painted in Etruscan taste.

The *Guide* showed two designs, for such tables, one oval-shaped, the other rectangular (Fig. 50), but a type with serpentine edges was also popular (Fig. 128).

COMMODES

Commodes lent themselves happily to the Adam approach to design, for their large surfaces were ideal for displaying the linear motifs of the neo-classical idiom. These articles include many of the loveliest creations of the Adam and Hepplewhite schools, and although few drawings by the architect himself survive (Figs. 114, 115 and 116), and are presumably only preliminary designs, they throw important light on several celebrated pieces in the Adam houses, and on the development of this class of furniture.

Although drawing-room commodes are among the most representative and often the most beautiful articles of the Hepplewhite school, only one design appears in the *Guide* (Fig. 117). This single design is for a semi-circular shaped example on curved bracket feet, but it is the precursor of innumerable pieces of

[1] Gloag, p. 355.

this form (Fig. 127). More usually they were made with feet of different character, round and fluted, or vase-shaped, and often carved with leaves. In many examples the feet are square in section, tapering, of greater or lesser length, sometimes even quite stumpy, and often having the faces of the legs recessed. It is probably on account of their having this kind of foot that so many semi-circular commodes are called 'Sheraton', although this designer did not illustrate the type at all in his first book of designs, the *Drawing Book* of 1791 or its subsequent editions. It is true that Sheraton made much use of the square, tapering foot, but the type had been established many years before by William Gates who made for King George III the superb pair of semi-circular satinwood commodes, inlaid with vases, which are at Buckingham Palace today.[1]

The height of charm in the semi-circular commode was probably attained in some of the painted examples, such as one in the Lady Lever Art Gallery.[2] This delightful piece is painted with oval panels containing figure subjects after Angelica Kauffmann, and has unusually shaped short legs carved with leaves, and having a square block faced with rosettes above the round tapering feet.

SIDEBOARDS

In the mid-eighteenth century sideboards had consisted merely of tables without drawers. One example illustrated in Chippendale's *Director* shows tapering legs of square section, and of the sturdy dimensions found in early Georgian furniture. They differed from ordinary side-tables in having mahogany tops instead of marble. After introducing at Kedleston in the 1760's, the idea of a unified sideboard composition with three small separate tables in the dining-room apse (see page 40) (Fig. 2), Adam developed the theme by adding pedestals with urns to provide formal equipment of great dignity for the important ceremonial function of the dining-room in his houses (Fig. 142). The large neo-classical sideboard, with its flanking urns and pedestals and with an oval wine-cooler below, provided by Chippendale for the dining-room at Harewood in 1771 is one of the most famous examples of this important type (Fig. 136). Several other designs survive. One, intended for the Duke of Cumberland and dated 1773,[3] has decoration in the 'Etruscan' style, with panels and bands of figures, and was presumably

[1] R. Edwards and M. Jourdain, Fig. 183.
[2] R. Edwards, *Dictionary*, Vol. II, Fig. 37.   [3] E. Harris, Fig. 34.

intended to be painted (see page 163). This treatment was frequently adopted for urns, pedestals and sideboards. It is interesting to note that a single sideboard-table was usually placed at the opposite end of the dining-room from the sideboard and pedestals. Even in small Adam houses, such as Marlborough House at Brighton, in 1787, the sideboard was fitted into a tiny apse of the dining-room.

In the later Adam period brass or bronze back-rails were fitted to sideboards, the uprights often being finished with small urns (Figs. 26 and 137). Candle-branches were sometimes attached to the rails. These galleries were intended to support silver dishes for display.

Hepplewhite's suggestions for sideboard-tables, pedestals and urns (or vases, as the compilers of the *Guide* preferred to call them) remained unchanged in the three editions of that work. Their one design for a large formal sideboard was a handsome one with four front legs and elaborately shaped front (Figs. 45 and 46). The *Guide* recommended that pedestals should be made to the same height as the sideboard, which was from twenty-eight to thirty-two inches, and were to be sixteen to eighteen inches square. Urns and pedestals of the earlier Adam period, about 1770, especially those from the firm of Chippendale, were often of a different proportion, the urns being taller and the pedestals lower than was the practice later. One pedestal would be fitted up as 'a plate warmer, being provided with racks and a stand for a heater'. It was lined with sheet iron for protection against the heat. The other pedestal sometimes served as a pot-cupboard, for elegance and coarseness existed simultaneously in the dining-rooms of the late eighteenth century just as they did in the drawings of Rowlandson in that age. The urns or vases were made either to serve as holders for cutlery, in which case the interiors were fitted with circular sacks with slots, or as water-cisterns 'for the use of the butler', or 'to provide iced water for drinking', the containers being lined with lead and furnished with a tap (Fig. 45).

A distinctive Hepplewhite creation derived from the sideboard and flanking urns has become one of the most characteristic articles of English furniture. This is the self-contained sideboard, consisting of a shallow centre-section (usually containing a drawer) supported on each side by two deep pedestals with drawers and cupboards (Fig. 135). One of the latter could be fitted for bottles, and other with a lead lining to hold water used for rinsing glasses or cutlery. The centre drawer was used for table linen. Under the Hepplewhite influence fillets or spandrels linking the centre portion with the pedestals were often elegant features sometimes treated as a fan or shell ornament (Fig. 135). In some instances there would be a horizontally sliding tambour-front covering a shelf below the central drawer.

Knife cases, intended to stand separately on sideboards or sidetables, were highly ornamental, being made in veneers of mahogany selected for their beautiful grain, and with sloping tops and fronts of bowed, serpentine, or concave-convex shape. These were featured in all editions of the *Guide*.

CELLARETS AND WINE-COOLERS

Cellarets and wine-coolers are identical in their outside appearance. The former are divided into compartments for bottles, and were intended for storing wine in the dining-room. Wine-coolers were lined with lead and the bottles were kept in them surrounded by ice during a meal. Under the Adam influence cellarets and coolers assumed an oval form, with serpentine fluting on the sides and with lion-paw feet, deriving from the decoration on the sides of ancient sarcophagi (Fig. 166), but it was not until later that the term 'sarcophagus' came into general use for these articles. The lids were often fluted radially like a shell, and finished with a knob of pineapple design.

A handsome mahogany wine-cooler now in the Wernher Collection at Luton Hoo, Bedfordshire, and once at Kenwood, appears in the engraving of the sideboard composition for the latter house in *The Works* (vol. 1, no. 2, Plate VIII).[1] It was probably made by William France about 1770 and differs from the engraving in having lion-masks instead of human-masks, round instead of square feet, and in having round the lid an egg-and-dart moulding of a kind that Adam never used after his early days.

There are no designs for cellarets or wine-coolers of a neo-classical character in Hepplewhite's *Guide*. The only illustrations are for the simple tub-like articles similar to those included in Chippendale's *Director*; oval or hexagonal in shape, and made of mahogany encircled with bands of brass, and standing on four sturdy square-section splayed legs of square section.

STANDS, PEDESTALS OR TERMS

Adam drew strongly upon early Georgian inspiration in the design of his early term-pedestals, especially upon examples such as those designed almost certainly

[1] Illustrated as executed in E. Harris, Fig. 20.

by William Kent for Rousham House, Oxfordshire, about 1735–40, which they follow very closely in shape, the chief differences being in the scale, though not the character, of the classical ornament. These have already been fully discussed in Chapter two (Fig. 19).

Pedestals associated with the Adam houses were usually painted to accord with the decoration of the room. But by 1788, when Hepplewhite's *Guide* was published, they were 'generally made of mahogany with the ornaments carved', although examples in satinwood with inlaid decoration or with mounts of ormolu are also found (Fig. 143); these may date from the 1770's or later.

The popularity of terms for the display of busts may be judged by the fact that eight designs were included in the *Guide*, most of them closely following Adam's designs, such as those already mentioned.

TRIPODS

The various types of tripod-stands that evolved in the time of Robert Adam have already been fully described in Chapter two. It is remarkable that although tripod stands of various types were in such evidence in Adam rooms and still survive in considerable numbers, no designs appear in the *Guide* for articles of this kind. The candlestands shown therein are chiefly of the simpler single-stemmed sort, more elaborate examples of which are the palm-tree pedestals in the bedroom at Kedleston (Fig. 37). One design for a tall, slender three-legged stand bears no relation to Adam's classical types, neither do two other stands with multiple candle or lamp-holders. This type however, became extremely popular and must have been made in very large numbers, to judge by the many beautiful examples that survive today, displaying extreme beauty of line and richness of decorative invention.

TAMBOUR WRITING TABLES

Tambour writing tables were usually articles of extreme delicacy on square tapering or round-section fluted legs, and were often handsomely decorated with inlaid neo-classical motifs (Fig. 175). The table top had one or two shallow drawers, and fitments for papers at the back. As illustrated in the *Guide* the sides are made of quadrant shape in front, and the tambour shutter runs over the top in grooves at the sides. Some examples were fitted with a shelf above and a brass gallery. In many instances the tables opened on both sides which were of similar quadrant shape. A beautiful specimen of such a table, possibly by Langlois (see page 88) is at Syon House.[1]

LIBRARY TABLES

The two magnificent library tables at Nostell and Harewood (Figs. 166 and 167) are among the masterpieces of the Adam movement, yet no drawings for such pieces from the hand of Robert Adam himself survive. Their design, which may owe more to the makers than to the architect, represents admirably the unfolding of tradition in the work of four or more great designers and craftsmen over three-quarters of a century.

Hepplewhite's *Guide* has only three designs for library tables, and these are of plain character and moderate size, obviously intended for more modest house-holds (Fig. 54). In this sphere his designs belong once again to the furniture of private domestic character with which Adam does not seem to have concerned himself. The most elaborate of the Hepplewhite library tables follows the traditional kneehole pattern of a plain top with a central drawer, supported on pedestals with plinth bases (Fig. 54). Like one of Chippendale's designs, both sides of the top are recessed in the centre. The pedestals have cupboards with a drawer above, and are framed with pilasters carved with scrolled leaf capitals and pendants of husks. Two other designs in the *Guide* have drawers, or mock-drawers in the pedestals; in one example they are bow-fronted. All these follow the style of the *Director* very closely.

LIBRARY BOOKCASES

Library bookcases have always, and especially in the days of William Kent and of Thomas Chippendale, provided a vehicle for the display of the characteristic decoration of their period, even though the form of the bookcase itself has changed little since about 1720 until modern times. Hepplewhite illustrated

[1] R. Edwards, *The shorter dictionary*, p. 563, Fig. 29.

four designs for large bookcases, ranging in height from six to thirteen feet, of conventional form with cupboards and drawers in the lower part, and a plinth base. The shelves above were fronted with glass doors from four to eight in number according to the length of the bookcase (Fig. 55). Many library bookcases incorporated a secretaire in the central portion, which was often of break-front form. The wings were frequently lower than the centre, but occasionally of the same height. As in the case of bureau-bookcases, library bookcases gave limitless opportunities for delightful variations in the patterns of glazing-bars, of which the *Guide* showed several examples.[1] These were often of rectangular or lattice design, the crossings sometimes ornamented with rosettes and other devices. Arched designs of Gothic character were popular, and so were neo-classical patterns based on scrolls of foliage, swags, and the outlines of vases with drapery. Adam is not known to have designed furniture of this class.

BUREAU-BOOKCASES

Once more it is with a type of furniture with which Adam seems not to have concerned himself directly, that the elegance and refinement of the Adam movement permeated the world of domestic furniture, for bureau- or secretaire-bookcases are among the most numerous surviving examples of the Adam and Hepplewhite style. They are also among the most charming specimens, especially on account of the delicacy and variety of the glazing-bar designs. In general form, however, they represent a development of the tradition embodied in Chippendale's *Director*.

The bookcase tops were either divided by two glazed doors, or made with a central section flanked by smaller wings (Fig. 173). The sloping desk-front opened flat and rested upon slides. The feet were usually of bracket form or splayed in the mid-century manner, but the neo-classical influence was seen in the treatment of the bookcase top, upon which 'when ornamented, is placed, between a scroll or foliage, a vase, bust or other ornament, which may be of mahogany, or gilt, or of light-coloured wood'. As shown by Hepplewhite, this decoration was fairly reticent and of small, delicate scale. One design shows only a simple *cavetto* moulding. What appear to be Gothic dentils in the cornice are seen in another. With Sheraton, from 1791 onwards, there was a return

---

[1] R. Edwards, *Hepplewhite furniture designs*, Fig. 44.

to swan-neck pediments and other elaborate features of the *Director* period.

The secretaire-bookcase was distinguished from the bureau-bookcase only in 'not being sloped in front' (Fig. 53). The desk-flap was upright and finished as a drawer-front, and the writing surface was 'produced by the face of the upper drawer falling down by means of a spring and quadrant' thus providing 'the same usefulness as a flap to a desk'. The recommended proportions for the bureau- or secretaire-bookcase were: 'length 3 feet 6 inches, depth 22 inches, height of desk 3 feet 2 inches, including 10 inches for the inside of the desk; total length about 6 feet; depth of bookcase about 12 inches'. It is evident, however, that in many examples the recommended height was exceeded.

BEDS

Robert Adam left only seven designs for beds, and of these only two appear to have been executed (see page 48). Such splendid creations as the state bed at Kedleston and the beds at Hampton Court,[1] Nostell[2] and Harewood (Fig. 177), probably owe more to the imagination of the individual craftsmen, John Linnell and Thomas Chippendale, who are presumed to have made them.

A bed believed to have been made in the Chippendale workshops about 1770 for David Garrick, the actor, and a friend of Robert Adam, is in the collections of the Victoria and Albert Museum, together with a pair of wardrobes and chairs of simulated bamboo *en suite*. The posts are fluted and tapering, and swell slightly where they join the square bases. The canopy is coved, with a flat top. Like the accompanying furniture, the bed is japanned in chinoiserie style with designs in green and gold on a cream ground and the hangings are of Indian silk (see also page 83).

A bed believed to have been provided for David Garrick's villa at Twickenham, presumably by Chippendale, about 1770–5 is now preserved at Claydon, Bucks. This delightful piece has a *cavetto* cornice painted with a Vitruvian scroll design of foliage in green on ivory. The posts are round, gently swelling in vase-like form towards the base, where there is leaf-carving, and they are painted with a naturalistic design of foliage and flowers in colours on an ivory ground. The bed

---

[1] R. Edwards, *The shorter dictionary*, p. 43, Fig. 33.
[2] *Country Life*, May 23, 1952, p. 1574, Fig. 6.

is hung with flowered chintz, and is one of the least pretentious and most charmingly domestic pieces of furniture ever devised in the Adam spirit.

It was left for Hepplewhite to disseminate the influence in the design of beds which Adam had excited by means of so few examples and even fewer drawings. The number of beds made from 1785 onwards in the spirit of Hepplewhite's designs must come next in number to the quantity of Hepplewhite chairs produced. So complete was the refurbishing of bedrooms in this period that little further replacement in this sphere was necessary during the Regency era and until the all-conquering Victorian brass and iron bedsteads swept away the elegant and graceful mahogany or painted four-poster in the name of hygiene. As a result, therefore, not a large number survived in their original form. When the advance of science destroyed the respect which earlier generations had for draughts and 'dangerous night air', and the tester bed fell from favour, countless beautiful Hepplewhite bed-posts were converted into vase- or lamp-stands.

The *Guide* showed seven designs for beds, and eight for bedposts, all of which remained unchanged throughout the three editions. The bed designs range from the simple ones with a narrow moulded cornice or with a carved cornice painted with leaves and with the tester surmounted with a small carved urn, to more elaborate patterns having richly carved arched cornices with delicate carved ornaments of urns, foliage and swags of husks, and surmounted by domes. The nine separate designs for cornices were extremely elaborate in the refined Adam manner, several of them being arched, and mostly had important central features such as urns, a motif of ostrich feathers or a cresting of delicate scroll-work. These designs for bed cornices were equally applicable as window pelmets: indeed, very seldom do these elaborate suggestions seem to have been executed for beds. Most of the richest surviving beds have comparatively simple mouldings, of which the *cavetto* variety was one of the most popular. The *Guide* suggested that 'The cornices may be either of mahogany carved, carved and gilt, or painted and japanned'. Even when the last treatment was adopted for the rest of the bed the pillars were often left as mahogany 'with the enrichments carved'.

The posts are shown as carved more or less elaborately but are almost all of the type originated by Adam — turned and tapering, plain, fluted or reeded, and usually slightly vase-shaped in the lower part and ornamented with leaf-patterns or chequered carving. The bases, which were covered by the valance, were usually square and fairly plain. Much confusion exists over the difference between Hepplewhite and Sheraton where beds are concerned. The cornices of the latter are invariably straight; the former are often curved. The bedposts of Sheraton design are much more ornate than Hepplewhite's, and when embodying vase-shaped lower portions, these are of octagonal section, like the shafts themselves.

A bed of about 1780, with carved and fluted mahogany posts and a semi-elliptical pedimented cornice, painted with trophies and leaf-scrolls is at Hedingham, in Essex.[1] At Chatsworth there is one of about ten years later, having a very elaborate cornice with an arched end, painted with floral designs and festoons.[2]

It was recommended in the *Guide* that 'Arms or other ornaments to stuffed head-boards, should be carved in low relief, gilt and burnished'. The design and carving of bed-posts probably reached their zenith not in England, but in the eastern and southern states of America where very elaborate designs were executed with great delicacy of carving. The Hepplewhite motif of the wheatear was especially popular in America, no doubt because of its double significance, as a classical and republican emblem and as a symbol of the fertility of the new land opened up by the pioneers. On the other hand, few woodwork cornices are found in the United States, so few in fact that it must be concluded they were not popular, perhaps because of their fragility. Instead, fabric valances are universal.

The hangings of a bed were of such importance that fashion offered no hindrance to the use of the widest variety or richness of material. The editors of the *Guide* observed that 'Bedsteads may be executed of almost every stuff which the loom produces' — 'and', they might have added, 'that the painter and printer of textiles could produce, for of course, European printed cottons, Indian chintz, and Chinese painted silks were at this period much in favour for bed-hangings. For formal state bedrooms plain or figured silks and satins, and fringed velvets were recommended. The heavier figured velvets and damasks so typical of the baroque age had now gone out of fashion for furnishing. 'In one case dove-coloured satin curtains with a lining of green silk was used with good effect.' In less pretentious domestic bedrooms, printed cottons and linens were suggested.

The forms of the festooned drapery were less elaborate in design than became customary some years later, but it was specified that 'The Vallance should always be gathered full, which is called a Petticoat Vallance'. Curved frames or 'sweeps' for the tops of field beds, or small portable beds were also shown in the *Guide*, but the Hepplewhite firm did not offer so many patterns of the smaller kinds of

---

[1] R. Edwards, *The shorter dictionary*, p. 45, Fig. 37.
[2] R. Edwards, *The shorter dictionary*, p. 45, Fig. 36.

bed as did Thomas Sheraton later on. The press bed, which folded away into a cupboard or wardrobe, was in very common use where accommodation was scarce, and the compilers of the *Guide* purposely omitted to include any designs, 'their general appearance varying so little from wardrobes as to make the inclusion unnecessary'. It was explained that their design for 'The wardrobe has all the appearance of a Press Bed; in which case the upper drawers would be only sham, and formed part of the door which may be made to turn up all in one piece, and form a tester; or may be open in the middle, and swing in each side; the under-drawers are useful to hold parts of the bed-furniture.'

A good example of a mahogany press bedstead of about 1780 is described and illustrated by E. T. Joy in *The Connoisseur* for September 1963.

BEDROOM AND DRESSING ROOM FURNITURE

The influence of the Adam style seems hardly ever to have been manifested in this class of furniture, except in the famous examples at Nostell and Harewood. Those at the former house, although very splendid, are none the less only of transitional character, but the superb dressing-commodes made by Chippendale for Harewood and Renishaw are among the masterpieces of any type of furniture (see page 81).

Hepplewhite did little to extend the Adam spirit into this particular domestic field, his designs for such pieces as chests of drawers, dressing-chests and commodes, dressing-tables, tallboys and wardrobes being somewhat plain in style, deriving from the mid-century manner of Chippendale's *Director*, although some of the pieces, probably those intended for the use of ladies, are shown as highly decorated with painting or inlay.

DRESSING COMMODES

Dressing-commodes differed from ordinary commodes in having the central drawer fitted for toilet articles. The commode then became an article of furniture for the dressing-room instead of taking its place in the drawing-room in the centre of one wall, as recommended in the *Guide*.

CHESTS-OF-DRAWERS

Chests-of-drawers were of several classes. When so referred to in the *Guide* they were plain, and made of mahogany, with straight sides and front, and with bracket-feet and a plinth-moulding of the mid-century Chippendale type or with splayed feet united with a central apron-piece in a sweeping curve, sometimes indented in the front (Fig. 169). The outer curve of the splayed feet ran smoothly into the vertical line of the chest at the corners. These curved bracket feet, curved apron-pieces, and shaped sides and front are distinctive of innumerable charming domestic pieces of the Hepplewhite period. Frequently chests with curved feet had bowed or serpentine fronts, and sometimes serpentine sides as well, and in one design the front corners were given a forward curve deriving from the typical form of mid-century French commodes.

The double-chest, or tallboy, which had been common since early Georgian days was less popular during the latter years of the eighteenth century, and wardrobes increasingly took over their functions. The cornices of these high pieces, which were otherwise plain, lent themselves to decoration which in the Hepplewhite era took the form of fluting or inlay. One of several examples given in the *Guide*[1] has a very traditional dentil cornice. Another design is unusually elaborate for Hepplewhite, and lacking in the grace of his best designs. The piece is framed with heavy fluted pilasters, of narrowing width in the upper stage.[2] The base is in the form of a cut-out plinth, the cornice has a heavy frieze, and is surmounted by an urn with heavy pendants of carved leaves and by smaller urns at the ends.

Dressing-drawers were similar to chests-of-drawers, but the top drawer was fitted inside with a folding mirror and receptacles for various toilet articles. In many examples a slide of similar size to the top was fitted, on which to stand toilet articles. Although usually plain, both chests and commodes were 'sometimes elegantly ornamented with inlaid or painted work. Some made of satinwood, with the ornaments of suitable colours.' The dimensions generally recommended for chests were three feet six inches long and twenty inches deep.

Wardrobes were 'usually made plain but of best mahogany'. The dimensions could be four feet wide, twenty-two inches deep, and five feet six inches high or more. They varied little in form, there being two long drawers (or occasionally

---

[1] R. Edwards, *Hepplewhite furniture designs*, Fig. 49. [2] *Op. cit.*, Fig. 50.

one only) with two small drawers above, in the base, and a cupboard with two doors in the upper part. The cupboard contained sliding trays or 'press-shelves' for the storage of clothes.[1] The hanging wardrobe hardly came into use until the Sheraton period when it became customary, in the case of large break-front wardrobes, for clothes to be hung in one of the flanking cupboard-sections.

DRESSING-GLASSES

Dressing-glasses to stand on chests were illustrated by Hepplewhite as oval-shaped mirrors between curved supports on a box-shaped base with a shallow drawer. The front could be bowed or serpentine, and they were sometimes decorated with inlay in designs of urns or shells. Some dressing-glasses were made of enchanting shield- or heart-shaped outline on open 'skeleton' stands with tiny urn finials,[2] and examples of these are to be seen at Melbourne Hall, Derbyshire, and Harewood.

SHAVING-TABLES

A type of man's dressing-table which remained popular well into the nineteenth century was the shaving-table. This was cubical in shape, on four square tapered legs. A tilting mirror could be drawn upwards from a slot at the back. The top opened on either side to form trays for toilet articles, and the interior was fitted for a basin, tumblers and other objects. Beneath were a small cupboard and drawers. When not fitted with a sliding glass the article was a commode dressing-table. Although ingenious, and probably useful on board ship, they must have been tiresome in use because of the tendency for objects to accumulate on the top flaps when shut. Similar shapes were adapted to contain a bidet in a sliding portion underneath, fitted with legs.

Night-tables resembled small chests-of-drawers, rather square in form and supported on splayed bracket feet, which concealed a night convenience behind imitation drawer-fronts.

Another form of man's dressing-table shown in the *Guide* was 'Rudd's Table, or

[1] R. Edwards, *Hepplewhite furniture designs*, Fig. 51–4.
[2] R. Edwards, *The shorter dictionary*, p. 383, Fig. 18 and p. 384, Fig. 20.

reflecting Dressing-Table'.[1] Two side drawers in the top opened outwards on hinges, and from one a looking-glass opened out; from the other a flap was hinged on a quadrant. It was remarked that 'This is the most complete Dressing-Table made, possessing every convenience which can be wanted, or mechanism and ingenuity supply. It derives its name from a once popular character for whom it was reported it was first invented.'

LADIES' DRESSING-TABLES

These were popular articles of furniture, usually larger than a man's shaving-table, and some examples opened with flap-trays in the same manner. They were more elegant in form, with a shallow top fitted for toilet articles, and made with imitation drawer-fronts. They stood on square straight or tapering legs, sometimes fitted with a stretcher-shelf. One type had the top in a single piece with serpentine-shaped sides, and hinged at the back. Another variety was in the form of a chest-of-drawers with a plinth base.

Fitted dressing-tables of this kind abound in the designs of Thomas Shearer, who seems to have delighted in mechanical devices in furniture. A design from the *Book of Prices* shows an elegant specimen on slender outward-curving legs, the top opening to reveal toilet receptacles and two swivelling mirror-frames which lifted into position at the sides by an arrangement of counter-weights.[2] These articles were made either of plain mahogany or veneered.

FIRE-SCREENS

'Horse fire-screens' on four-legged stands, of the Hepplewhite era, like many of the smaller domestic articles, have more in common with the furniture in Chippendale's *Director* than with the forms of the Adam school. Tribute was paid to the new fashion, however, by the provision of urn finials to the top of the uprights. The latter supported an oval screen which in one example is shown as sliding to permit of adjustment to different needs.

Two of Hepplewhite's three designs for pole-screens[1] are more closely linked

[1] R. Edwards, *The shorter dictionary*, p. 547, Fig. 22.
[2] R. Fastnedge, *Shearer furniture designs*, Pl. 10, Fig. 2.

to Adam, with their classical leaf-carving and urn-shaped stems, and screens of circular, oval and shield shape[1] (Fig. 159). Another design with a square screen, and with curving tripod-feet, continues the domestic tradition of the *Director*.

All types of fire-screen were described as capable of being 'ornamented with maps, Chinese figures or needlework, etc.'

HANGING SHELVES

These delightful articles, with their delicate carved openwork fret-pattern sides, of which two designs appear in the *Guide*, again derive rather from the *chinoiserie* designs of Chippendale's *Director* than from the classical idiom of the Adam school. Chinese, rococo and Gothic patterns were followed for the sides, and the bottom shelf was usually fitted with drawers. Those shown in the Hepplewhite plate have bowed fronts.

CABINETS, CUPBOARDS AND PRESSES

Adam's early designs for cupboards and presses were massively architectural, in the manner of Kent's great bookcases and cabinets, but overlaid, as the earlier masters were not, with small-scale ornament. A drawing of a 'Cloathes Press for the Earl of Coventry' (Soane, vol. 17, no. 212) of 1764, is based on a triumphal arch design, the pilaster-shaped supports carrying female busts, and the panels of the basement were given the serpentine sarcophagus-fluting that was seen in the dado panels of the gallery at Syon a few years later. The cabinet was converted, apparently into a pair of smaller ones in clumsy and ponderous fashion, probably in accordance with a 'Design for altering the great cloathes press £11:0:0:' entered in the Croome accounts, 6 May 1767.[2]

A cabinet designed by Adam for 20 St. James's Square in 1776 (Soane, vol. 17, no. 222) on a stand having square, tapering legs with block capitals and feet expresses his later more sophisticated manner. The frieze of both stand and cabinet are deep, giving a sense of stability to a somewhat stilted design. The cabinet doors are painted with grotesques in Adam's later manner, within a

---

[1] R. Edwards, *Hepplewhite furniture designs*, Fig. 67. [2] E. Harris, Fig. 37.

border.[1] Adam made few designs for such furniture, however, and Hepplewhite showed no examples of cupboards or cabinets other than the characteristic glass-fronted types which served as, or were combined with bookcases, chests and secretaires. As we have noted these derived their form from the types in Chippendale's *Director* rather than from Adam.

MIRRORS AND GIRANDOLES

The output of mirror designs from the Adam brothers and from their contemporary John Linnell, as well as of the numerous craftsmen and furnishing firms of the Adam era is so vast that it cannot adequately be treated in such a general work as this. However, the chief developments in style expressed in Adam's mirror-designs have already been remarked upon, and may be studied by referring to the illustrations and notes at the end of this book. Hepplewhite's upright rectangular pier-glasses and his oval mirrors with ornaments of scrolling foliage are close in spirit to Adam's designs, but with a heightened nervous intensity in the extreme delicacy and attenuation of their forms. As already mentioned (see page 105) he did not represent at all mirrors with crestings of human or animal figures, or Adam's distinctive innovation of the tripartite mirror. He does illustrate, on the other hand, a fresh type of upright mirror, with scrolled cresting and broad vertical borders at the sides only, containing delicate ornament overlaid on the glass.

[1] E. Harris, Fig. 37.

MATERIALS AND PROCESSES

PRINCIPAL CABINET-MAKING WOODS

AMBOYNA

This wood is as puzzling to botanists, who usually identify it with *Pterocarpus* or *Pterospernium*, as it often is to furniture collectors, who are sometimes known to confuse it with Thuyawood. Originally imported from the West Indies, and later from the islands of Amboyna and Ceram in the East Indies, it has a rich, light, slightly reddish-brown colour with a fine 'bird's-eye' curl. Thuyawood is more yellowish brown in colour. Amboyna was used in the late eighteenth century occasionally as a surface veneer, and more often as a banding.

EBONY

From Ceylon and the East Indies. It is one of the heaviest woods, black and close-grained. It was very much used as an inlay, especially at the end of the eighteenth century.

HOLLY

This is a white or light greyish wood, fine-grained and hard, which was frequently used as an inlay and marquetry, also for small solid fancy articles. It was often stained in different colours.

KINGWOOD

From Brazil. This wood is often confused with satinwood, especially of the East Indian variety, because of its light yellowish-brown colour and the strongly contrasting darker streaks of its figure, regularly spaced. It was sometimes known in the eighteenth century as 'pimes wood'. It was used for plain veneered surfaces, and also for inlays and crossbanding.

MAHOGANY

Through the influence of Robert Adam, and the reaction against the use of the dark-toned woods which had been fashionable up to about 1760, furniture that was gilt or painted became more and more popular, especially in the great houses, but as the neo-classical characteristics became absorbed into the English furniture tradition through the influence of designers like Hepplewhite and Shearer, and cabinet-makers such as the firm of Seddon and Sons, the qualities of this noble wood caused it to maintain its appeal for its quiet dignity and durability.

Mahogany is the name given to a wide range of woods, including innumerable varieties which have been brought from Africa in modern times. Here we are concerned only with the true mahogany, the *Swietenia mahogani* from Central America and the West Indies. The first mahogany to be imported in quantity into Britain, about 1730, was called 'Spanish mahogany' because it came from the Spanish Islands of the West Indies, especially San Domingo. This wood, from which has been formed some of the finest articles of furniture of the early and mid-Georgian periods, was very dense and heavy, of straight grain with little figure, and dark, often almost black in colour. The fine crisp, sharp and vigorous carving in mahogany of the Kent and Chippendale schools owed much to the qualities of this wood. Spanish mahogany was also imported from Jamaica, Porto Rico and Haiti.

By the beginning of the Adam period, about 1760, the accessible growths of Spanish mahogany from San Domingo had become depleted, and mahogany from Cuba had almost entirely taken its place. This was redder in colour than the Spanish wood, and worked more easily, being less hard in texture. Above all it possessed a fine figure, with variations of grain that were given such names as splash-mottle, roe and mottle, fiddle-back, plum, snail, blister and cross-bar.[1]

By the 1790's Cuban mahogany itself was becoming scarce and expensive, and was in turn superseded by mahogany from the Bay of Honduras, which gave the wood its alternative name of Baywood. This was lighter in tone and browner in colour than the other varieties; also it was straighter in grain, and lacking in the handsome figuring of the Cuban wood.

[1] Howard, *Timbers of the World*, 1920, pp. 317–46.

Spanish wood from Hispaniola (San Domingo) was spoken of by the firm of Gillows as 'the safest sort of mahogany to turn out good', and Spanish mahogany from Jamaica was also favoured by some, but was very liable to great variations in quality. By 1803, as Sheraton stated in his *Cabinet Dictionary*[1] of that year, Honduras mahogany was 'the principal kind of mahogany in use among cabinet-makers'.

PEAR-WOOD

It is a light reddish or yellowish-brown, hard and fine textured, much used as an inlay.

ROSEWOOD

French: *Palissandre*.

Brazilian rosewood, the species mostly used in the late eighteenth century, comes from *Dalbergia nigra* and *D. Cearensis*, large trees in Brazil and the West Indies. Later, *D. Catifolia* from India and the East Indies came to be used. The former wood is reddish-brown with dark brown or black streaks. East Indian rosewood is violet-brown. Mostly used as a veneer, and for bandings, inlay and marquetry, but also in the solid for small objects such as drawer knobs. In the early nineteenth century it was used in solid form for table tops. It should not be confused with tulipwood (q.v. French: *Bois de rose*. Portuguese: *pau rosa*).

SATINWOOD

By the 1770's mahogany was being displaced by satinwood for fashionable furniture, although the former wood remained in favour in the more modest households, and in such masculine preserves as the study and the library. From that date until the end of the century the lovely qualities of this wood became so richly associated with the art of Adam, Hepplewhite and Sheraton that the Age of Satinwood has taken its place with those of Oak, Walnut and Mahogany, as one of the four chief periods into which the great years of English furniture have been grouped.

The finest late eighteenth century satinwood furniture was made almost invariably from the West Indian species (*Zanthoseylum*), which was introduced into Britain about 1760, chiefly from Porto Rico. This wood was of a beautiful golden-yellow, that has matured over the years into a rich, mellow honey-like

[1] T. Sheraton, *Cabinet Dictionary*, pp. 253–4.

tone never dreamed of by the eighteenth century users. Sheraton mentions in the *Cabinet Dictionary*[1] of 1803 that satinwood had been very much used for the last twenty years, and he admired a 'fine, straw colour' in this wood as having 'a cool, light and pleasing effect in furniture'. The grain is smooth, hard and usually straight, without prominent fibres, but sometimes has a rich bold irregular figure. The wood was almost always used as a veneer on mahogany, or on pine in the less expensive pieces. Used in the solid it had a tendency to split. Sheraton, however, advised the use of solid satinwood for chairs, and it was used in this form for the honeysuckle-back chairs at Kedleston (see page 87) and by Chippendale for the dining-table urns at Newby (Fig. 140).

About 1780 satinwood began to be imported from the East Indies, chiefly from Ceylon. This wood is the *Chloroseylon swietenia*, and is of a lemon colour, sometimes even of a brownish hue, and figured in fairly regular and rather small streaks. East Indian satinwood did not come into general use until the early years of the nineteenth century, and examples of its use exist in the chairs made for Stourhead by Thomas Chippendale the Younger.

The satinwood furniture made in the Adam and Hepplewhite styles during the late Victorian and Edwardian periods by such firms as Edwards and Roberts of London, although of extremely fine craftsmanship and showing careful attention to period character, may often be distinguished by their use of East Indian satinwood, which in addition to the pronounced streakiness of the grain, is lacking in the bright luminosity of the West Indies wood. However, the striped grain caused it to be much used in early times for banding and inlays.

SYCAMORE

This English wood, almost white in colour and smooth in grain, was occasionally used in the latter half of the eighteenth century as a surface veneer, but usually for inlay, when its pale colour contrasted with other woods. When stained a greenish-grey colour with iron-salts sycamore became harewood, and was much used for marquetry work and for bandings. It was sometimes called silverwood.

THUYA-WOOD

From Africa. Rich, golden brown, with small 'bird's eye' figure. Used as a veneer and for inlay and bandings.

[1] T. Sheraton, *Cabinet Dictionary*, pp. 314–15.

TULIPWOOD

French: *Bois de rose*.

From Brazil: *Dalbergia frutescens* var. *tomentosa*.

The wood is of a rose-red to carmine colour, with yellow stripes, but fades after exposure. Not to be confused with rosewood (q.v.) or with tulip-tree wood, *Liriodendron tulipifera*, from North America, sometimes known as Canary white-wood. When freshly cut it is a greenish colour, but after exposure becomes greenish or yellowish-brown. The grain is not prominent.

YEW-WOOD

English: *Taseus baccata*.

It is a fairly open-grained hard wood, reddish-brown in colour. When first cut is slightly violet. Cross-cut yew, from the root or near, was often used as a burr veneer.

ZEBRA WOOD

From Guiana. This is a heavy wood, of light brown colour, close-grained, with vivid streaks of much darker brown. It is chiefly used as a veneer.

VENEERING, INLAY AND MARQUETRY

In the last three decades of the eighteenth century the arts of veneering and inlay reached heights of beauty and craftsmanship under the influence of Adam, Hepplewhite and Sheraton unsurpassed even with the lovely inlaid furniture of the mid-century *rococo* taste.

Veneering was a process introduced into this country from Holland in the late seventeenth century, and has almost continuously since then been popular as a method of displaying the rich colours and handsome figure of scarce and expensive woods by mounting them in thin sheets upon a carcase of less rare wood. The process called for great skill, and in good pieces almost invariably the veneers were mounted upon straight-grain mahogany or other good quality plain wood. In the Adam and Hepplewhite period, the main surfaces of inlaid furniture were usually of satinwood and mahogany, sometimes used by themselves, but often in conjunction, and with decorative designs inlaid with such distinctively coloured or contrasting woods as sycamore, tulipwood, kingwood, rosewood, zebra-wood, pear-wood, holly, yew and ebony. Harewood is sycamore stained grey or green with iron salts.

These inlays often took the form of banding, which consisted of a strip or border of veneer round the edge of a panel or drawer. The richness and variety of the woods used for banding was increased by their being cut at an angle to the grain, giving a feathered figure to the wood.

The tops of commodes, side- and pier-tables, and of Pembroke and card-tables offered unrivalled opportunities for the displays of inlays, on which the familiar motifs of paterae, swags, festoons of husks, vases, and other details from the neo-classic repertory were often varied by running scrolls of foliage and flowers, and by patterns of shells.

Marquetry is inlay-work in which the design forms a prominent part of the aspect of a piece of furniture. It was introduced from Holland in the seventeenth century and was popular up to the age of Queen Anne, going out of fashion during the early Georgian period, when the fine-grained Spanish mahogany that was then being imported lent itself especially to the deep, crisp carving which then became popular. Marquetry revived with the increasing popularity of the French taste, and the fondness for floral design on furniture at the middle of the eighteenth century. With the Adam movement marquetry remained fashionable, the designs only undergoing a change from naturalistic floral patterns to the more formal classical motifs.

The Adam inspiration produced such masterpieces of marquetry work as the magnificent furniture made by Chippendale for Harewood (Fig. 165) and Panshanger (Fig. 172). In some instances, as in the commodes made for Corsham Court by John Cobb, neo-classical designs of urns appear inlaid upon a commode of rococo form.[1] In other examples, such as the commode in the Lady Lever Gallery, believed to be by Chippendale, naturalistic floral designs, though admittedly of a somewhat classical stiffness, are inlaid on a work of neo-classical form (Fig. 125).

Towards the end of the eighteenth century the art of pictorial marquetry inlay was diminishing in popularity, and the reticent and dignified effects of surfaces of beautiful woods set off by simple bandings of contrasting woods came to be

[1] R. Edwards and M. Jourdain, *Georgian cabinet-makers*, Fig. 71.

more highly esteemed. In small articles such as work-tables, boxes and cabinets, the veneered surfaces of satinwood or sycamore were often relieved by medallions of darker woods like Thuya-wood, rosewood or mahogany.

The doors of large pieces such as bookcases, cabinets and wardrobes were often made with oval centres of figured wood with banding of feathered veneers in a contrasting wood. Hepplewhite recommended in the *Guide* the use of 'fine waved or curled wood', and richly grained panels with both straight-grain and feathered banding are seen in the plates.[1]

JAPANNING AND LACQUER

Japanning is properly the term applied to English lacquer work. It is distinguished from the true Chinese or Japanese lacquer in that it is carried out not with the gum of the *lac* tree, the *Rhus vernicifera*, but with a form of gum varnish called gum-lac, seed-lac or shellac. These are various forms of a resinous substance secreted from certain trees when they have been attacked by the insect *Coceus lacca*. It is produced in Burma, Bengal, Assam and Siam, and is used in the manufacture of various varnishes, French polish and sealing-wax. Some of the best japanned work carried out by skilled craftsmen was almost indistinguishable from oriental lacquer. Its excellence depended, as it did in the East, upon the patient building up of the surface which was to receive the design, with many layers of lacquer, each one being carefully rubbed down before the next was applied. When practised, however, as a domestic craft, especially as an elegant amusement for young ladies, japanning was responsible for the production of much inferior work. In the *Description* (1782) of his celebrated Gothic villa at Strawberry Hill, Horace Walpole mentioned a cabinet japanned by Lady Walpole, but elsewhere he referred to 'two vile china jars, that look like the modern japanning by ladies'. Much of this domestic work soon deteriorated, however, and comparatively little of it seems to have survived. By the beginning of the Adam period the craft was seriously declining in popularity, according to Robert Dossie, whose book *The Handmaid of the Arts* was published in 1758. In it he stated that japanning was 'not at present practised so frequently'. In the same or following year (the exact date of the first edition is unknown) appeared a work entitled *The Ladies Amusement, or Whole Art of Japanning made easy* was published by Robert Shayer, of the Golden

[1] R. Edwards, *Hepplewhite furniture designs*, Fig. 51–4.

Buck, Fetter Lane, Fleet Street, London. Although it contained over 1,500 motifs for japanning, including some designs by Pillement, it gave little technical advice.

Japanning had been popular in England since the seventeenth century, and was usually carried out with the aid of the famous work published by John Stalker and George Parker in 1688, entitled *Treatise of Japanning and Varnishing . . . With the best way of making all sorts of Varnish for Japan.*

The most notable and beautiful examples of japanning in the Adam period are among the articles which Thomas Chippendale supplied to Harewood House and Nostell (Fig. 120), and the commodes made for Osterley about 1770 (Fig. 122) (see page 100). Hepplewhite's *Guide* referred to japanning as a fashion 'which has arisen within these few years' but he was alluding to a simplified form of the process in which much of the tedious work of building up the surface was omitted. Dossie remarked that 'one principal variation in the manner of japanning is the using or omitting any priming or undercoat on the work to be japanned. In the older practice such work was always used . . . but in the Birmingham manufacture it has always been rejected'.[1]

The 'Birmingham manufacture', to which he refers, was the then still quite small lacquer industry in which the technique was being applied, not only to wood, but to *papier-mâché* and tinware, under conditions of mass-production — an industry which was to increase greatly in size in the early nineteenth century.

Generally, by Hepplewhite's day japanning had come to mean little more than paint-work carried out with a high proportion of varnish, and in consequence little of it is found today in a good state of preservation.

GILDING

Great variations will be noticed in the character and quality of the gilding of furniture. These are chiefly due to the differences in the two processes mostly used — oil-gilding and water-gilding.

For both processes the preparation of the ground was similar. The parts to be gilded were coated with a fine white composition of whiting and glue or size made up into a thin smooth paste called gesso. Six or seven coats were given, the earlier coats containing more glue than the later ones, until a thickness of about

[1] Dossie, *Handmaid of the arts*, 1758.

a sixteenth of an inch was built up on the wood work. Any decorative shaping or ornament was then worked by the fingers, or with chisels and gouges, to keep the edges of the design sharp and clean, with a care and skill almost equal to that devoted to carved work.

When the gesso ground was ready, a mordant, or adhesive, which would bite on to the gold and make it adhere, was applied. This consisted of a glue composed of a mixture of oil gold-size and parchment-size. For water-gilding parchment-size alone might be used. The mordant also contained colouring matter of red or yellow ochre to give depth and richness to the final appearance of the gold. The traces of red showing through worn gold add greatly to the beauty of old gilding. In the process of water-gilding, when the mordant was hard the surface was liberally wetted, and the gold-leaf gently applied so that it floated out on the moist surface without any wrinkles, and was absorbed into the smooth surface of the ground.

After some hours the gold was hard and ready for burnishing, which was done with a piece of agate or other hard stone, set in a long handle. This was known as a 'hound's tooth' from the fact that the tooth of a dog or other long-toothed animal was used originally and indeed is so used today. Smoothing of the gold with this produced a brilliant lustrous effect. Some parts were often left matt for contrast, and these were dulled by painting the unburnished gold with vermilion or yellow ochre in gold-size or white of egg. The ground might sometimes be given a different effect by being punched with tools to produce a diaper or similar pattern.

CARVING
AND APPLIED ORNAMENT

Wood-carving, which had reached such heights of skill and beauty by the middle of the century, began to wane in popularity as marquetry and applied ornaments of ormolu increasingly took its place.

The robust character of carving was also inappropriate in the delicately tinted and modelled interiors of the fully developed Adam school. In the early years of the period a limited amount of carved work survived, especially in such articles as those supplied by the firm of Chippendale, and also on the richly carved pedestals for urns in some of the Adam dining-rooms. The urns at Nostell have boldly worked ornaments of fruit in dark Spanish mahogany contrasting with the yellow satinwood bodies, but more often such carving as existed was in the shallower relief of classical paterae, fluting, husks and delicate swags. On mahogany furniture like sideboards, small carved details such as plaques with representations of a vase, an urn, or a lion, might appear, but before long most of this carved work gave place to details modelled in the patent composition which Adam used, consisting of a mixture of resin, whiting and size. This was pressed into moulds while hot and plastic, and, when the composition had set, the ornaments were fixed to the furniture by means of pins or glue. From 1770 onwards, as the bold forms of Adam's early style developed into the attenuated patterns of his later manner, carving went out of use for the frames of looking-glasses, and the delicate designs of festoons and airy scrollwork were carried out in composition built up on cores of wire.

Again, as Adam's decorative style came to consist less of a small number of boldly formed ornaments, as in the case of such articles as the side-table at Osterley (Fig. 15), and instead more and more of small-scale motifs in shallow relief closely set in repetitive patterns (Fig. 105), mechanical methods instead of hand carving and modelling were less resorted to, and ornaments cast in composition and in soft metals such as lead were increasingly used. The adoption of such methods as these was assisted by the production of ornaments by industrial methods on a large scale in factories that were now developing rapidly through the influence of the growing Industrial Revolution. Plaques of Wedgwood pottery lent themselves with especial ease and appropriateness to the decoration of Adam furniture because of the facility with which they could be applied, and because of the suitability of the neo-classical subjects depicted in them. They filled the place in English furniture occupied in French furniture by plaques of Sèvres porcelain, which was a much favoured adornment during the Louis Seize era.[1]

PAINTED FURNITURE

The vogue for painted furniture developed strongly after 1770, when Robert Adam's decorative work passed out of the early phase with its bold carving and modelling of ornament, and moved into a new phase in which decoration was

[1] F. J. B. Watson, *Louis XVI furniture*, pp. XLV and 12.

more superficial, with ornament in very light relief. The painting of furniture was encouraged also by the increasing fondness for furniture and decorations in light tones and delicate colours (see also page 34).

The painting of furniture had been popular in earlier times — in the seventeenth century and even back to the Gothic period, and it was for centuries a popular process in Germany and Italy. In England the craft was closely associated with the techniques of painting the panels of coaches with decorations of figures, flowers and formal ornaments. The painter Cipriani, who executed decorative work for Robert Adam at Syon, Lansdowne House and elsewhere, had carried out painted decorations on the panels of the coach of King George III. This had been built by Joseph Wilton, a sculptor of French descent, who carved the marble fireplaces at Osterley. He had been brought to England from Rome, together with Cipriani, by the designer of the King's coach, the architect Sir William Chambers. Both of these artists would have become acquainted in Rome with the beautiful Italian painted and japanned furniture. The latter process differs from the former in that various gums and resins are used which cause the decorative surface to dry with a peculiar porcelain-like hardness.

The figure paintings in oval or circular medallions which appear within veneered or painted surrounds on the panels and doors of commodes and cabinets of the Adam period were executed both in full colour and *en grisaille*. They are often attributed to such famous decorative painters of the day as Angelica Kauffmann, William Hamilton, Cipriani or Pergolesi. However, it is only in comparatively rare instances that such attributions may be depended upon, as they can be in the case of the inlaid sycamore commodes in the drawing-room at Osterley, with circular and oval medallions painted by Angelica Kauffmann (Fig. 122). More frequently these painted groups of figures in classical, pastoral or biblical scenes have been copied from canvases by her or by another gifted woman artist, Lady Diana Beauclerk. The engravings of paintings by Cipriani were another source of inspiration. Such paintings of figures, groups and scenes, were never represented in the designs of Hepplewhite, and only sketchily in drawings of some minor furniture in Sheraton's first book. This agreeable kind of decoration derives directly from the influence of Robert Adam.

Occasionally the panels of furniture were painted with the flying figures of girl musicians and similar subjects against backgrounds of black or Etruscan red, copied from the wall-paintings in the Naples Museum, which had been taken from the excavations at Herculaneum.

The finer quality figure-paintings were usually executed on oval or circular sheets of copper let into the fronts of the commodes or cabinets, while the associated decoration of flower garlands, wreaths and sprays was painted directly on to the surface.

Painting was a technique of especial importance in the Adam system in exercising the unifying effect of colour. Pier-tables, side-tables, sideboards, urns and pedestals were eminently suitable for this treatment as permanent decorative fittings of an interior. The earlier chairs, particularly those of the dining-rooms, were usually of mahogany, but the drawing-room chairs tended at first to be gilded, and later to be painted.

Beds, which were generally so expressive of the elegance of the Hepplewhite period, lent themselves admirably to the beauties of painted work (Fig. 175). Often the cornices were painted while the posts were of carved wood.

Especially distinctive of the late 1780's and the 1790's are the handsome articles made in satinwood, such as cabinets, bureaux, wardrobes and smaller pieces like pembroke tables, side-tables and card-tables, upon which have been painted designs of floral swags, garlands and sprays, or of strings of husks, in bright naturalistic colours. Some of the plain satinwood pieces of the Adam period have had this kind of floral decoration added in modern times in an attempt to enhance their value, but these decorations usually betray themselves by their excessively heavy treatment, which often appears to overwhelm the object itself, and by the solidity of the colouring which lacks the clear brilliance and transparency of early work. The same remarks apply to the painted decorations on the numerous Victorian and Edwardian imitations of eighteenth century satinwood furniture.

Modern painted decoration of this kind may also sometimes be detected by a close examination of the *craquelure* which is a feature of old painted work. Spurious paint-work sometimes has imitation crackled lines painted in with a fine brush, or it may be created artificially by means of varnishes that shrink while drying and produce crackling. The unwary collector may easily be deceived by such expedients.

A fruitful source of motifs for the painting of furniture was *A New Book of Ornaments*, published in 1775 by the Italian decorator P. Columbari. It was described as containing 'a variety of elegant Designs of Modern Pannels Commonly executed in Stucco, Wood or Painting'. Columbari's style was similar to that of Pergolesi, Zucci and Cipriani. His designs lacked the spare, rarefied classical character of Adam's own work, and consisted more of intricate scrollwork.

METALWORK

Decorative mounts of *ormolu* (gilded bronze) or brass were used during the third quarter of the eighteenth century on furniture in the French taste such as commodes and cabinets, usually as mounts of naturalistic leaves in the rococo manner at the angles of these pieces. With the coming of the neo-classical taste these mounts took on a more formal character as capitals in the form of ram's-heads with drooping swags, on the pilaster supports of the pieces, as may be seen on the commodes and library tables made by Chippendale for Harewood (Figs. 121 and 167). The large sideboard, wine-cooler and urns on pedestals at Harewood are also highly enriched with ormolu (Figs. 136 and 138).

Many ornaments of this kind were made by the firm of Matthew Boulton, who established his factory at Soho, outside Birmingham, in 1762. He was spoken of as the 'first and most complete manufacturer in metal', and at one time employed thirty-five metal workers, a number of them being foreigners. His wife, who was connected with Elizabeth Montague, the head of that intellectual côterie the 'Bluestockings', encouraged him to 'triumph over the French taste and to embellish your country with . . . elegant productions'. In 1770 James Adam urged Boulton to manufacture articles of ormolu 'in an elegant and superior style' and soon Robert Adam was supplying him with numerous designs for candelabra, perfume burners and other articles in what came to be called 'English Ormolu'. However, these were ancillary decorative objects, and after the early 1770's the use of ormolu mounts diminished during the later years of the Adam and Hepplewhite period, metal castings of more stereotyped character being used to a greater extent where metal ornaments were desired. Metal galleries and applied enrichments and mouldings for the edges of shelves were made in a great variety of the familiarly classical patterns of anthemion (honeysuckle alternating with palm-leaf), running scrolls, sometimes interrupted with vase motifs, acanthus, and palm-leaves.

HANDLES AND LOCKS

The D-shaped drop-handle fixed to two small circular back-plates which had been common in the 1750's retained its popularity, and is shown in one or two of Hepplewhite's plates in the *Guide*, and in several of Shearer's designs in the

London Book of Prices. In the years of the French taste drop-handles had often been elaborately chased in the form of naturalistic foliage in the rococo form. The same form was now ideally adaptable for shaping in classical fashion as a drooping swag of leaves or reeds hanging between circular or oval paterae (Fig. 173).

The circular drop-handle on a circular back-plate of the same size was especially favoured by Hepplewhite. These handles seem to have developed naturally out of the neo-classical scheme of ornament, since the ring could be chased to represent a wreath of bay-leaves and the back plates could be stamped in the centre as classical paterae (Fig. 175) or with the representation of an urn.

A gracefully shaped oval handle is shown in several of Shearer's designs, but the semi-elliptical handle on an oval back plate which is such a charming feature of much late eighteenth century furniture was certainly much used, and may have been invented by the firm of Seddon and Sons, for such handles appear in several authenticated pieces supplied by them (see page 127). They were possibly produced with the aid of the hand-operated metal-press which was supplied to Seddons by the Birmingham firm of Pickering. With such a press, handles of various kinds could be stamped out of sheet metal and at the same time impressed with suitable ornament, instead of being made by the much more expensive process of casting in solid metal. The tradesmens' pattern books of metal furniture fittings of the period show numerous examples of metal handles, keyhole escutcheons, knobs and ornaments of different kinds. These oval handles, which are not shown in any of the designs of Hepplewhite, Shearer or Sheraton, seem frequently to be found in Seddon furniture, such as the articles at Ulefoss Manor already mentioned (see page 127).

Towards the end of the century small knobs tended more and more to be adopted instead of drop-handles. In some articles the knobs were stamped from sheet brass, often with the familiar neo-classical ornaments of paterae or a small vase. In other pieces the knobs were of wood, and for small interior drawers of ebony, ivory or bone.

The distinctive type of lock named after its inventor, Joseph Bramah, was patented in 1784, and its appearance may help in the dating of a piece. Instead of being operated by levers, the lock was turned by a tubular key, the end of which was cut into slots that could be reproduced only with difficulty. These locks usually bore the name of Bramah, and in the early nineteenth century the impress of a crown and the Royal initials, G.R., W.R., or V.R., but not in the late eighteenth century.

MARBLE AND SCAGLIOLA

The use of solid marble for table tops, or 'slabs' as they were almost invariably called by designers and craftsmen, continued throughout the Adam period. The side-tables with terminal figures (Fig. 98) at Nostell have tops of pink *fleur de pêche* marble, and numerous other examples of solid marble table tops exist. 'Statuary' marble was often specified for solid tops, and referred to white marble of the greatest purity as used for sculptured statues.

Nevertheless, the employment of solid marble for the tops of side-and console-tables and similar articles diminished considerably by comparison with its popularity in earlier years. The great cost of solid marble, which mostly came from Italy, with the attendant risks of breakage and long delays on the journey discouraged its use, although the desire for economy sometimes favoured the practice of using thin sheets of marble glued on to a slate core. Other factors than these, however, caused solid marble to fall into disfavour. The deep toned *verde antico*, porphyry and Breccia marbles which were suited to the richly coloured rooms of the great Palladian houses were often too heavy in tone for the new delicate Adam interior, and furthermore, it was desired to have table tops to embody designs that would repeat the decorative motifs of the rooms. For these reasons an imitation marble known as 'scagliola' was found preferable. It had the advantage that it could be produced easily, cheaply and quickly in this country, and with it table tops or 'slabs' could be made either to represent any of the well-known marbles, or with an inlaid design of neo-classical motifs to accord with the surroundings.

Scagliola is said to have been known in ancient times, and to have been re-invented in Italy during the early seventeenth century. The name derives from the Italian word *scaglia*, meaning scales or chips, and basically the material consists of pieces of marble imbedded in plaster. There were innumerable recipes, and the process was often supposed to be shrouded in mystery, but principally it consisted of small pieces of marble in a mixture of plaster of paris together with colouring matter and various substances added to accelerate or retard the setting of the material. It was built up with a fine outer layer upon a coarser foundation, and it could be coloured and polished so successfully that it was often indistinguishable from the best marble.

A recipe compiled by the architect Sir William Chambers in 1767[1] was as follows:

'The composition for the foundation is Bitts of Tile or well-baked brick and bitts of marble mixed with Lime of River flints — a Sufficient quantity to bring the whole to a Consistency of a paste. Then a finer paste of the same composition but with less of the marble is laid on . . . and having beat it for some time then strew in bitts of Marble of different kinds and beat them in the paste, then when dry put on a paste composed of Powder of tiles, lime and soapwater, for otherwise it never takes a polish . . . smooth and polish it with a clean polished trowel before it drys, then rub it with linseed oil and a woollen cloth. N.B. The Italians give what colour they please by mixing with the paste Brown, Red Vermilion, Yellow Occar, or any colour that agrees with Lime.'

While James Adam was touring Italy in 1760, he noted with wonderment in his diary 'The scagliola is curious, and could be used to answer different purposes, for columns representing different marbles, for tables resembling mosaic work, and for most elegant floors for baths and low apartments, or for linings to any place damp, etc., and likewise for imitating different marbles in cabinet-work and such like things.'

The floor of the ante-room at Syon is scagliola, inlaid with an elaborate pattern. Such slabs as those for the Nostell tables and those of the side-tables at Syon were executed in white statuary marble, incised and channelled to receive a design in small pieces of coloured marble and cement paste. Table slabs of inlaid marble or of mosaic work were invariably obtained from Italy, as in the instances of the mosaic marble tops of the great side-tables of the red drawing-room at Syon (Fig. 93), and those of the commodes in the state bedroom at Woburn (Fig. 119). During the nineteenth century the technique came to be practised in England as well.

Scagliola was used by James Wyatt in the Pantheon in Oxford Street, which was opened in January 1772, and it was afterwards widely adopted by the Wyatt family. In 1783 it was stated[2] that the columns of the Pantheon were formed of a 'newly invented composition which rivals the finest marbles in colour and hardness'.

Something of a monopoly in its production was held by the firm of Richter and Bartoli of Great Newport Street, London. They supplied to Nostell the two

---

[1] Quoted by R. B. Wragg in *The History of scagliola*.
[2] Ralph Cuheal, *Observations on the marble buildings in London*, 1783.

slabs of white marble inlaid with scagliola which were made to Adam's design. They also supplied '2 Tables of Scagliola at £65 each' to Croome Court in 1768, and several articles to the Duke of Northumberland, probably for Syon.

During the last war, one of the magnificent *verde antico* columns in the ante-room at Syon, which, like some columns at Newby, were for long been said to have been dredged up from the bed of the Tiber, was damaged by a bomb-fragment and found to be made of scagliola. It is possible that one or two of the columns were indeed made of this material in order to make up the number necessary for the room, but it has not so far been thought desirable to run the risk of spoiling the other columns to discover whether they are genuine *verde antico* or scagliola, so the question may never be satisfactorily resolved whether the Duke of Northumberland (and William Weddell of Newby also) were tricked in this way by the Italian purveyor of antique marbles from whom the columns were obtained.

A highly individual type of marble inlay was practised by another Italian, Signor Bossi, who was established in Dublin between 1785 and 1798.[1]

He was described as an 'inlayer in marble and stucco worker' and it is said that eventually he had to leave the city because he was implicated in the revolutionary movement. Bossi's process was a closely guarded secret, and it was carried out behind closed doors in the actual houses of the Irish gentlemen who were his principal clients. Bossi's work is said to be of extremely high finish and accuracy, and on this account somewhat hard and unsympathetic in appearance. The remarkable way in which it has survived is believed to be due to the fact that the inlay filling (being presumably composed of marble particles) possessed the same rate of expansion and contraction as solid marble.

[1] Georgian Society's Publication, Dublin, Vol. 1, p. 22.

GLOSSARY

Acroters: Triangular-shaped ornaments at the upper corners of cabinets, bookcases, cupboards, etc. Originally statue-platforms on Greek buildings.

Anthemion: A form of ornament related to the honeysuckle flower. Properly applied to a frieze in which honeysuckle alternates with palmette ornament (q.v.).

Caryatides: Supports for a table, cabinet, etc., in the form of female figures. Male supports of this kind are called Atlantes, Persians or Telamones.

Colonnettes: Slender column-shaped supports, with turned or carved ornaments. They are attenuated to a length in proportion to their diameter to a far greater degree than is permitted for an orthodox column. Their length is often broken up by annular mouldings.

Console: A bracket or support in the form of a double scroll.

Cornice: The projecting, top member of an entablature (see below), also the moulding that covers the angle where a wall joins the ceiling.

Entablature: The upper part of an architectural order, consisting of architrave, frieze and cornice: the horizontal beam or member which is carried on the columns of an order.

Frieze: The broad band, either plain or sculptured, between the cornice and architrave of an entablature. Also the upper part of the wall of a room below the cornice. In furniture, applied to the band or border beneath a table-top, or below the cornice of a cabinet.

Gadrooning: A form of ornament consisting of a series of short convex ribs, usually of a swollen tear-drop shape, and sometimes twisted in S-form. Also called nulling or lobing.

Guilloche: A form of ornament used for borders, friezes, etc., consisting of a series of interlaced circles or ovals.

Palmette: A form of ornament based on the hand with its outstretched fingers, similar to the honeysuckle.

Patera: A flat circular, square or oval ornament, usually applied or carved, but sometimes painted, of a floral design.

Pediment: A classical feature, usually triangular, like a shallow gable-end, surmounting the tops of bookcases, cabinets, cupboards, etc. A broken pediment has the central angled portion omitted.

Pilaster: A support shaped as a flat column applied to the front of a cabinet, etc.

Rosettes: Raised circular ornaments consisting of a rose design.

Terms, or terminal figures: Supports or pedestals shaped as figures with natural heads, busts and feet, and with the legs and lower bodies formed as tapering columns.

Pelta: An ancient type of leather-covered shield of kidney-shape, much used as a decorative ornament by Adam, and other exponents of neo-classicism.

Vitruvian scroll: A wave-like ornament, much used by William Kent and other Palladians, and also by Adam in his early designs.

Volutes: Spiral-shaped ornaments, used in the capitals of Ionic columns and in chair-backs, etc.

NOTES

1. (p. 84)   The library table from the Gallery at Harewood House was sold at Sotheby's on July 1st, 1965, for £43,050. It has been acquired by Leeds Corporation and is now part of the magnificent collection of furniture at Temple Newsam House.

2. (pp. 91, 188, 213)   An engraving for the drawing was published as Plate 4 in John Vardy's *Some designs of Mr. Inigo Jones and Mr. William Kent*, where it is wrongly ascribed to the former. See Peter Ward-Jackson *English Furniture Designs*, 1958.

3. (p. 49)   Adam's adoption of grotesques in the decoration of rooms provides another instance of the inspiration of William Kent, who used this form of ornament in the ceiling of the Presence Chamber at Kensington Palace (1720) and at Rousham Hall, Oxon (1738–41).

4. (p. 65)   The tapestries at Nostell are not Gobelins, but from the Brussels workshops after Van der Borcht, and represent the story of Cupid and Psyche. Any question of possible influence from French sources through this channel does not consequently arise.

5. (p. 66)   By a misprint, the date of Mayhew and Ince's bill for these commodes has wrongly been stated in the catalogue as 1761, instead of 1765.

6. (p. 72)   An intriguing instance of the influence of English fashions upon French taste exists in connexion with '10 Neat Bamboo Chairs with loose seats . . .' which Linnell supplied for £2:5:0 each on 29 May 1767. These chairs were of Chinese Chippendale pattern with trellis backs and sides, all the members being carved in round section as bamboo, and corresponded almost identically with some *fauteuils* stamped by Georges Jacob, at one time at the *Folie Saint James* in Paris, and more recently in the collection of M. Christian Dior.[1] The great French *menuisier* is well-known to have been an exponent of the *style anglais*, especially of the *chinoiserie* designs of Chippendale, and possessed a copy of the *Director*.

7. (p. 72)   With regard to the authorship of the pier-tables supplied by Henry Holland to Carlton House, which I suggested in my *Regency Furniture* must have come from the workshop of Weisweiler, Mr. F. J. B. Watson wrote on 24 June 1964; after a visit to New York:

> 'I took the opportunity to examine very carefully the secretaire stamped by Weisweiler which belongs to Mrs. Linsky, and which is illustrated as Plate 90 in the English edition of my *Louis XVI furniture*. There is to my mind no doubt at all that the hand which made this piece made the side-tables from the Chinese Drawing Room at Carlton House which are now at Buckingham Palace.'

[1] Catalogue of Exhibits at the Musée des Arts Décoratifs, Paris, 1955–6, 'Grands Ebénistes et Menuisiers Parisiens du XVIIIme siècle'.

8. (p. 82) No accounts or other documents relating to these cabinets are to be found in the Panshanger papers at the Herts. County Records Office. Nor are there any references to furniture supplied by any of the well-known cabinet-makers of the Adam and Hepplewhite periods. From 1753 to 1789 the third Earl Cowper lived entirely in Florence.

9. (p. 49) This bed is kept in the taffeta room on the first floor and is not at present on view to the public. It is of simpler form than the state bed, executed in polished yellow wood with a painted design.

10. (p. 130) The motif of a single feather appears in Prince Arthur's cupboard (early sixteenth century) at the Victoria and Albert Museum, and frequently in glass candelabra of the late eighteenth century.

11. (p. 206) Since going to press, some interesting information has come to light regarding the authorship of the Woburn commodes. They are identical with a commode in the Fitzwilliam Museum, Cambridge, which bears the signature of a Daniel Langlois, who was apprenticed in London in 1770. Any relationship between Daniel and Peter Langlois, although highly probable, has not been confirmed. (See *Furniture History*: the Journal of the Furniture History Society, Vol. 1. p. 62, Leeds, 1965, Anthony Coleridge: *The Chippendale Period in English Furniture*, Faber and Faber, 1966, and Ralph Edwards: *The English Furniture at Woburn Abbey*. Article in *Apollo*, December, 1965.)

BIBLIOGRAPHY

ROBERT and JAMES ADAM, *The works in architecture*, facsimile edition, Tiranti, 1959.

Le antichità de Ercolano, 8 vols., Accademia Ercolense, Naples, 1757–92.

GEOFFREY W. BEARD, 'New light on Adam's craftsmen.' Article in *Country Life*, 10 May 1962.

'Robert Adam at Croome Court.' Article in *The Connoisseur*. Vol. 152, 1953, p. 73.

'Adam's craftsmen.' Article in *The Connoisseur Year Book*, 1958.

ARTHUR T. BOLTON, *The Architecture of Robert and James Adam (1758–1794)*, 2 vols., *Country Life*, 1922.

OLIVER BRACKETT, *Thomas Chippendale*, London, 1930.

R. BUCKLE, *Harewood: a guide book*, English Life Publications Ltd., Derby.

COMTE DE CAYLUS, *Recueil d'antiquités égyptiennes, étrusques, grecques et romaines*, 7 vols., 1752–67.

C.-N. COCHIN, *Mémoires inédits*, Paris, 1880.

Observations sur les antiquités de la ville d'Herculanum, 1754.

ANTHONY COLERIDGE, 'Chippendale: interior decorator and house furnisher.' Article in *Apollo*, April 1963.

H. M. COLVIN, *A biographical dictionary of British architects: 1660–1840*, John Murray, London, 1954.

'The Connoisseur' Period Guides, vol. 3, The late Georgian period, 1760–1811.

LORAINE CONRAN, 'Robert Adam's influence in furniture design.' Article in *Apollo*, January 1951.

ANTONY DALE, *James Wyatt*, Basil Blackwell, 1956.

ROBERT DOSSIE, *The Handmaid of the arts*, 2 vols., London, 1758.

CARLE DREYFUS, *Le mobilier français*, Musée du Louvre, Paris, 1921.

RALPH EDWARDS, *The dictionary of English furniture*, 3 vols., *Country Life*, London, 1954.

English chairs, V.A.M. Publications, H.M.S.O., London, 1951.

Georgian furniture, H.M.S.O., London, 1958.

Hepplewhite furniture designs, Tiranti, London, 1947.

The shorter dictionary of English furniture, *Country Life*, London, 1964.

RALPH EDWARDS and MARGARET JOURDAIN, *Georgian cabinet-makers*, *Country Life*, 1955.

G. ELAND, *Shardeloes papers*, Oxford University Press, 1947.

SVEND ERIKSEN, 'Early neo-classicism in French furniture.' Article in *Apollo*, November 1963.

'Lalive de Jully's furniture "à la grecque".' Article in *The Burlington Magazine*, August 1961.

'Marigny and "Le goût Grec".' Article in *The Burlington Magazine*, March 1962.

The Farington Diary, ed. by James Grieg, 1923.

RALPH FASTNEDGE, *English furniture styles*, Penguin, 1955.

Sheraton furniture, Faber and Faber, London, 1962.

Shearer furniture designs, Tiranti, London, 1962.

MAURICE FENAILLE, *Etat général des Tapisseries de la manufacture des Gobelins*, Paris, 1907.

JOHN FLEMING, *Robert Adam and his circle*, John Murray, London, 1962.

JOHN GLOAG, *Short dictionary of furniture*, Allen and Unwin, London, 1952.

EILEEN HARRIS, *The furniture of Robert Adam*, Tiranti, 1964.

'Robert Adam and the Gobelins.' Article in *Apollo*, April 1962.

J. H. HAYWARD, *Commodes*, V.A.M. Publications, H.M.S.O., London.

'A library writing table by Thomas Shearer.' Article in *The Connoisseur*, June, 1961.

AMBROSE HEAL, *The London furniture makers*, Batsford, London, 1953.

A. L. HOWARD, *Timbers of the world*, Macmillan, 1948.

G. BERNARD HUGHES, 'George Seddon of London House.' Article in *Apollo*, May 1957.

MARGARET JOURDAIN, *English decoration and furniture of the later XVIIIth centuries*, 1760–1820, Batsford, 1922.

'The furniture at Woodhall Park.' Article in *Country Life*, 26 April 1930.

'Unpublished accounts of furniture supplied to Dumfries House.' Article in *Country Life Annual*, 1949.

E. T. JOY, 'Chippendale in trouble.' Article in *Country Life*, 24 August 1951.

ALISON KELLY, *Wedgwood plaques in furniture, Country Life*, London, 1965.

FISKE KIMBALL, 'Les influences anglaises dans la formation du style Louis XVI.' In *Gazette des Beaux Arts*, 6th series, vol. V, 1931.

   'The beginning of the Style Pompadour, 1751–9.' In *Gazette des Beaux Arts*, 6th series, vol. XLIV, 1954.

   The creation of the rococo, Philadelphia, 1943.

Decorative art from the Samuel H. Kress Collection at the Metropolitan Museum of Art, Phaidon Press, London, 1964.

JOHN LEES-MILNE, *The age of Adam*, Batsford, London, 1947.

H. LEFUEL, *Georges Jacob*, Paris, 1923.

PERCY MACQUOID, *A history of English furniture: the age of satinwood*, Lawrence and Bullen, London, 1908.

J.-F. NEUFFORGE, *Recueil d'architecture*, 10 vols., Paris, 1757–77.

JEAN NICOLAY, *Maîtres ébénistes français*, Paris, 1956.

E. H. PINTO, 'Woburn Abbey furniture.' Articles in *Apollo*, November 1955 to February 1956.

H. REPTON, *Fragments of the theory and practice of landscape gardening*, London, 1816.

F. DE SALVERTE, *Les ébénistes du dixhuitième siècle*, Paris 1953.

SOPHIE VON LA ROCHE, *Sophie in London*, translated by Clare Williams, London, 1933.

SIR JOHN SOANE, *Lectures in architecture*, ed. A. T. Bolton, Soane Museum, London, 1929.

EDITH A. STANDEN, 'Croome Court: the tapestries.' Article in Metropolitan Museum of Art Bulletin, November 1959.

SIR JOHN SUMMERSON, *Architecture in Britain, 1530–1830*, London, 1958.

JOHN SWARBRICK, *Robert Adam and his brothers*, Batsford, London, 1913.

   The works in architecture of Robert and James Adam, Tiranti, 1959.

R. W. SYMONDS, 'Adam and Chippendale: a myth exploded.' Article in *The Connoisseur Year Book*, 1958.

G. S. THOMSON, *Family background*, Cape, London, 1949.

HORACE WALPOLE, *The Letters*, ed. by Peter Cunningham, 9 vols., Edinburgh, 1906.

PETER WARD-JACKSON, *English furniture designs of the eighteenth century*, H.M.S.O., 1958.

   Osterley Park: a guide, Victoria and Albert Museum, H.M.S.O., London, 1954.

BIBLIOGRAPHY

F. J. B. WATSON, *Louis XVI furniture*, Tiranti, 1960.

'Painter and furniture designer: reflections in taste in the decorative arts in France around 1760.' Article in *The Antique Collection*, December, 1960.

The Wallace Collection. Catalogue of furniture. London, 1956.

GEOFFREY WILLS, 'Robert Adam at Saltram.' Article in *The Connoisseur Year Book*, 1958.

R. B. WRAGG, 'The history of scagliola.' Article in *Country Life*, 10 October 1957.

NOTES TO THE ILLUSTRATIONS

A. Drawing by Robert Adam for the state bed at Osterley Park, Middlesex. Soane Museum, vol. 17, no. 157, dated 16 May 1776. It is from this design that the bed (Fig. 109) was finally executed, another design having blue upholstery of slightly different design having been rejected (Soane, vol. 17, no. 156). The valance is embroidered with the crest of Robert Child, the owner of Osterley, and a flower ornament on alternate tabs.

The design is one of Adam's most splendid and richly coloured drawings, and displays the liveliness and charm with which he endowed figures, such as those of the delightful sphinxes at the corners of the bed-canopy, and of the putti of the headboard, in the drawings of his mature period. The counterpane was made from Adam's design of 19 August 1776 (Soane, vol. 17, no. 159) and the interior of the dome from one of 18 October 1776 (Soane, vol. 17, no. 158). The headboard is similar to Adam's mirror-crestings, having a central portrait medallion surmounted by figures of putti and dolphins, and supported by female figures.

B. Commode or commode-chest. Harewood and satinwood veneers, with marquetry in various woods. About 1773. This remarkable and very handsome piece is of unusual form, and may have been intended for the dining-room, the drawers being suitable for the storing of cutlery, and the space beneath the hinged top for the keeping of table linen. The concave top may relate to similar features in the music-cabinets provided by William Vile for King George III about 1763. A chest of very similar form and character, but with a flat top, is in the gallery at Syon House.[1] In describing the present commode Mr. E. T. Joy[2] suggests that both commode and chest are the work of Chippendale's firm, on the basis of the inlaid linked rosettes in the frieze of both pieces being exactly similar to rosettes in the frieze of a pair of side-tables in harewood which were supplied to Mersham-le-Hatch where the furniture was provided by Chippendale, and whose bills survive. Furthermore, the character of the marquetry-work in both the articles is similar to that of the dressing-commode which Chippendale is known to have supplied to Harewood in 1773 (Harewood accounts) (see page 81). Another point of similarity is in that of the bold inlaid anthemion motif within a leaf-shaped line which appears in the small 'bonheur-du-jour' writing-table at Stourhead (Fig. 164) which is believed to have been supplied to the house by the younger Chippendale.

Colour transparency supplied by Hotspur, Ltd.

C. The tapestry room at Osterley Park, Middlesex. Victoria and Albert Museum. Designed by Robert Adam and completed about 1776. Horace Walpole described the room in 1778 as 'the most superb and beautiful that can be imagined' at the same time criticizing Adam for 'sticking diminutive heads in bronze, no bigger than half-a-crown, in the chimney-piece's

[1] R. Edwards, *The shorter dictionary*, p. 210, Fig. 40.
[2] E. T. Joy, 'A marquetry commode of c. 1775'. Article in *The Connoisseur*, January 1965.

hair'! These offending ornaments, which appear also in the friezes of the door-cases, are in fact of composition, and represent Adam's attempt to obtain effects of delicacy and refinement by means of small-scale decoration.

The ceiling is characteristic of Adam's best work in his mature middle period. Although the ornament is in low-relief, unlike his earlier work, it is still bold and satisfying in form, and given its full effect by its careful disposition in space. The central ornament is shaped as a Greek cross with a central painted roundel, and smaller roundels in the corners. As in so many of Adam's best rooms, the ceiling-design is echoed, though not exactly reproduced, by the carpet, made by Moore, for which a design by Robert Adam exists dated 1775.

The tapestries bear the signature of Jacques Neilson, manager of the Gobelins manufactory, together with the date 1775 woven into them in the panel above the fireplace. The medallions in gold against a background of rich crimson represent 'The Loves of the Gods' after designs by Boucher, while the sofa, chairs and screen are covered with tapestry *en suite* decorated with designs from the same artist representing *Les Enfants Jardiniers*. The flower ornaments on the seats are after designs by Maurice Jacques, as also are the vases, garlands of flowers and trophies in the wall-hangings, and by his colleague Tessier. The gilt tripod-stand, one of a pair, is a fine example of one of Adam's most beautiful types (see page 52). The tripod-shaped perfume-burners on them are most probably the work of Matthew Boulton. For the chairs see Fig. 64.

D. The gallery at Harewood House, Yorkshire. The Earl of Harewood. Completed about 1769, the date of Adam's drawing for the ceiling, which was executed by Joseph Rose. It is of an extremely complex design consisting of ovals alternating with octagons surrounded by crosses and lunettes, and eighteen panels painted with classical scenes by Biagio Rebecca. It is somewhat distracting in its intricacy, and the profusion of small-scale ornament is of the kind that caused Adam's work eventually to be criticized by Sir William Chambers as 'filigraine toywork'.

The great pier-glasses, presumably supplied by Chippendale about 1770, represent this craftsman's interpretation of Adam's tripartite design for mirrors. In these the oval crest-panels also are painted. The pier-tables themselves are of the early Regency style rather than that of Adam, being supplied by the younger Chippendale in 1796 (Harewood accounts). In the window-bays are gilt window-seats in the Adam style with high scroll-shaped arms. The most astonishing feature of the room however, are the curtain valances. Hanging from carved gilt curtain-boxes of great richness, they are not of silk taffeta, as they appear, but are carved in wood and painted with remarkable skill. They are not merely a *tour-de-force* of the carver's art, but have been executed with such breadth of form, and endowed with such sculptural quality, even the marks of the carver's tools on the work being visible without destroying the illusion, that they have become satisfying works of art in themselves. And yet this masterpiece of three dimensional *trompe l'oeil* is functional, for silk material would soon have become dusty and would have been difficult to clean at that height, and would moreover have perished quickly, and the work of replacement every few years would have been both difficult and costly. In the foreground are two of Chippendale's chairs combining the rococo in their cartouche-backs and curved back-legs with the neo-classical spirit of the straight fluted front-legs. The black lacquer table and cabinet are of the Queen Anne period.

Colour transparency supplied by English Life Publications, Ltd.

1. The dining-room apse at Kedleston Hall, Derbyshire. The Viscount Scarsdale. Robert Adam's first sideboard composition, the design for which is dated 1762, and is illustrated in Fig. 2. This sectional drawing preserved at Kedleston shows the half-dome painted in red, blue, green and gold; it is now pale blue with ornaments in white. The three small separate tables represent a more primitive arrangement than the later Adam sideboard groups, such as those at Saltram. They are painted white, with gilt ornaments. The apse reproduces the arrangements in ancient Roman baths, even to the wine-cooler of Sicilian marble that takes the place of the *labrum* or marble head-bath in the apse of a Roman *calidarium*. Adam did not design the wall-lights or the mirror; these were added in comparatively modern times, but it seems that Adam intended there to have been some other decoration on the walls of the apse.

2. 'Drawing at large of the sideboard in the nich [sic] of the Dining-Room at Kedleston.' Signed and dated 'Robt. Adam Architect 1762.' The Viscount Scarsdale's Collection. This is Adam's first neo-classical furniture design and is clearly based on a drawing by James Stuart for the painted room at Spencer House (Fig. 3) dated 1759 and one for the hall at Kedleston, where Stuart is known to have been employed before 1758 (see E. Harris, *Adam furniture*, Fig. 1). The pedestals, tripod and other accessories are no longer displayed in a united group, but are dispersed in various positions in the dining-room and elsewhere.

   Separate drawings exist for the wine-cooler (Soane, vol. 25, no. 80) the tripod candela-brum (Soane, vol. 25, nos. 89, 91) and the two urns and basins (Soane, vol. 25, no. 83) and were apparently made a year before the table, in 1761.

3. Design attributed to James Stuart, for the painted room at Spencer House, St. James's, London. British Museum. The drawing bears the date 1759 in Roman numerals in a tablet over the door. The decorative details of painted roundels and panels on the walls, the 'flowing rainceau' of the pilasters, and the ornament of an urn flanked by sphinx supporters above the door are features familiar in Adam's subsequent work. The table is obviously the forerunner of Adam's classical tables with straight, square-section tapering fluted legs at Kedleston and those at Syon made several years later. The lion-paw feet closely resemble those of a marble table which Stuart may have seen at Pompeii (see page 31). The lion support is an ancient feature not generally adopted until much later in the eighteenth century, and like many elements in Stuart's architecture and furniture design, more commonly found during the Regency period (see page 31).

4. Side-table in the dining-room at Kedleston Hall, Derbyshire. One of a pair, carved and gilt. The Viscount Scarsdale. These tables, which stand in the window-piers, correspond more closely in some aspects to Adam's sideboard drawing than the tables of the niche themselves, especially in the richness of the frieze and of the foliated ornaments of the feet (see Figs. 1 and 2). They also have additional ornaments of festoon drops depending from rosettes in the capitals of the legs, and small ornaments in the angle of the legs and the frieze. An interesting departure from Adam's drawing, however, both in these tables and those of the niche, is that the moulding beneath the marble top instead of being of an acanthus leaf-top design, has been executed in a tongue and dart pattern, which Adam never used in his furniture designs but which appears in James Stuart's early neo-classical furniture (Fig. 5). The maker may have been Linnell, who is known to have made other furniture at Kedleston. The marble tops have serpentine shaping, and may not originally have belonged to the tables.

5. Pier-table from Spencer House, St. James's, London, now in the great room at Althorp,

Northants. The Earl Spencer. One of a pair, carved and gilt, with marble tops. These pier-tables, associated with tall pier-glasses, were most probably made to the design of James Stuart, about 1759–61, and possess features found in Adam's straight-legged side-tables of later years, especially in the triple fluting of the legs, the block capitals with rosettes, and the guilloche moulding of the stretcher, which became a favourite frieze ornament of Adam's. The tongue and dart moulding beneath the frieze, the central female mask, and the heavy swags of flowers, are surviving baroque elements. The delicate feet, with their concave fluting, suggest the form of the very characteristic feet and legs of commodes and other articles in Chippendale's neo-classical furniture of some ten years later (Figs. 120, 123, and 126).

6. Design for a window pier. Detail from a drawing for a great hall and attributed to James Stuart. The Viscount Scarsdale's Collection. Although the drawing is unsigned, its stylistic similarity to the Spencer House drawing (Fig. 3) justifies the ascription to Stuart. Also it is known that he was producing designs for Kedleston in 1758 or just before (see page 40). Apart from the straight-legged classical pier-table, an important feature is the tripod candelabrum, which is the forerunner of a type designed by Adam in 1760–1 for the dining-room at Kedleston (see Fig. 2). The baroque scroll-feet of the pedestals have a similarity to those of the pedestals made for Spencer House, now at Althorp, and almost certainly designed by Stuart (Fig. 9).

7. Tripod from Spencer House, St. James's, London, now at Althorp, Northants. The Earl Spencer. One of a pair, carved, painted and gilt. These tripods, almost certainly designed by James Stuart, embody the classical formula of straight tapering fluted legs of square section, with lion-paw feet and fluted frieze, as expressed in Stuart's drawing for Spencer House dated 1759. The honeysuckle capital is of distinctive character and is found in other neo-classical furniture from Spencer House. This tripod may have influenced the design of certain side-tables later made under Adam's influence for Syon House (Fig. 8).

8. Side-table in the gallery, Syon House, Middlesex. The Duke of Northumberland. One of a pair, carved and gilt, with marble tops. No drawing by Robert Adam appears to exist for these side-tables, although the pendent frieze-ornament of half-rosettes corresponds closely to Adam's design (Fig. 18) for the gilt side-table of 1767 in the eating-room at Osterley, but the present tables must be rather earlier in date. The theme of the classical tripod embodied in the articles from Spencer House has obviously been a strong inspiration, as it obviously was to Adam in his use of it in the stucco ornament of the gallery walls at Syon. The scale and character of the table legs are very similar to those of the small tripods from Spencer House (Fig. 7) and the lion-paw feet are almost identical. The handling of the interlace ornament on the curved stretcher suggests Linnell as the maker. He is known to have carried out work at Syon. Again the un-Adam-like tongue and dart moulding found in the side-tables at Kedleston appears beneath the table-top.

9. Tripod, pedestal and candelabrum from Spencer House, St. James's, London, now at Althorp, Northants. The Earl Spencer. One of a pair, the pedestals carved, gilt and painted, the candelabra of ormolu, on marble bases. Presumably designed by James Stuart c. 1759. The candelabra are similar to those shown in Stuart's drawings (Figs. 3 and 4) and later adopted by Adam. The highly characteristic anthemion ornament of the Spencer House gilt-wood tripods is seen again in the scrolled base of the pedestals. The painted decoration of winged female figures on a dark Etruscan-red ground was apparently influenced by late

Roman wall decorations, such as those of the painted figures from the House of the Dancing Faun at Herculaneum, which were widely reproduced in England. Stuart must have seen decoration of this kind during his visit to Pompeii in 1754.

The scroll-shaped feet of the tripods provide a link between the baroque and the classical, as exists in most of Stuart's furniture, and the gryphons have the taut stiffness of Kent's and Flitcroft's[1] animal supports of thirty years earlier. Later, Adam was to adapt this design, moving the gryphons to a lower stage of the piece (Fig. 145).

10. Side-table at Rousham House, Oxfordshire. Carved and gilt. T. Cottrell-Dormer, Esq. Presumably designed by William Kent, who remodelled the house in 1738–41. A typical example of Kent's advanced classicism of the earlier part of the eighteenth century, with the straight, square-section tapering legs, with strings of husks on the outer face, key-pattern frieze with rosettes, and square, block feet, so frequently to be followed thirty and more years later by Adam and Chippendale. The console tops to the legs, the heavy swags and the shell are the baroque features indicating the true age of the piece.

11. Side-table, in the dining-room at Syon House, Middlesex. One of a set of four, carved, painted white and gilt, and with marble tops. The Duke of Northumberland. Designer unknown. Two of the tables are larger, with four front legs, but of similar design. The precedent of William Kent's early neo-classicism has obviously been followed in the designing of these tables for Syon, which was Adam's first completely neo-classical interior, created by him 1762–9. A drawing by Robert Adam (Soane, vol. 17, no. 12) dated 1765, and described as being intended for Syon, shows a side-table with straight, square-section legs having the baroque feature of a console-shaped upper part, although other elements are purely neo-classical. This design was illustrated in *The Works* as intended for the Earl of Bute, but there is no evidence that it was ever executed as drawn. The smaller dining-room tables at Syon reproduce closely the Kentian form of the Rousham table, and also the precise shape of the block-feet (see Fig. 10). The frieze however has been given Adam's acanthus-tip moulding denied him in the Kedleston side-tables. In view of these indications it seems reasonable to suggest that Adam must have had a hand in the designing of these tables.

12. Side-table at Rousham House, Oxfordshire. T. Cottrell-Dormer, Esq. Carved and painted. Probably designed by William Kent, *c.* 1738–41. The neo-classical spirit introduced by Kent some twenty years before Adam is apparent in this piece with its key-pattern frieze, straight, square tapering legs and square block feet. The 'pelta' or shield-form motif seen in the block capitals, later became a favourite motif in Adam's work, and indeed in much neo-classical decorative work throughout Europe. It was extremely unusual at this early date. This type of traditional English classicism was a strong influence in Chippendale's early classical furniture.

13. Side-table from Stanmer House, Brighton, about 1755. The Earl of Chichester. Now at Brighton Art Gallery. Pine, carved, painted white and gilt. Siena marble top. This side-table is of a traditional English type informed by William Kent's early neo-classicism, and has the familiar leaf-ornamented console scroll. Similar side-tables are to be found at Newby Hall, Yorkshire, belonging to James Paine's era. The form has been closely followed in Adam's foregoing design (Fig. 15) but the ornament is there more delicate and of less baroque character.

14. Design of a sideboard-table in Chippendale's *Director*, third edition, 1762, Plate LXI. Two

[1] R. Edwards, *The shorter dictionary*, Fig. 24, 25, 27 and 29.

types of leg are shown, both of renaissance classical origin, with small Ionic capitals and two forms of block feet. One pair of legs is fluted, the other panelled in the early Georgian manner but with classical husk-ornament.

15. Drawing of a 'Table frame for the Dining-Room at Sion' dated 1765, Soane Museum, vol. 17, no. 3. This design was followed with some minor modifications for the tables now in the ante-room at Syon (Fig. 95). It shows Adam's fondness for giving greater importance to the upper part of a table leg than would be obtained by a capital only. This treatment, and the acanthus leaf motif of the decoration appear to have derived from a design by the French architect Neufforge (vol. 5, 1763, Plate 297). Even though Adam's designs of this period are ponderous by comparison with his later creations, they are infinitely lighter than those of the Frenchman, and this greater refinement of character is probably Adam's chief contribution to furniture design. Adam has made an important advance upon the baroque character of Neufforge's style, and of much English furniture of the baroque era (Fig. 13), by making the leaf-ornamented feature of the legs straight instead of the scrolled, console-shape customary in early French and English furniture.

16. Design of a 'Sopha for Sir Laurence Dundas, Bart,' by Robert Adam. Soane Museum, vol. 17, no. 73. It was apparently rejected by Sir Laurence Dundas for Moor Park and accepted by Lord Coventry for Croome Court before February 1765, if this is indeed the article mentioned in Adam's bill of that date as 'Another design of a Sopha or Scrol Chair,' and it may thus be dated to 1764.

    Adam's earliest surviving fully neo-classical design for seat-furniture, it shows an adaptation of the straight-legged formula to be seen in the Syon side-tables, the legs here being of round section however. It is a development followed in the work of several crafts-men subsequently (see Fig. 58). Although such features had appeared in isolated French designs, they were by no means common at that early date. The stool itself is illustrated by E. Harris (Fig. 104).

17. 'The front and side elevation of a design for a Table Frame for the two porphyry tables.' Part of a drawing signed by Robert Adam, dated 1765, and inscribed with the name of the client, Sir Charles Farnaby. Soane Museum, vol. 17, no. 6. This is Adam's earliest known design embodying the classical elements found in early French neo-classical designs appearing in Neufforge's *Recueil*, especially in the use of triple fluted straight legs of square section with bolt-heads above the flutes, heavy festoons, small Ionic capitals, and Vitruvian scroll moulding (Neufforge, vol. 5, 1763, Plate 310). However, all these elements existed in English as well French and Italian Renaissance furniture, where they are moreover treated with far greater delicacy than in Neufforge's designs. The drawing is important also in being the forerunner of an interesting group of Linnell's writing and library tables at Alnwick, Osterley (Fig. 39) and elsewhere. These are associated with Linnell's drawings of c. 1775 (Victoria and Albert Museum: E236–1929 see Fig. 36).

18. 'Design of a table frame for the Sideboard in the Eating-Room at Osterly' by Robert Adam. Signed and dated 1767. This design, preserved at Osterley Park, was published as an engraving in *The Works*, vol. III, Plate IX, wrongly inscribed as for Syon House, and showing also the accompanying pedestals and urns, and a wine-cooler which has not been traced. The design indicates a step further towards the baluster leg which became fully developed in Adam's chairs made about 1777 for the bedroom at Osterley (Fig. 66). This type of leg, which began to be common during the 1770's in England, and was one of the distinguishing

marks of chairs in the Louis Seize style in France, first appears in English furniture with Chippendale's library chairs for Nostell of 1768 (Fig. 62). Their only known French fore-runner is in the chair made by Georges Jacob as his masterpiece in 1765 (see page 67).

By permission of the Victoria and Albert Museum.

19. Design of a term-pedestal by Robert Adam, about 1765. Soane Museum, vol. 17, no. 59. Inscribed 'Design of a Term for Candles for Sir John Griffin Griffin.' Executed in the form of six pedestals, two ornamented and four plain, which are now at Audley End, where Robert Adam re-decorated a room, 1763–5. The form is akin to those designed by William Kent for Rousham. A similar pedestal made for Sir Laurence Dundas and once at 19 Arlington Street, is in the Victoria and Albert Museum (see E. Harris, *Adam furniture*, Fig. 131). It corresponds closely with the same Adam drawing, and with another (Soane, vol. 17, no. 58) of a pedestal made for Sir John Astley, of Patshull, Staffordshire. These articles are typical of Adam's bold early classical style, and at the same time provide instances of the scaling-down and refinement of such decorative details as the festoons, paterae and mouldings by comparison with the more ponderous earlier Georgian types, and there is nothing to correspond with the wildly exuberant acanthus ornament found on Kent's pedestals.

20. Design of a tripod-stand, by Robert Adam, dated 1778, inscribed 'Design of a Tripod for Lady Home', Soane Museum, vol. 17, no. 63. A number of designs exist by Robert Adam for tripod pedestals of this very beautiful type, adapted by him from the ancient model revived presumably by James Stuart with the pedestals for Spencer House (Fig. 9). Adam has narrowed and attenuated the base almost into the form of a triangular column, but retaining the concave panelled sides. He has also copied the gryphons of Stuart's and earlier pedestals, but has brought them down from the upper part to form supports for the super-base with paw-feet and a plinth. Tripods executed to a similar design (Soane, vol. 17, no. 62) dated 1773 and intended for 20 St. James's Square are now at Alnwick Castle (illustrated in E. Harris, Fig. 137). Another tripod-stand of similar form but with variations of detail is at Osterley (Fig. 146).

21. Design for a 'Table-Frame for Sir Laurence Dundas Baronet' by Robert Adam. Dated 1765. Soane Museum, vol. 17, no. 5. A table was executed to this design, presumably by Samuel Norman, for 19 Arlington Street. A similar table but with different mouldings was made for Moor Park and eventually brought to Arlington Street (see E. Harris, Fig. 8). The design shows a Vitruvian scroll in the frieze and stretcher, and scale-moulding in the supports, both of them early Georgian features. Neo-classicism enters with the rams' heads, festoons, and delicate festoons, but the basic design of this type of table, with four curved supports gathered into a small stretcher, derives from early eighteenth century English and French types, such as the baroque console-table of similar form, with hoofed feet made for the Château de Bercy about 1715, and now in the Louvre.[1]

22. 'Design of a Glass Frame to be placed over the Chimney in Lady Bathurst's Dressing Room', by Robert Adam. Soane Museum, vol. 20, no. 171. Dated 31 January 1778. The design represents the excessive delicacy and nerveless refinement of Adam's later versions of the tripartite 'Venetian window' type of looking-glass. The elongated terminal figure supports are stiff and characterless, and have lost the life and charm of the figures in his earlier mirror-designs such as that for Luton (Fig. 27).

[1] C. Dreyfus, *Le mobilier français*, Plate 8.

23. Design for a 'Sopha for Mr. President Dundas' by Robert Adam, dated December 1770. Soane Museum, vol. 17, no. 77. This is one of an interesting series of designs made by Adam between about 1765 and 1773 for sofas which are all of great length in relation to their height, and are presumably intended as permanent features in a wall-composition. In this piece there is a strong resemblance to Adam's first neo-classical seat-design but the legs mark an advance to a more elegant form, being of attenuated vase-form with narrow 'therm' necking, and finely fluted. The outward scrolling ends still retain a hint of early Georgian design, although they are much more delicate, and the medallion crest derives from examples in the designs of Neufforge (e.g. Fig. 40).

24. Design of a 'Harpsichord for the Empress of Russia', by Robert Adam. Dated 1776. Soane Museum, vol. 25, no. 9. The design was published in *The Works*, vol. I, Part 5, Plate VIII, but in plans and elevations instead of perspective, and with female instead of male goat-legged figures.

    Adam seems to have sacrificed the traditional and functional harp-shape of a harpsichord in the interests of classical symmetry, creating a rectangular shape in which much space must have been wasted.

25. 'Design of a Slab [table-top] for Sir Abraham Hume, Baronet' by Robert Adam. Soane Museum, vol. 17, no. 34, dated 1779.

    The drawing represents a type of design for table-tops much favoured by Adam, embodying plaques and medallions with figures, arranged as focal points detached from the centre of the designs, and linked by festoons. Compare with Hepplewhite's table-top designs (Fig. 52).

26. 'Design of a Sideboard Table and Wine-Cistern for the Right Honble. W. G. Hamilton's Dining Room at Brighton,' by Robert Adam. Soane Museum, vol. 6, no. 116. Undated, probably 1787, when Adam was designing Marlborough House. The table has the somewhat attenuated tapering legs of square section frequently adopted by Adam for his dining-room sideboard tables in his later years. Here they are rather unusually ornamented for this date with a tiny Ionic capital. The frieze ornament is in the form of a vine-leaf and grape meander almost exactly as executed in the sideboard at Newby Hall (Fig. 136) which is believed to be from the firm of Chippendale.

    The bronze back-rail became increasingly popular for sideboards from the later Adam period into the Regency age. The wine cistern has a band of serpentine 'sarcophagus' fluting and lion-mask handles, of a kind frequently found in a more or less developed form (Fig. 168).

27. Engraving of a mirror, table and tripods in *The Works*, vol. III, 1822, Plate VIII, from a design inscribed 'Glass and Table frame and Tripods for the Drawing Room at Luton', dated 1772, Soane Museum, vol. 20, no. 116. The engraving is wrongly described as 'Furniture for Sion House'. It is one of Adam's finest tripartite mirror designs with a flat centre portion and female terminal figure supports. The table has tapering legs of an unusual type for Adam, being reeded instead of fluted, and without capitals, similar to those of the sideboard at Newby Hall (Fig. 136). A pair of sideboards made to this design are now at Mount Stuart, Rothesay, the seat of the Marquess of Bute, for whose ancestor the articles were first designed and made. A mirror corresponding closely to the design, but differing slightly in the dimensions, is now at Sledmere, Yorkshire, the seat of Sir Richard Sykes.

The tripods are a development of the antique sacrificial incense-burner type of tripod introduced by Adam in the 'Water-stand' design for Lord Coventry, Sir Laurence Dundas and the Duke of Bolton (Fig. 28 and see page 51) which was based on French originals. The tripods in this engraving represent the more slender and delicate forms of Adam's middle period. A year later than Adam's design such tripods had been given the name of 'athéniennes' in France, after J.-B. Vien's painting, 'La vertueuse Athénienne' of 1763, which represented a young priestess offering incense at such a tripod (see page 71).

28. Engraving of a mirror, table clock and tripods, etc., in *The Works*, vol. I, no. I, 1773, Plate VIII, entitled 'Design of a glass and commode table upon which is placed a clock and vases with branches for candles.' Engraved by B. Pastorini. The design for the mirror (Soane, vol. 20, no. 97) is inscribed 'Glass frame for Messrs. Adam at the Adelphi' and is dated 1772. No design appears to exist for the table, but it is of similar character to a design for a table at Luton (Soane, vol. 17, no. 9) illustrated in E. Harris, Fig. 23. A pair of small tables of similar type, presumably executed for Luton, are now at Mount Stuart, Rothesay, the seat of the Earl of Bute.

The reclining female figures upon the upper curve of the mirror represent an adaptation by Adam of a baroque theme, in a more graceful and relaxed spirit (see page 43). The horizontal moulding and the crest, supporting scrolled foliage and other ornaments is again very characteristic of Adam's mirror designs. The tripod to the left is described in *The Works* (vol. I, part I, page 12) as 'tripod for the Earl of Coventry executed in ormolu for Sir Laurence Dundas and afterwards for the Duke of Bolton.' The design was based on a sketch by Adam (Soane, vol. 6, no. 177), illustrated in E. Harris, Fig. 134. It is inscribed 'Lord Coventry's Tripod (?) for' with the words 'Water Stand' heavily written over.

An entry in Adam's bill to Lord Coventry (Croome accounts) for 6 May 1767 refers to 'A Tripod altered from a French design for a Water Stand £1.1s.'. Adam's design for this and for the tripod on the right of the engraving thus represent his earliest application of the classical tripod adapted as an article of furniture, and are clearly inspired from French neo-classical sources (see page 51). James Stuart's earlier tripods made for Spencer House (Fig. 9) are much earlier but are of different form. The tripod to the right is described in *The Works* (*loc. cit.*) as 'Tripod for the Earl of Coventry with a base for candles'. It does not appear to have been executed.

29. 'Design of a Sofa for Lord Scarsdale & also executed for Mrs. Montagu in Hill Street,' by Robert Adam, dated 1762. Soane Museum, vol. 17, no. 69. This drawing has similarities to another in the Soane Museum (vol. 17, no. 70) which was followed very closely in a sofa now in the Philadelphia Museum of Art (illustrated in E. Harris, Fig. 100). The drawing was presumably never accepted by Lord Scarsdale, but taken by John Linnell as a point of departure for the sofas in the drawing-room at Kedleston which were made by John Linnell (Fig. 34). Adam's drawing is strongly baroque, with its Kentian back, gadroon moulding of the seat rail and use of supporting figures, although the massiveness of the baroque idiom is no longer present.

30. Design of a sofa, signed *J. Linnell*. Victoria and Albert Museum. E140–1929. Strong similarities to Adam's drawing (Fig. 24) are obvious in the shape of the back with its medallion, the character of the supporting triton figures, and in the form of the legs, although they have been made more stumpy.

31. Design of 'Lord Scarsdale's Sofa at Kedleston in Derbyshire' by John Linnell. Victoria and Albert Museum, E129–1929. This drawing marks a considerable advance towards the sofas at Kedleston as finally executed by Linnell. The figures of mer-folk are almost exactly as realized, although they differ in each of the four sofas. The use of these figures originated immediately with Adam in his ceiling decoration of mer-folk in the drawing-room at Kedleston, and earlier in the ceilings of Hatchlands (1758–61), although massive gilt figures of mer-folk were used as supports of Roman baroque seventeenth century furniture, such as the great harpsichord with flanking figures in the Metropolitan Museum, New York.[1]

32. Drawing of a Triton, by John Linnell. Victoria and Albert Museum, E119–1929. This drawing is a delightful example of Linnell's vigorous, lively and engaging manner.

33. Detail of Triton end-support of sofa in the state drawing-room at Kedleston Hall, made by John Linnell (see Fig. 29). The craftsman seems to have received inspiration in the final designing of the figures from those of mer-folk in the coach designed by Sir William Chambers for the coronation of King George III in 1762[2] (see page 86). They are also akin in style to the massive figures of mer-folk used as supports of baroque seventeenth century Italian harpsichords and other furniture.

34. Sofa in the state drawing-room at Kedleston Hall, Derbyshire. The Viscount Scarsdale. Carved and gilt, by John Linnell. The sofa is one of a set of four, with the supporting figures of tritons and sirens differing in each piece. The gadrooning of the seat rail is exactly as in Adam's original drawing (Fig. 29), and the design of the back-rail and medallion closely follows it. The motif of twisted dolphins in the front feet derives from sixteenth century Italian renaissance furniture, as well as from ancient models (see also Fig. 31). The general form and scale of the sofas are very similar to those at Woburn Abbey, where, as already noted (page 43), are many examples of baroque furniture that could have provided Adam with inspiration for his early designs.

35. Sketch of a pleasure-boat, by Robert Adam. The Viscount Scarsdale's Collection. The sketch is on the back of a drawing of a rustic building by Adam. The bridge and boat-house or fishing-house at Kedleston were among the first works carried out by Adam at Kedleston, while Paine was still engaged there, and the sketch for the boat would seem to belong to this phase. The palm-tree motif was a fairly common baroque idea, appearing at the early date of 1665 in a drawing by John Webb for an alcove and bed for King Charles II (see page 86).

A connexion between Adam and Spencer House again arises for the palm-tree motif appeared in 'Athenian' Stuart's designs for the painted room there dated 1759 (Fig. 3, and page 40) and in decoration carried out by John Vardy about 1760. Adam also used the motif in the tea pavilion at Moor Park about 1763. It is of course an ancient device, appearing in the decorations of the House of Modestus at Pompeii.

36. Design for a pier-table by John Linnell. Victoria and Albert Museum, E236–1929. This drawing is closely related to one by Robert Adam of a table for Sir Charles Farnaby (Fig. 17), and both may derive from a design by Neufforge (*Receuil*, vol. 5, 1763). These designs, and another by Linnell (Fig. 31) would appear to provide the basis for the writing-tables at Alnwick and Osterley, and for the library table also in the latter houses (Fig. 39). The

[1] *Illustrated London News*, 9 March 1963.
[2] R. Croft-Murray, 'Three famous state coaches'. Article in *Country Life* (Coronation number), 1953.

character of the Vitruvian scroll ornament, which reverses in the centre, is identical, and the treatment of the festoons is also similar.

37. Torchère of palm-tree design in the state bedroom at Kedleston Hall. The Viscount Scarsdale. One of a pair, carved and gilt, by John Linnell. The palm-tree columns flanking the doors of Chambers's coronation coach seem to have served as a model for these torchères as well as for the palm-tree posts of the state bed itself (see Fig. 37, also page 86 and Fig. 38).

38. The state bed at Kedleston. The Viscount Scarsdale. Carved, painted and gilt, by John Linnell. In its form and decorative treatment the bed is strongly baroque in design, even to the ostrich-feather plumes of seventeenth century type at the angles of the canopy. Although the suggestion for the palm-tree treatment seems to have been Adam's, at this early stage his neo-classical style was insufficiently formed to permit of a successful design being carried out without having a basis in an established style.

39. The library, Osterley Park, Middlesex. Victoria and Albert Museum. Designed by Robert Adam in 1766 (the drawings may be seen at the house) and finished by 1773. The ornament of the bookcases is bold in scale and is beautifully detailed. The large library table and the writing table, both veneered with mahogany and harewood and inlaid with emblems of the arts of architecture, sculpture, music and painting, are believed to have been made by Linnell together with much other furniture of the house, including the lyre-back chairs which are just visible (see also Fig. 62). The Vitruvian scroll in all the library furniture is of the same character as in the drawings of Linnell and Adam (Figs. 17 and 36), the direction of the scroll being different on each side and the join made in a characteristic and unusual manner.

40. The centre-bay of the long gallery at Syon House, Middlesex. The Duke of Northumberland. Completed 1769. This interior represents the beginning of Adam's mature period in its most beautiful form. The ornament is more delicate, smaller in scale and in lighter relief than earlier, but is not yet of the excessive refinement that caused his work to be criticized later. The enchanting sphinx-mermaid figures above the door are similar to ornaments frequently used by Adam in his furniture, such as the state bed at Osterley (Fig. 109) and several of his mirror designs (Fig. 100).

The gilt side-tables show the still satisfying but more elegant form of Adam's furniture-designs of this period, with an early type of the baluster leg, and with the urn-mounted stretcher deriving from earlier French models (see Fig. 97 and page 89). The painted and gilt armchairs with their cartouche backs and slender curving legs, covered, like the sofa, with contemporary embroidery, are typical of the extreme elegance achieved by English craftsmen in their adaptation of French rococo forms which enjoyed a revival of popularity during the Hepplewhite period about 1770 to 1780 (see page 107). The sofa, one of a pair, has the delicate baluster leg of the Adam style (see Fig. 83).

41. Designs for chairs from Hepplewhite's *Guide*, 1788, 1789 and 1794 editions. Plate 2, c and d, first published 1787. Two shield-back designs. Design c shows splayed legs of a type that was to become increasingly popular in the Sheraton period. In design the plainness of the legs contrasts strongly with the rich carving of the back.

42. Designs for chairs from Hepplewhite's *Guide*, 1788 and 1789 editions only. Plate 6, K and L, first published 1787. An oval-back and a shield-back design. The legs show the influence of traditional English classicism as developed by Chippendale rather than the spirit of later

Adam design. In the third edition (1794), Plate K was exchanged for a more modish square-back design.

43. Designs for chairs from Hepplewhite's *Guide*, 1788 and 1789 editions only. Plate 1a and b, first published 1787. Plate 'a' is for a design often followed for the simpler kind of furniture in the Hepplewhite style, especially by provincial and rural craftsmen. In the 1794 edition design 'b' was replaced by one for a chair of more fashionable square-back type. The splayed legs in plate 'b' should again be noted (see also Fig. 41).

44. Designs for chairs from Hepplewhite's *Guide*, 1788 and 1789 editions only. Plate 12 W and X, first published 1787. These two designs are in the rococo style which persisted quite strongly during much of the Hepplewhite period. Plate W shows a back of cartouche form, with legs of square-section but curved and splayed in what may be called a semi-classical manner. Design X is for a richer type of chair, of fully rococo form with cabriole legs and French scroll feet, but with neo-classical decoration of an urn, husks, wheat-ears and formalized leaf and flower sprays. In the third edition the plate was replaced by one of six designs for chair-backs, four of them square.

45. Designs for pedestals and vases from Hepplewhite's *Guide*, 1788, 1789 and 1794 editions. Plate 36, first published 1787. The oval and pear-shaped forms for vases seem to have been Hepplewhite's own contribution; there are no designs of this kind among Adam's drawings. One pedestal is shown fitted up as a plate-warmer with racks and a stand for a heater. It would have been lined with tin. The height of the vases was about 2 feet 3 inches.

46. Design for a sideboard from Hepplewhite's *Guide*, 1788, 1789 and 1794 editions. Plate 34, first published 1787. Again the influence of traditional English classicism, transmitted through Chippendale, is apparent in the robust vigour and scale of the carved frieze ornament, and in the moulding of the legs. Adam's influence is seen in the small urns in the frieze above the legs. The ornaments to the front could be carved, painted or inlaid in various coloured woods.

47. Design for a sofa from Hepplewhite's *Guide*, 1788, 1789 and 1794 editions. Plate 24, first published 1787. This design expresses the characteristic elegance of the Hepplewhite settee, combining fulness of form in the great depth of back and seat, with the delicacy of the slender legs. These are of the baluster type originating in England about 1768 (see page 38), with concave necking, but are shown presumably painted, with a surface design of spiralling garland instead of the carved or painted pendent leaf-ornament usual on late Adam settee and chair-legs.

48. Design for a chair-back settee from Hepplewhite's *Guide*, 1788, 1789 and 1794 editions. Plate 26, first published 1787. Described in the *Guide* as a 'Bar-back sofa', this type of settee is one of the most graceful and popular pieces evolved by Hepplewhite. The legs are shown as of smooth baluster form with a lotus-leaf capital.

49. Designs for window stools, from Hepplewhite's *Guide*, 1788, 1789 and 1794 editions. Plate 18, first published 1787. Both designs are strongly Adamesque in their general graceful and feminine form, especially in the reversed leaf-capping of the legs in Plate A. Distinctive Hepplewhite features are the string of leaves along the frieze and the smooth turned legs in the upper design, and the moulded and panelled leg in the lower example. The 'curtain' ornament in the latter design is very unusual. The dimensions of window stools were 'regulated by the size of the place where they are to stand: their height should not exceed the height of the chairs'.

50. Designs for Pembroke tables from Hepplewhite's *Guide*, 1788, 1789 and 1794 editions. Plate 62, first published 1787. Tables of this elegantly simple character are often regarded as 'Sheraton', but that designer does not in fact illustrate any comparable types. Hepplewhite features which should be noticed are the shell and festoon decoration, the string of husks in the recessed leg faces, and the tapering block or spade-feet. The bowed frieze of the oval table is a refinement which should not be missed.

51. Designs for pier-tables from Hepplewhite's *Guide*, 1788, 1789 and 1794 editions. Plate 64, first published 1787. The two attitudes prevailing in Hepplewhite's designs, within the general Adam influence, are clearly expressed in these two designs; the upper embodying the more rugged Chippendale type of traditional classicism in the square sectioned, tapering leg with sunk face and husk ornament, the lower exhibiting Hepplewhite's extreme refinement of the Adam manner in the undecorated smoothness of the straight turned leg. Both designs exhibit an individual rendering of neo-classical mouldings and ornaments. It was specified that pier-tables should rise equal to or above the dado of a room.

52. Designs of tops for dressing tables and commodes from Hepplewhite's *Guide*, 1788, 1789 and 1794 editions. Plate 78, first published 1787.

The upper two designs well-express Hepplewhite's characteristic refined elegance. The bottom example is a less graceful design, but all have a character that is very different from Sheraton's nervously taut patterns.

53. Design for a 'Secretary and Bookcase' from Hepplewhite's *Guide*, 1788, 1789 and 1794 editions. Plate 44, first published 1787. One of the most typical and most frequently executed of Hepplewhite's designs, the glazing bars being diversified in a great variety of patterns (Fig. 173). The curved splayed feet in a single piece with the base are especially characteristic.

54. Design of a library table from Hepplewhite's *Guide*, 1788, 1789 and 1794 editions. Plate 49, first published 1787. As so often in Hepplewhite's designs for more purely domestic types of furniture, this simple library table derives from Chippendale (*Director*, Plate LXXXIII), rather than from Adam. The strings of husks in the pilasters are typical of the former, and the capitals consisting of a leaf-ornament and a scroll closely resemble characteristic details in the Harewood library table and the Firle bookcase (Figs. 167 and 172), and earlier in a design for a library table in Chippendale's *Director* (third edition), of 1762, Plate LXXXIII.

55. Design for a 'Library Case' from Hepplewhite's *Guide*, 1788, 1789 and 1794 editions. Plate 48, first published 1787.

Long library bookcases such as these did not figure among the articles designed by Adam, as far as is known; and Hepplewhite was inspired instead by examples in Chippendale. The secretaire portion, which is found in most of Hepplewhite's designs, seems to have been an innovation of his own, so also apparently is the elliptical broken pediment.

56. Arm-chair at Alnwick Castle. Duke of Northumberland. Wood, carved and painted white with gilt details. Executed between 1777 and 1780 for the chapel at Alnwick, where Adam had created an entirely Gothic interior in 1770–80 (demolished in the nineteenth century). Made after a design which was a 'copy of one of the Chairs in the Church at Croome for the Earl of Coventry' by Robert Adam dated 1761, which is in fact Adam's earliest furniture design (Soane, vol. 50, no. 21). It is also the only example in Adam's furniture designs of that fascinating but much neglected early phase in his career in which he was producing

drawings of Gothic buildings of great charm, originality and picturesqueness (see page 39). In this interest Adam was again following the example of Kent, who revived the Gothic style early in the eighteenth century (see J. Summerson, *Architecture in Britain*, page 239).

57. Arm-chair. Carved and gilt. Executed for Sir Laurence Dundas at 19 Arlington Street, London, presumably by Samuel Norman, and corresponding to a design for a sofa by Robert Adam dated 1764 (Soane, vol. 17, no. 74). Adam's bill of charges for the house refers on 18 July 1765 'To Design of sopha Chairs for the Salon £5' (Bolton, vol. 2, page 345). The chair is part of a set of which three chairs and a sofa of corresponding design (Fig. 81) were sold at Sotheby's on 6 June 1947, and again on 5 July 1963. Another identical sofa and some chairs are still in the possession of the Marquess of Zetland, a descendant of Sir Laurence Dundas. The form of both chairs and sofas is early-Georgian, overlaid with neo-classical ornament of honeysuckle and sphinxes. A cresting of honeysuckle takes the place of the crest of a shell of feathers that would have been found in an earlier piece. The maker is believed to have been Samuel Norman on the grounds that he is known to have carried out large orders for Sir Laurence.[1] The velvet covering is presumably modern. Originally these chairs and sofas were more likely to have been covered with a silk damask.
Photograph supplied by Sotheby & Co.

58. Arm-chair from Croome Court. The Earl of Coventry. Carved, San Domingo mahogany. One of a set of eight made for the gallery at Croome in 1764 by John Cobb.

Described in the accounts at Croome for 1764–5 as having 'carving all the arms and front feet [by John Cobb] all the rest by Mr. Alken.' Seferin Alken was a carver employed at Croome for especially fine work on doors, windows, architraves and bookcases. He had executed the carved work in the library at Shardeloes, and must have been well-known to Adam. It would appear that the anthemion back-splat and top rail of the chairs were carved by him, and the rest by Cobb.

The chairs seem almost certainly to have been made to some extent in accordance with a design by Robert Adam similar to that of the 'Sopha for Sir Laurence Dundas'. The legs of the chair closely follow this design (Fig. 16), especially in the somewhat thin straight tapering fluted form, and in their relation to the rather large block capitals, with rosettes.

The use of padded arms in conjunction with an open carved wooden back instead of a stuffed back is a highly unusual feature.

59. Chair in the dining-room at Harewood House, Yorkshire. The Earl of Harewood. Mahogany, carved. Supplied presumably by Thomas Chippendale, about 1767. The chair is based on a traditional pre-Adam design, having square tapering legs with panelled faces and block-feet. Chippendale has attempted to adapt this type to a neo-classical interior by giving it a top-rail and back supports with straight lines instead of the flowing curves of the rococo. The top-rail is also fluted, and minor neo-classical details of paterae and husks have been added, including a string of husks around the seat. It is the precursor of later square-back chairs of Chippendale (Fig. 69) which anticipated a characteristic type of the late Louis Seize period (see page 69); but this is a tentative effort, owing more to traditional English classicism than to neo-classical ideas.

60. Lyre-back chair in the eating-room, Osterley Park, Middlesex. Victoria and Albert Museum. One of a set of ten, carved, of Cuban mahogany, the seat upholstered with leather, and with narrow brass moulding around seat frame. They were executed presumably in 1767 when

[1] R. Edwards and M. Jourdain, p. 39.

C   The Tapestry Room at Osterley Park, Middlesex

Adam was designing the sideboard and urns on pedestals for the room (Plates 20 and 141). The craftsman was almost certainly John Linnell, who made not only the latter articles, but who supplied to Shardeloes in 1767 '2 Mahogany elbow chairs with harp-backs. £5:10:0'. Adam's drawing of a 'Chair for Robert Child Esq.' (undated, but assigned to 1767 on the above evidence) was followed except for the legs, which in the drawing are of Adam's primitive classical type, of square-section with large triple-flutes.[1] Aspirations towards increasing elegance are expressed in the impossibly delicate foliated feet of the drawing. The chairs were eventually made with legs of round-section, straight and tapering, with narrow concave necks, and a more practically robust leaf-and-ball foot.

Adam's design is the first known design for a lyre-back chair. The back-rails are still of the early bow-shaped Chippendale *Director* type.

61. Arm-chair from the tapestry-room at Moor Park, now in the Philadelphia Museum of Art. Carved and gilt, and upholstered with tapestry. One of a set of six arm-chairs, two sofas (Fig. 82), two window-stools and a screen, executed about 1770, presumably by Samuel Norman who is known to have supplied furniture 'to the amount of over ten thousand' to Sir Laurence Dundas. The tapestry wall coverings for the seat furniture, of a similar kind to those at Croome Court, Newby Hall, Osterley and Weston Park, were supplied by the Gobelins manufactory in Paris between 1765 and 1769, but it is extremely doubtful if they were intended for oval-back chairs, but were meant instead for chairs with cartouche-backs (see page 65), for which the design seems more suitable. No comparable design for chairs by Robert Adam exists. Except for the oval backs, the design is different from that of the furniture in all the other tapestry rooms, the legs being of a primitive classical type, of square-section with block capitals, and having recessed faces containing, like the arms also, an ornament of paterae overlapping in the manner of early Georgian coin-moulding. Furthermore, the design of the arms does not seem to have taken into account the small oval Gobelins tapestry arm-pads.

62. Lyre-back arm-chair in the library, Nostell Priory, Yorkshire. Lord St. Oswald. San Domingo mahogany, carved. One of a set of six supplied by Chippendale to Nostell. His bill of 22 January 1768 records '6 Mahogany Chairs with arms for the library the carving exceedingly rich in the antique taste the seats covered with Green Cloth £36.' The chairs display a wholly individual interpretation of Adam motifs, carried out with a robust vigour that is distinctive of Chippendale's work.

The lyre-back and oval patera of the back-rail are of a similar kind to those in Adam's design for the Osterley lyre-back chair (Fig. 60), and the moulding of the seat-rail is in the spirit of typical Adam frieze ornaments. The most significant feature, however, is the round and fluted baluster leg with leaf ornament forming the capital. This is the earliest known manifestation of the leaf-ornamented, fluted baluster leg in English furniture, made a year before its appearance albeit in a less rugged form, in the chairs made by Ince and Mayhew for the tapestry room at Croome (Fig. 63). Even the nulled ball feet of the Chippendale chairs are not unlike the more-vase-shaped feet of the Croome chairs. The design is an advance upon that of the legs of the side-table at Osterley made to Adam's design of 1767 (Fig. 18).

The feet are much more practical than in any of Adam's surviving chair designs, in which this feature possesses a highly unpractical delicacy. A slight awkwardness is

[1] R. W. Symonds in *Country Life Annual*, 1958, p. 54.

apparent in the splaying of the back legs, for which the round tapering style is not suited so well as legs which are of square section.

The lyre-motif carved in the back-splat was introduced by Adam a year earlier, in his design of 1767 of the eating-room chairs for Osterley (Fig. 60).

63. Arm-chair from the tapestry room at Croome Court, now in the Metropolitan Museum, New York. One of six armchairs, carved and gilt, covered with Gobelins tapestry of floral design on crimson imitation damask ground, *en suite* with two settees, made by Mayhew and Ince (see Fig. 102). The accounts at Croome record: 'Oct. 5, 1769. To Mayhew and Ince . . . 6 Large Antique Elbow Chairs with oval Backs carv'd with Double husks and ribbon knot on top, Gilt in the Best Burnish'd Gold, Stuffed with Best hair, in Linen — Backt with Fine Crimson Tanning — proper for covering with Tapestry in the Country . . . the patterns included £77:8:0.'

The final words of the account, which curiously enough appear to have been added subsequently, suggest that Mayhew and Ince provided the design, and not Adam (see also page 66). The legs of the chairs are of the round-sectioned fluted and leaf-ornamented baluster form typical of the Louis Seize style in France. This type of leg had already appeared in Chippendale's library chairs at Nostell in 1768 (Fig. 62). It does not appear generally in France, however, until many years after. It can be conceded that the oval chair-backs may have been inspired by the oval shape of the tapestry medallions, but the strings of husks round the backs and seats must have been inspired from another source, because in the tapestries the crestings are floral sprays (Fig. 102). Crestings of husks were first used in the frames made for Marigny in 1760. As Mrs. Harris mentions,[1] there must have been a 'French design' for the room which Adam saw (see page 64) and which is assumed to have shown furniture. There is no certain evidence, however, that the design did show furniture, or if it did, that it was of neo-classical character. The furniture of all the tapestry rooms differs in the design of the legs; the only constant factor is the oval backs. The tapestry chair-panels however were designed, not for oval backs, but for cartouche backs (see page 65) and the sofa for the Croome tapestry-room is of cartouche shape, as is necessitated by the character of the design (Fig. 102).

64. Lyre-back arm-chair in the library, Osterley Park, Middlesex. Victoria and Albert Museum. One of a set of eight, *en suite* with a large library table and two writing tables (see Fig. 39) of rosewood inlaid with satinwood and ornamented with swags and medallions in ormolu. The shape of the back represents a more sophisticated interpretation of the lyre-theme than the earlier examples at Nostell and Osterley with bow-shaped back rails (Figs. 60 and 62). Like the library-table and writing-tables at Osterley and Alnwick, the design of the frieze and legs — the former with an inlaid Vitruvian scroll, the latter with triglyphs, and festoons — are related to Adam's design dated 1765 of a table frame for Sir Charles Farnaby (Fig. 17) and also to Linnell's drawings (Fig. 36) and Linnell must again be presumed to be the craftsman, as for other furniture at Osterley. The medallion in the chair-back is of comparable character to the metal plaques in the drawing-room commodes there (Fig. 122), and also to the medallions in the backs of the great sofas at Kedleston which are indubitably by Linnell (Fig. 34).

65. Arm-chair in the tapestry room, Osterley Park, Middlesex. Victoria and Albert Museum. One of a set of eight, *en suite* with a sofa carved and gilt and upholstered in Gobelins

[1] E. Harris, *Adam furniture*, p. 10.

tapestry; the backs with Boucher's *Enfants Jardiniers*, the seats with floral designs on a rose-pink imitation damask ground. The chairs were probably executed in 1776, when the tapestry room was formed. By that date this type of chair with oval-back and straight legs was possibly established in France, although no dateable specimens of this period are known. The oval-back has become more refined in form than in the Croome Court examples (Fig. 63). The husks of the cresting have diminished to a tiny string. The legs are of a form rarely if ever seen in France, and the splayed back legs are typically English. The seat-rail, although rounded, has not the almost circular curve favoured in French examples. No comparable design by Robert Adam exists.

66. Arm-chair in the state bedroom, Osterley Park, Middlesex (see also Fig. 109). Victoria and Albert Museum. One of a set of six, carved and gilt. Executed to a design by Robert Adam dated 24 April 1777 (Soane, vol. 17, no. 97). The chairs embody Adam's favourite device of female sphinxes which appear so frequently upon his mirror crestings, as they do in this room and at the angles of the bed itself. Approaching the style of Adam's later period, the leaf ornament of the legs is beginning to lose its crispness and vigour of modelling. In 1779 a similar design was executed for Sir Abraham Hume (Soane, vol. 17, no. 86) with more elaborate and delicate urn-shaped capitals (see E. Harris, Fig. 122). The silk covering shown is not original.

67. Arm-chair in the Etruscan Room, Osterley Park, Middlesex. Victoria and Albert Museum. Beechwood, painted grey-green with ornaments in black and terra-cotta. One of a set of eight executed to a design by Robert Adam dated 6 March 1776 (Soane, vol. 17, no. 95). An earlier design (Soane, vol. 17, no. 96), which was not carried out, was of more elaborate character, with an openwork scrolled back and arm supports in the form of fabulous birds: it has a fierce intensity in its rhythm that is very different from the smooth plainness of the design eventually adopted.

68. Hall-chair at Nostell Priory, Yorkshire. Lord St. Oswald. Mahogany, carved. Provided by Thomas Chippendale 1766 (Nostell accounts). One of Chippendale's most engaging designs, it combines his characteristic vigour with a nervous elegance. The fluted shell motif in the back with the surrounding looped circle of husks is especially pleasing. A ribbon-bow as crest survives from the rococo phase. The legs are a development of Chippendale's characteristic early neo-classical form — straight, fluted, tapering and of round section, with graceful leaf-ornaments, knob-feet, and the tops of the flutes curling outwards to form a corona-like capital. Chairs of similar form were supplied by Chippendale for the Entrance Hall at Harewood about 1767.

It would be interesting to learn the source of this circular-back design. Adam leaves no drawing of this form earlier than 1774 (for Lord Stanley, Soane, vol. 6, no. 157) and there is another drawn in 1778 for Sir Abraham Hume (Soane, vol. 17, no. 98). A circular, or rather oval back does not otherwise appear in English neo-classical furniture until 1769, in the Croome Court suite (Fig. 63).

69. Chair in the tapestry room at Nostell Priory, Yorkshire. Lord St. Oswald. Carved and gilt. Presumably supplied by Thomas Chippendale about 1774. The early type of classical design introduced by Chippendale in the Harewood dining-chairs (Fig. 59) has now reached a more mature and well-integrated form. The back-supports are now columnar and enclose a carved trophy of a lyre, trumpets and a wreath. The chair anticipates the type popular in France about 1785, when backs of this type containing similar trophies or a monogram

were made by such craftsmen as P. Bernard and N. S. Courtois, including important pieces for Marie Antoinette's boudoir (see page 69).

70. Arm-chair in the music room, Harewood House, Yorkshire. The Earl of Harewood. Supplied presumably by Chippendale about 1771. This chair marks the height of sumptuousness attained by Thomas Chippendale in the making of chairs. The back is of the oval shape introduced in the Croome Court tapestry room chairs in 1769, but the cresting is of especially handsome form. All the features and details are of great richness, the front rail enhanced by a tablet. The sheath-like leaf-ornament of the legs is highly individual, and has been interestingly simplified in the back legs. The tapestry is presumably of later date.

71. Arm-chair in the gallery at Harewood House, Yorkshire. The Earl of Harewood. Supplied presumably by Chippendale about 1770. Carved and gilt. The square back, although common in earlier stuffed-back chairs is now in accordance with the rectilinear influence that was later to become general. The legs again have great richness and individuality, especially in the ribbed-leaf ornament above the feet, and in Chippendale's characteristic corona-like leaf capital.

72. Arm-chair, carved and painted, c. 1770. The chair is one of a distinctive class in which the oval back is open, with an oval panel in the centre containing a painted decoration. Other examples of this type of back and decorative treatment are the chairs and sofa in the Lady Lever Art Gallery, and a set once belonging at Upton House, Essex. The present chair has an affinity with the oval-back chairs made for Croome Court in 1769 by Ince and Mayhew (the first in England of their type) in having a baluster-shaped vertical arm-support rising from the side-rail (Fig. 61).
Photograph supplied by H. Blairman & Son.

73. Chair, from the dining-room, Heveningham Hall, Suffolk. The Hon. Andrew Vanneck.
One of a set of eighteen; mahogany, carved, c. 1785. The backs exhibit the bold character of Wyatt's furniture designs, being formed of two interlaced ovals within a third oval, the central portion containing a carved ornament of a bowl with rams'-heads on a pedestal surmounted by anthemion. The legs derive also from the Adam inspiration, but the smooth unfluted lower portion has more of the spirit of the Hepplewhite phase.

74. Oval-back arm-chair, mahogany, carved. The chair is characteristic of the Hepplewhite school in having straight, fluted legs of square section, in the fondness for leaf-carving, and in the use of Prince of Wales's feathers in the back (see page 130). It represents however the more modest middle-class type of furniture provided for by Hepplewhite rather than the richer examples of the Adam school shown in the previous examples.
Photograph supplied by Philips of Hitchin, Ltd.

75. Shield-back arm-chair, painted, c. 1790. The back and seat caned; painted yellow with peacock feathers and with leaf-and-flower ornaments in green. A highly simplified but graceful design, with plain tapered legs of square section. It is interesting to compare this specimen with Adam's painted chairs in the Etruscan room at Osterley Park (Fig. 67).
Photograph supplied by Trevor Antiques.

76. Shield-back arm-chair, c. 1790, painted a buff colour with a leaf-and-flower ornament in colours. The lobed back is of particularly pleasing form, incorporating the Prince of Wales's feathers, and representing an original exercise in the Hepplewhite school of

design, although not based on any plate in the *Guide*. The square-section legs are enriched by leaf capitals from which spring the arm supports.

Photograph supplied by H. Blairman and Sons.

77. Arm-chair, carved and painted. The chair is a handsome, and presumably early example of the use of a large honeysuckle motif in a chair-back, a type of design not uncommon in the 1780's and later. Robert Adam made use of a large-scale ornament of this kind in his hall-chair design for Sir Abraham Hume of 1778 (Soane, vol. 17, no. 98). A well-known example of the same theme, strikingly executed in deep toned satinwood, but with rococo cabriole legs of a sort that were still current in the Hepplewhite period, is to be seen at Kedleston.

Photograph supplied by H. Blairman and Sons.

78. Shield-back arm-chair. Mahogany, carved. About 1790. A graceful example of a type developed from Hepplewhite's designs. This specimen is of unusually high quality.

Photograph supplied by H. Blairman and Sons.

79. Oval-back arm-chair, *c.* 1780. The Lady Lever Art Gallery. Carved and gilt, with painted splat. The upholstery modern. An important and extremely elegant example of the open oval-back design containing a central medallion (cf. Fig. 72).

80. Sofa from the painted room, Spencer House, St. James's, London, designed presumably by James Stuart, about 1759, now at Althorp, Northants. The Earl Spencer. From a set of two large sofas, two smaller ones, and six arm-chairs, carved and gilt. Stuart's design for the painted room is dated 1759 (Fig. 3). In this impressive suite the masses and proportions are still strongly baroque in feeling. The lion-forms however correspond very closely to classical originals which Stuart must have seen in Rome. In this respect Stuart displays a truly neo-classical approach, several years before Adam arrived at a convincing formula. In 1762 Adam was still struggling to lighten baroque forms, and with uneasy assimilations of neo-classical motifs (Fig. 29). Even in his more assured design of 1764 (Fig. 81) neo-classicism is for Adam still chiefly a matter of surface decoration. His forms are still an amalgam of ideas drawn from Kent, Chippendale and Neufforge. In his close adaptation of ancient furniture observed at first hand Stuart was more original. In his use of existing forms Adam was more a man of his own time.

81. Sofa. Carved and gilt. Executed for Sir Laurence Dundas at 19 Arlington Street, presumably by Samuel Norman, to a design by Robert Adam dated 1764 (Soane, vol. 17, no. 74) which is referred to in Adam's bill of charges for the house: 18 July 1765 'To Design of sopha Chairs for the Salon £5' (Bolton, vol. 2, page 345). The sofa is *en suite* with a number of chairs, one of which is now in the Victoria and Albert Museum, and another is illustrated in Fig. 57.

Photograph supplied by Sotheby & Co.

82. Sofa in the tapestry room from Moor Park, at Philadelphia Museum of Art. Part of a set (see Fig. 60). Carved and gilt. Made *c.* 1770 probably by Samuel Norman, who provided large quantities of furniture for Sir Laurence Dundas. The legs of square section with block capitals are of a type somewhat earlier in character than was usual at this date, by which time the baluster leg was well established in England (cf. 58 and 62).

83. Sofa in the gallery at Syon House, Middlesex. The Duke of Northumberland. Carved, painted and gilt. An example of a richly ornamented and finished Adam settee of palatial quality. Its date could be 1769, by which year the gallery was finished, and the fluted baluster leg

with leaf ornament had appeared (cf. Fig. 62). The embroidery must have been professional work of the period and was clearly made for this sofa. The formal elements of the design are of neo-classical character, but the flowers are still drawn in the traditional baroque manner.

84. Confidante, carved and gilt. The sofa of this type designed by Adam for Sir Abraham Hume in 1780 (Soane, vol. 17, no. 83) was of extreme delicacy,[1] having very slender baluster legs with vase-shaped capitals, and the piece represented in Hepplewhite's *Guide* of 1788 is almost of the same degree of refinement. The example shown here has the more practical and sturdy elegance often adopted by craftsmen interpreting the Adam style.
Photograph supplied by Mallett and Son.

85. Sofa, carved and gilt, *c.* 1785. The baluster legs with leaf capitals, the guilloche-pattern frieze and moulded back-rail with its sweeping curve mark this piece as fine example of the Adam period.
Photograph supplied by Mallett and Son.

86. Duchesse, carved and painted, *c.* 1790. The *Duchesse* was a composite article intended for a boudoir or ante-room, formed by two facing 'Barjier chairs [*bergères*] of proper construction, with a stool in the middle'. This example possesses the sturdy elegance given by the square tapering legs so often favoured by Hepplewhite. It will be noticed that the two chairs have backs of unequal height. A distinction between the French examples and the English articles is that the former were invariably equipped with loose cushions.
Photograph supplied by Mallett and Son.

87. Sofa, painted with bell-flower and other flower designs in black, green and gold, *c.* 1790. The straight back for sofas appeared in the first edition of Hepplewhite's *Guide* (1788) following numerous Adam precedents, but it became one of the distinctive forms of the last years of the century. Tapering legs of square section are numerous in Hepplewhite's designs.
Photograph supplied by Mallett and Son.

88. Chair-back settee from Upton House, Essex. Carved and painted, *c.* 1780. One of the most elegant manifestations of the attractive open oval-back designs with central medallion applied to settees (cf. Figs. 72 and 79). The central panel represents the story of Damon and Musidora, from Thomson's *Seasons*. The plain, square tapering legs set off the gracefulness of the backs probably better than would the more sophisticated baluster leg. The leaf-ornamented term necking, the rosettes, and the scrolled arms, give a touch of subdued richness.
Photograph supplied by H. Blairman and Sons.

89. Chair-back settee. Mahogany, carved. About 1790. One of the loveliest examples of a settee of Hepplewhite character. The backs are extremely delicate and graceful, with beautiful detail in the carved drapery, leaf-ornament and mouldings. As so often in Hepplewhite furniture the legs are of the simple square-sectioned, tapering fluted type.
Photograph supplied by M. Harris and Sons.

90. Window-seat, carved and gilt, *c.* 1775. The high ends of earlier years have diminished to the lower height more commonly found in the later Adam period. The baluster legs are of an unusual form, and the acroters at the angles are an enriching feature.
Photograph supplied by Sotheby & Co.

91. Window-seat, mahogany, carved with inlaid panels of marquetry, *c.* 1790. The simple

[1] E. Harris, *Adam furniture*, Fig. 124.

fluting of the legs is carried into the arms, with a slight elaboration of leaf ornament above the seat frame. The serpentine curve of the seat is another refinement expressing the simple elegance of the Hepplewhite influence.

Photograph supplied by M. Harris and Sons.

92. The Eating-room at Osterley Park, Middlesex. Victoria and Albert Museum. Designed by Robert Adam, *c.* 1767. (See page 97. See also Figs. 60, chairs; 139, urns; 18, sideboard.) The pillar-and-claw dining-table is of the Sheraton period, *c.* 1795.

93. Side-table in the Red drawing-room at Syon House, Middlesex. The Duke of Northumberland. One of a pair, carved and gilt, with inlaid marble top in a reeded brass moulding, *c.* 1765. The tables represent the height of richness attained in the side-tables of Adam's early period, using his initial neo-classical formula of straight, square-section legs. The bold vigour of this splendid design is not lost, despite the sumptuous and complex ornament of rams'-heads, festoons, and mouldings of flower and overlapping leaf patterns. The tops are of marble mosaic in geometrical patterns. No specific drawing by Robert Adam survives, but the tables together with pier-glasses are illustrated in *The Works* (vol. III, Plate XI), wrongly inscribed as designed for the Earl of Bute. The mistake was probably due to the engraver or publisher, for the third volume was published by Priestly and Weale in 1822 and was compiled of material rejected from the earlier volumes. The festoons shown below the frieze in the engraving either were never executed, or were too fragile to survive. The Roman mosaic tops are recorded as having cost £300, and are said to have been 'found in the Baths of Titus'.

94. Side-table in the music room at Harewood House, Yorkshire. The Earl of Harewood. Supplied by Thomas Chippendale, *c.* 1765–70 (see page 89). Wood, carved and gilt; the top of rosewood veneer inlaid with contrasting woods. Chippendale here shows his mastery of the new classical idiom with his own version of the great rectangular side-tables of the early Adam period. It falls no way short of Adam or Adam's own craftsmen in excellence of design and in perfection of workmanship, and there is as well the masculine quality that is distinctive of Chippendale. Something of the influence of traditional English classicism is discernible — in the recessed faces of the legs, in the boldly projecting mouldings of the block capitals, and in the surviving baroque feature of a satyr mask in the frieze. The festoons of husks are of a scale also seen in early Georgian furniture. The sunken panels on the faces of the legs are of course a common feature of Chippendale's designs in the *Director*.

95. The ante-room at Syon House, Middlesex. The Duke of Northumberland, *c.* 1761. The most splendid room in Adam's first completely neo-classical interior, and one of the most magnificent rooms in Britain. The green of the scagliola columns and pilasters admirably sets off the gilding of Adam's beautifully detailed Ionic capitals, and frieze. According to a tradition, the columns were of verde-antico marble 'dredged from the bed of the Tiber', but damage from a flying-bomb in the 1939–45 war revealed that they were of scagliola. The tradition presumably originated in the sales-talk of the Italian merchant who sold them. A similar tradition exists at Newby, Yorkshire. The table is one of a set of three, of wood carved and gilt, and with mosaic tops (see Fig. 15). The stool is of the Regency period made by Morrell and Hughes about 1825.

96. Side-table in the gallery at Syon House, Middlesex. The Duke of Northumberland. One of pair, carved and gilt, with white inlaid marble tops. Made probably by John Linnell (see page 89) about 1769, the date of the completion of the gallery, and soon after the intro-

duction of the fully formed baluster leg (Fig. 62). Early in Adam's mature period, the form combines a satisfying boldness of scale and detail with elegance of line. The same bold character is evident in the design of the inlaid marble top, contrasting strongly with the extreme delicacy and small-scale ornament of his later designs (Fig. 25).

97. Pier-table in the saloon at Nostell Priory, Yorkshire. Lord St. Oswald. One of a pair, carved and gilt, with semi-circular inlaid marble tops. Executed with slight modifications from Robert Adam's design, dated 1775 (Soane, vol. 17, no. 28) of two tables with 'statuary marble slabs for Nostell' (see page 93). These extremely beautiful tables embody the unusual features of oval medallions set in the legs, below the square capitals which are especially fine and of composite form. The curved stretchers with urns supported by cupids, and the exquisite detailing of the frieze and legs contribute to the sense of elegance. The rich anthemion frieze was adopted from the design for the tables in the hall, which have fluted legs, and for which the fluted frieze originally proposed for these tables is obviously more suitable (Fig. 98). These must obviously be 'two statuary Tables inlaid of Scagliola According Messrs. Adam's Disaing for the Salon at Nostel' supplied by the firm of Richter and Bartoli in 1777 for 75 guineas each (Nostell accounts).

98. Pier-table in the hall at Nostell Priory, Yorkshire. Lord St. Oswald. One of a pair, carved and gilt with solid *fleur de pêche* marble tops, executed with minor alterations from a design by Robert Adam, dated 1775 (Soane, vol. 17, no. 28), of '. . . two tables for the Hall to have Statuary slabs at Nostel'. The terminal figures appearing here are a remarkable baroque survival, or revival, comparable with Adam's use of terminal figures as mirror supports (Fig. 27). Here he has adopted the form in order to give interest and importance to the upper part of a table leg.

99. Side-table in the tapestry room at Osterley Park, Middlesex. Victoria and Albert Museum. Carved and gilt, with semi-circular inalid marble top. Executed to a design by Robert Adam inscribed 'Table Frame and slab for the Tapestry Room at Osterley' dated 1775. The table combines a bold three-dimensional form with a sense of elegance, and owes its richness to the fine detailing of the frieze with its pendent anthemion ornament and inset tablets with painted medallions. The ornament of the capitals, stretchers and feet is also of the highest quality, and the table well represents the summit of beauty and excellence in Adam's mature period.

100. Side-table and pier-glass in the Velvet drawing-room, Saltram House, Devonshire. The National Trust. One of a pair, carved and gilt, with shaped marble tops, executed by Joseph Perfetti. John Parker's account book records '31st March 1772. To Perfetti for Table Frames in the Velvet Room - - - £41.' The tables were executed to a design by Adam inscribed 'Glass and Table Frame for John Parker, Esq.' dated 1771 (Soane, vol. 20, no. 70).

    The mirror is of the type having a crest of a medallion with supporting figures, typical of Adam's middle period.

101. Side-table and pier-glass in the saloon at Saltram House, Devonshire. The National Trust. One of a pair, carved and gilt, with rectangular marble tops, provided by Joseph Perfetti. John Parker's account book records 'Jan 29, 1771. Pd. Perfetti for Table Frames for the Great Room Saloon - - - £41.1s.'. The tables were probably designed by Perfetti himself to accord with those of the Velvet room, for no related drawings by Adam exist. The absence of the master-hand is apparent in the ungraceful treatment of the festoons, which

pass in front of the table legs, and in the clumsy ornament of the frieze. The mirrors, however, are among the most charming examples of Adam's crested looking glasses, having a central ornament (an urn) supported by female figures. These mirrors, of which there are four, were made with slight modifications from a design by Adam of a 'Glass Frame for the Great Drawing Room at Saltram', dated 1769 (Soane, vol. 20, no. 69).

102. The tapestry room from Croome Court, now at the Metropolitan Museum, New York. The room was transferred from Croome Court in 1922.[1] The Gobelins tapestries with figure subjects after paintings by Boucher were purchased by Lord Coventry in 1765. The chairs and settees were made for him by Ince and Mayhew in 1769 (Fig. 63). It will be noticed that the crestings of the oval furniture backs are strings of husks, while the medallions have rococo crestings of flowers: also that the back of the settee is not oval, as in the tapestry room furniture from Moor Park (now in the Philadelphia Museum of Art) but more square, corresponding to the cartouche backs of earlier furniture. This shape is enforced by the design of the settee back covering. In fact, the chair-back panels were originally designed by Jacques or Tessier in 1762 of cartouche-shape[2] (see page 65). There could thus at that date have been no intention at the Gobelins factory that the chairs on which the backs should be used should be of an oval shape. This pattern, adopted when the chairs were made by Ince and Mayhew in 1769, was most probably due to the firm's own designer (see page 65). The tapestry backs of the Moor Park chairs also were presumably not intended for oval-back chairs, to judge from the character of the design.

103. Side-table from the drawing-room, Woodhall Park, Hertfordshire. Carved and gilt, with marble top. Another table in a similar style, but with different ornament in the legs and frieze, stood in the same room. In their robust form the tables are in the same class as Adam's early neo-classical side-tables at Syon (Figs. 15, 93, and 95), but the legs, with their narrow necking, unlike those of Adam's tables, seem to derive from classical terms, as do William Kent's chairs of about 1735–40 at Rousham (see page 42). The architect of Woodhall Park was Thomas Leverton, but there is no evidence that he designed any furniture in the house. These particular tables seem to owe their character to a craftsman aware of Adam's innovations in furniture, but also deeply rooted in tradition. The workmanship and finish are of a very high order. The drawing-room at Woodhall Park, as it was before the dispersal of the furniture, is illustrated in A. Tipping, *English Homes*, *1760–1820*, p. 233, fig. 369 (see also page 103).

104. Side-table; one of a pair; the semi-circular top of satinwood inlaid with a fan design, scrolls and husk festoons in rosewood and tulipwood marquetry; the frame and supports carved and gilt. About 1770. Tables with caryatid supports were not unknown in the days of William Kent (see page 53) and appear in the designs of Robert Adam (Soane, vol. 20, no. 24) and Chippendale (*Director*, Plate CLXXVI). They represent an aspect of the established English classical tradition rather than any introduction of a new style, but the delicacy of the anthemion ornament of the frieze is a mark of the new spirit introduced by Adam.

Photograph supplied by Mallett and Son.

105. Side-table; carved and gilt, the semi-circular top of mahogany veneer, c. 1775. Typical of a large class of side-tables in the Adam phase, of great elegance and beauty, and of bold semi-circular form but delicate slender legs, this table has a frieze with a finely modelled

[1] Decorative art from the Samuel H. Kress Collection, 1964, p. 54. [2] *Op. cit.*

anthemion and wreath design, and the legs are beautifully worked with leaf ornament in the capitals and feet.

Photograph supplied by Mallett and Son.

106. Side-table; carved, painted and gilt. Another example of this large class of elegant side-tables favoured from 1770 onwards, here charmingly decorated with painted ornament. The semi-circular top is painted with a central shell ornament and a floral border.

Photograph supplied by H. Blairman and Sons.

107. Side-table in the library at Harewood House, Yorkshire. The Earl of Harewood. Carved and gilt, with marble top. Supplied presumably by Thomas Chippendale. About 1769. The scale of the frieze ornament is early Georgian in character, but the use of rosettes with the triglyphs is due to neo-classical influence, and the way the faces of the legs are carved as a single leaf with the upper ends curling outwards is a highly original feature. The sense of vigorous elegance is very characteristic of Chippendale.

108. Side-table in the Rose drawing-room at Harewood House, Yorkshire. The Earl of Harewood. Carved and gilt, the semi-circular top of satinwood bordered and inlaid with contrasting woods. Supplied presumably by Thomas Chippendale, *c.* 1773. This table marks an astonishing advance upon earlier neo-classical examples in elegance of design, the legs being of extreme slenderness in relation to the top, yet a harmonious relation between the top and frieze is achieved with the satisfying scale of the block capitals. This type of design was later followed in many small side-tables during the Adam period (see Figs. 105 and 106).

109. The state bedroom at Osterley Park, Middlesex. Victoria and Albert Museum. Designed by Robert Adam, about 1776. The walls are hung with plain green silk, to form a recessive background to the magnificent state bed. This was executed to a design by Adam of 16 May 1776 (Soane, vol. 17, no. 157) with dark green velvet hangings embroidered with flowers. The posts of the bed are of satinwood painted with black and green stripes and lines of bell-flowers; the plinths are inlaid, and the capitals are of gilt metal. The cornice is of carved and gilt wood, supporting at the angles charming figures of sphinxes in gilt metal, and has also carved and gilt ornaments like those seen on the cornices of fantastic ruins in the fresco paintings of Herculaneum and Pompeii. For the chairs, see Fig. 66.

110. Design of a console-table. Artist unknown. Victoria and Albert Museum, E1740–1912. Part of a drawing for a console-table and pier-glass. The table shown has much in common with Chippendale's gilt console-tables in the gallery at Harewood (Fig. 111) especially in the form, proportions and open spacing of the supports, in the hoofed feet, and in the close similarity of the leaf-ornamented fluted frieze in both tables. The drawing has pronounced French character, and may have come from the hand of Neufforge. Its identification might throw revealing light on the inspiration of Chippendale's neo-classical furniture.

111. Console-table in the gallery at Harewood, Yorkshire. The Earl of Harewood. Supplied presumably by Thomas Chippendale, about 1767. One of a pair, carved and gilt, the tops inlaid with various woods. These exceedingly fine tables are usually assumed to have been executed to Adam's designs (Fig. 21) but marked differences in style and character are obvious. They accord much more closely with the preceding anonymous drawing at the Victoria and Albert Museum (Fig. 110).

112. Console-table in the Green drawing-room at Harewood House, Yorkshire. The Earl of

Harewood. Supplied presumably by Thomas Chippendale, about 1770. One of a pair, carved and gilt, with inlaid marble tops. These tables mark a development from the austere neo-classicism of the gallery tables (Fig. 111) to a florid and sophisticated elegance, in which French influence is evident in the ribbon ornament and in the use of supports with female heads in the manner of French Régence and English console-tables, and their English derivatives of the 1740's (see page 44).

113. Console-table from Stanmer House, Brighton. The Earl of Chichester. Now in the Royal Pavilion, Brighton. One of a pair, carved and gilt with tops of Siena marble. These tables were made for the drawing-room at Stanmer House, which was decorated in the Adam style about 1777. The linked wreaths in the frieze are found also in the friezes of the door-heads, of the fireplace, and of the cornice of the room, and closely resemble a moulding in the frieze of the library fireplace at Goodwood Park, Sussex, which is believed to have been designed by James Wyatt. The stiffly upright form of the goat-legs seems to derive directly from a console-table design (Plate 54) in Piranesi's work on interior decoration (see page 54) in which this characteristic appears.

114. 'Design of a commode for Sir George Colebrooke, Bart.' by Robert Adam. Dated 1771. Soane Museum, vol. 17, no. 17. The form and proportions of this rectangular commode are still based on early Georgian models such as the writing-tables of William Kent, with their tapering pilasters, although ram's-heads now take the place of the earlier lion's-heads as capitals. The painted decoration in blue and green is of neo-classical subjects with pink figures and is confined within recessed panels; the large-scale motifs have the bold character of Adam's early style.

115. Design of a 'Commode for his Grace the Duke of Bolton', by Robert Adam. Dated January 1773. Soane Museum, vol. 17, no. 18. This design, Adam's first for a semi-circular commode, is the ancestor of innumerable bow-fronted commodes and chests of the later Adam and Hepplewhite age. It exhibits the increasing elegance of Adam's mature period yet retains a satisfactory solidity of form. The pilaster supports have become slenderer and less prominent and the decoration now spreads over the whole surface of the front instead of being confined within panels. The design, for which a preliminary sketch also exists, was followed, with modifications, for the pair of commodes in the drawing-room at Osterley (Fig. 122) although it was originally intended for Bolton House in Russell Square, London. The drawing also shows in outline a design for the semi-circular top.

116. Design of a 'Commode for the Second Drawing Room at Apsley House', by Robert Adam, dated June 1779. Soane Museum, vol. 17, no. 43. This is a finished and coloured version of a design dated 1777 in the Victoria and Albert Museum (E3225–1938). There is also a partly finished drawing in the Soane Museum dated 1778 (vol. 17, no. 35). The design for this commode has many similarities to the Countess of Derby's especially in the decoration of the frieze and the character of the pilasters and their ornament at the feet. The proportions of the commode have been lengthened, however, giving it the extreme elegance of Adam's later period.

The ornament has also been greatly simplified in character and reduced in scale, again heightening the impression of elegance. Decorations of this kind, consisting of widely spaced medallions with sparse and delicate strings of husks, correspond to the painted medallion ceilings of Adam's middle years at Harewood and Osterley. His style has now lost most of its early plastic vigour and relies almost entirely on surface decoration.

117. Design for a commode from Hepplewhite's *Guide*, 1788, 1789 and 1794 editions. Plate first published 1787. This single design for a bow-fronted commode represents that very beautiful type originated by Adam in his design of 1773 and in the corresponding articles made for Osterley (Figs. 115 and 122). Commodes like this were made in great numbers and with much variety of detail during the late 1780's and the 1790's (cf. Fig. 127). The design embodies distinctive features of Hepplewhite's style — the splayed feet curving in a continuous line with the shaped base, and the semi-circular top decorated with a radiating design of flowers and husks. The commodes were often made of satinwood and were usually 'elegantly ornamented with inlaid or painted work'.

118. Commode in the Green drawing-room at Harewood House, Yorkshire. The Earl of Harewood. Supplied presumably by Chippendale, about 1770. Mahogany, with marquetry in other woods. The beginnings of rectilinear form are here apparent in the straight lines of the corners and of the cupboard door. The commode in fact represents Chippendale's interpretation of the French Transitional commode. The somewhat vestigial ormolu mounts combine the sinuous line of the rococo with classical rams'-heads and festoons. The inlaid decoration is wholly neo-classical, consisting of formal garlands, leaf-sprays and a circle of husks or bell-flowers enclosing a stylized circular flower device.

119. Commode from Croome Court, Worcestershire. The Earl of Coventry. One of a pair, supplied by Mayhew and Ince, 1765. The firm's bill (Croome accounts, no. 25) reads: 'Augst. 15 and Sepr. 21. 2 very fine SattinWood and Holly Commodes, neatly grav'd and inlaid with Flowers of Rosewood, the one with drawers, the other with shelves to glide, lin'd with paper and Green Bays to do. brass nail'd. 40 ,, ,,'.

Although simplicity of form is inherent in the British tradition, anything approaching it in the degree exhibited in these commodes would be hard to match at any time in the eighteenth century. The full force of the change from the richness of rococo decoration to the severity of neo-classicism is expressed in a comparison of the Croome commodes with the chest at Longford Castle, Wiltshire, believed to have been made by William Vile.[1]

The underlying simplicity of form is identical in the different pieces, but the contrast between the old style and the new could hardly be more strikingly apparent. The character of the neo-classical marquetry of urns and flowers is truly astonishing for the date of 1765. Nothing remotely comparable is known to appear in English or French work for another five years. The alternating stripes of satinwood and holly veneer are a highly original and striking feature. The commodes were probably intended for architectural plans and drawings, many of which must have been accumulating at Croome Court during the remodelling from 1765 onwards. Beneath the tops are thin draw-slides to provide an enlarged working surface.

120. Commode in the state bedroom at Nostell Priory, Yorkshire. Lord St. Oswald. Presumably supplied by Chippendale in 1771 (see page 94). Japanned. The semi-rectilinear break-front form for commodes, that was general before Adam's introduction of the bow-fronted shape in 1773, has here been reached. The neo-classical decoration of husks at the corners has been much used by Kent, however, and was already a part of the English classical tradition. The voluted and outward-turned half-capital that is found in many of Chippendale's productions should also be noted, and the tapering, concave fluted legs with round block feet are also typical of his work.

[1] R. Edwards and M. Jourdain, *Georgian cabinet-makers*, Fig. 66.

The japanned decoration of green and gold in the Chinese taste seems to have been determined by the desire to harmonize this furniture with the Chinese wallpaper of the dressing-room and bedroom, although such *chinoiseries* were at that date somewhat out-moded in England, but not in France. This decoration corresponds exactly with the green and gold japanning of the 'Cloathes press or wardrobe' which stands in the dressing-room, and which is mentioned in a list of furniture at Nostell made by Chippendale.

121. Dressing-commode in the private apartments, Harewood House, Yorkshire. The Earl of Harewood. Satinwood, with marquetry of various woods. Supplied by Chippendale in 1773 at a cost of £86 (Harewood accounts). In the bill it is described as 'with exceeding fine Antique ornaments'. Few pieces in the whole realm of English furniture can compare with this fine commode in nobility of form and dignified beauty of ornament. The volutes and leaf-ornaments in the frieze of this attested Chippendale piece give authority for the attribution to the same craftsman of other articles possessing the same feature (see Figs. 125, 167 and 172). The form of the legs is also a conclusive feature. The dressing-commode at Renishaw Hall, Derbyshire, is almost identical except in having the semi-circular knee-recess flush with the front instead of being concave. The circular medallions in the Harewood piece represent Diana and Minerva, and the character of the inlay, with light woods contrasting strongly with an ebony ground, is similar to that in the commode at Stourhead which is believed to have been supplied by Thomas Chippendale the Younger after his father's death (Fig. 127). For this reason it seems likely that marquetry of this character, seen on various late Chippendale pieces at Harewood and elsewhere, was especially favoured by the son, and possibly even a mark of his authorship in various otherwise unattested works.

122. Commode in the drawing-room, Osterley Park, Middlesex. Victoria and Albert Museum. One of a pair, of harewood veneer, with the frieze in satinwood, and with marquetry and inlay of various other woods. The metal mouldings and other ornaments are of gilt brass. The central medallion has marquetry representing Diana with her hounds (the companion piece shows Venus and Cupid) and the ovals of the side panels depict female figures. The commodes are based on several designs for various parts: one for the tops (Soane, vol. 18, no. 63) dated 30 January 1773, showing a coloured design for painting instead of the inlay in which they were executed. Three others, undated, show ornaments for the side-panels (Soane, vol. 25, no. 210, and vol. 5, nos. 20 and 21). One of these (vol. 5, no. 20) is a design as executed. Another design dated 1773, for a 'Commode for his Grace the Duke of Bolton' (Soane, vol. 17, no. 18), which is in fact Adam's earliest surviving design for a semi-circular commode, seems in many respects to be a prototype of the Osterley commodes, especially in the circular central medallion and the side-ovals, in the character of the pilasters (despite differences of detail), and in the similarity of the pendent 'fringe' ornament in the lower part. This pendent ornament is very closely allied to a similar ornament of ormolu in a pair of pier-tables belonging to the Prince of Wales about 1791 (see page 72), and believed to have been made by the French craftsman Weisweiler, though not before about 1785. The central gilt plaque representing gryphons supporting a medallion is repeated above the doors of the drawing-room, and derives from a device in the ceilings of the Villa Madama in Rome. The commodes are the only authenticated Adam articles of the kind known to exist, and are among the very finest pieces of furniture of any type executed to his designs.

123. Bow-fronted commode in the state bedroom at Osterley Park, Middlesex. About 1774. Victoria and Albert Museum. The front, sides and top are formed of panels of Chinese lacquer; the mouldings of the top, frieze and base, the pilasters and ram's-head ornaments are carved in wood and gilt to simulate ormolu. The term-shaped pilasters with their ornament are similar to those on a commode designed by Adam for the Countess of Derby, illustrated in *The Works*, vol. 2, part 1, 1779 (see E. Harris, Fig. 47). The short legs of the piece also seem to follow that design but their robust character is similar to that of articles made by Chippendale. So also are the ram's-heads and festoons, and the blocks instead of ball-feet are again typical of that craftsman.

124. Commode in the state bedroom at Woburn Abbey. The Duke of Bedford. One of a pair, mahogany, with bandings of tulip-wood and kingwood, and marquetry of various woods, and ormolu mounts. The tops of inlaid marble. The commodes correspond very closely to the description in an inventory of Bedford House of 1771, which reads: 'An inlaid commode very richly ornamented with brass work, gilt festoon mouldings, etc., the tops of curious composition formed into a landscape of flowers.' The 'curious composition' no doubt refers to scagliola, for the tops are inlaid in coloured marbles, depicting harbour scenes with classical buildings, shells and foliage, medallions, flower sprays and butterflies, and the inscription 'Lambertus Christianus Gori F. Florentiae AD MDCCLXII'. It is extremely doubtful if the date of the marble tops is a true indication of the date of the commodes themselves. The date of the inventory in which they appear is likely to be closer to the year of their making. The ormolu mounts and festoons have something of the character of similar ornaments from Chippendale's workshop, but they are larger in scale, and more distinctively of French character, as also is the marquetry work with its design of beribboned flower sprays, which accords well with what was said of the character of the work of Langlois (see page 119, and Note 11, p. 174).

125. Commode in the Lady Lever Art Gallery. Satinwood banded with mahogany and with marquetry of other woods, and ormolu mounts, about 1770. The character of the ram's-heads and the small scrolled half-capitals above (see Fig. 120) suggest the hand of Thomas Chippendale. The sunk borders to the oval panels and the outswept bracket feet are very unusual, the latter apparently deriving from a detail in the third edition of Chippendale's *Director* (1762), Plate LXVIII. They are found also in a drop-front secretaire made by the French craftsman J.-F. Oeben about 1760, which is itself an early example of French neo-classicism.[1] The commode has a robust nobility that is very striking, and like most of Chippendale's work, is exquisitely made.

126. Bow-fronted commode in the drawing-room at Stourhead, Wiltshire. The National Trust. Mahogany with marquetry of other woods. Presumably supplied by T. Chippendale the Younger to Sir Richard Colt-Hoare about 1785. The suave elegance introduced into the form of commodes with those he designed for the Osterley drawing-room (Fig. 122) reaches its full development by this date. The pilasters hardly break the smooth surface of the front. The feet, similar to those in Fig. 123, seem to be distinctive of Chippendale work, and the strongly contrasting marquetry figures, white on a black ground, may be characteristic of the son's productions. Similar inlay appears in various attested pieces from his hand.

127. Bow-fronted commode: satinwood, with marquetry. About 1790. The completely

[1] S. Eriksen, 'Early neo-classicism in French furniture'. Article in *Apollo*, November 1963, Pl. II.

superficial treatment typical of the Hepplewhite era is apparent in this charmingly simple commode, in which the semi-circular form makes its effect without undue distraction of ornament. Inlaid vases take the place of ormolu mounts, and Hepplewhite's distinctive feature of curved feet in a continuous sweeping line with the base enhances the shape of the piece. This feature is of course a rococo survival. The commode closely follows the design in the *Guide* (Fig. 117), which was highly influential in popularizing articles of this type.
Photograph supplied by Mallett and Son.

128. Card-table, mahogany, carved and inlaid with satinwood and other woods: serpentine folding top, lined with baize. About 1785. The ornament of the legs is finely carved, but the flutes of the frieze are inlaid. It is a good example of the facility in the exercise of the Adam system attained by fashionable craftsmen. The shaped top, which appears in several designs in the *Guide*, became a characteristic feature of small tables in the Hepplewhite era.
Photograph supplied by Christie, Manson and Woods, Ltd.

129. Card-table, satinwood with marquetry of harewood and other woods. Semi-circular folding top, lined with baize. About 1785. The semi-circular shape lent itself admirably to card-tables. The feet are of a type common in the Adam period, and later assimilated in simplified form into the Hepplewhite style.
Photograph supplied by M. Harris and Sons.

130. Pembroke table: satinwood, with marquetry of rosewood, sycamore and other contrasting woods. About 1785. The shaped top is characteristic of the Hepplewhite period. The inlaid flutes, leaf-ornament of the feet, and the inlaid patterns are typical of the superficial treatment of Adam motifs after 1780 (see Fig. 131).
Photograph supplied by Mallett and Son.

131. Top of the Pembroke table illustrated in Fig. 130; satinwood, with marquetry in shell and vase designs.
Photograph supplied by Mallett and Son.

132. Side-table from the eating-room of No. 20 St. James's Square, London, now at Buscot Park, Berkshire. The National Trust and the Lord Faringdon. One of a pair, of San Domingo mahogany, carved, with marble tops, about 1780. The tables, the tops of which are curved, stood in the music room, latterly used as the eating-room, and their backs are shaped to fit the curve of the walls of the inner apse of the room, as they do today also at Buscot. The carving of the frieze and centre tablet and of the baluster legs with leaf-capitals is of remarkable quality.

133. Sideboard from the eating-room of 20 St. James's Square, London, now at the National Folk Museum, St. Fagan's Castle, Cardiff. Carved and painted. Executed from a design by Robert Adam dated 1773 (Soane, vol. 17, no. 21), inscribed 'Sideboard Table for the Eating Room for Sir Watkin Wynne Bart. of mahogany'. The original painted decoration of pale green with details in blue and white on the sideboard and on the pedestals and urns (Fig. 141),[1] was revealed when dark brown paint was removed in recent years. This had probably been applied at an early date to make the sideboard group match two side-tables of carved mahogany (Fig. 132) which were added to the room.
By permission of the National Museum of Wales.

134. Sideboard-table from Woodhall Park, Herts. Mahogany, carved. Woodhall Park was

[1] The complete group illustrated in E. Harris, Fig. 25.

built by Thomas Leverton (1743–1824), a follower of Robert Adam, in 1777–82, for Sir Thomas Rumbold. There is a very fine gilt side-table from the house now in the Royal collection, and a number of other pieces exist, but there is no evidence that Leverton ever designed furniture. All the known pieces would appear to have been the result of the general absorption of the Adam style by fashionable craftsmen.
Photograph supplied by Hotspur, Ltd.

135. Sideboard. Mahogany, inlaid with vases and strings of grapes and vine-leaves. About 1790. In the sideboards of the Hepplewhite period the pedestals have become incorporated in the table itself, as in this case. The pedestal cupboards held a wine cellarette, and sometimes a rack for plates, together with a spirit burner for warming them.
Photograph supplied by M. Harris and Sons.

136. Sideboard, urns on pedestals, and wine-cooler in the dining-room at Harewood House, Yorkshire. The Earl of Harewood. Supplied presumably by Chippendale about 1771. Mahogany with marquetry in various woods, and ormolu mounts. This group forms the most magnificent example in existence of the type of sideboard composition introduced by Adam, and represents Chippendale at the height of his genius. The craftsman's hand is to be seen in the legs of the sideboard, with their block and ball feet, and capitals having festoons issuing from rosettes: also in the sturdy nobility of design.

137. Sideboard in the dining-room at Newby Hall. Major E. R. F. Compton. About 1772. Satinwood, with marquetry of rosewood and other woods. The striking light colour and contrasting inlay of this fine piece and of the accompanying magnificent urns on pedestals (Fig. 140), together with the bold refinement of design, suggest Thomas Chippendale the Younger as the maker. The straight, round-section tapering legs are unusual in being reeded instead of fluted, but are seen in Adam's design of a 'Glass and Table frame and Tripods for the Drawing Room at Luton' dated 1772 (Soane, vol. 20, no. 116) which was published as an engraving in *The Works* (vol. III, Plate VIII) (Fig. 27) erroneously described as 'Furniture at Sion House'. The inlaid frieze ornament of vine leaves and grapes has its counterpart in the frieze of the sideboard in Adam's drawing for 'the Right Honble. W. G. Hamilton's house at Brighton' (Soane, vol. 6, no. 116 and 118, Fig. 26), and even the lion-mask capitals of the sideboard have their counterpart in the wine-cistern shown in Adam's drawing.

138. Urn and pedestal in the dining-room at Harewood House. The Earl of Harewood. One of a pair, mahogany and inlay of various woods, with ornaments of ormolu. *En suite* with a sideboard (Fig. 137). The quality of the mounts, and the perfection of the veneer inlay on the pedestals, are remarkable.

139. Urn and pedestal in the eating-room at Osterley Park, Middlesex. Victoria and Albert Museum. One of a pair, carved, painted white and partly gilt. The masks and handles are of gilt brass. Executed presumably by John Linnell, who made a similar pair for Shardeloes. A bill of his dated 2 October 1767 (Drake Papers: Bucks. County Record Office) states 'To making and carving 2 Coopers, the Tops in the form of Vases and large Brass Handles like Mr. Child's one lin'd with lead to hold water, and the other Top Sham and a pot cupboard underneath and painting the same all compleat. £30' (illustrated by E. Harris, *Adam Furniture*, Fig. 33). Unfortunately Adam's design for the Osterley urns does not survive but they are illustrated, together with the sideboard (Fig. 18), in *The Works*, vol. III, Plate IX, where they are described erroneously as 'furniture at Syon House'. Unlike

the Shardeloes pieces they both have lead-lined water-containers and taps, and are both fitted with cupboards in the pedestals.

140. Urn and pedestal in the dining-room at Newby Hall, Yorkshire. Major E. R. F. Compton. About 1772. One of a pair, the pedestals of satinwood with marquetry, the urns of carved wood, the swags of mahogany, the serpent handles of gilt brass. The urns and pedestals are *en suite* with a sideboard ascribed to Thomas Chippendale the Younger (Fig. 136) and the whole set is of unusual character, the bold forms and golden-yellow colour creating a very striking effect. The serpentine 'sarcophagus' fluting is a *tour de force*, and the vine-leaf inlay, which corresponds closely with a sideboard design by Adam (Plate 21), is especially beautiful. The articles contrast with the Harewood sideboard group (Fig. 137) in being without ormolu ornament (except for the urn handles), and they richly express the Chippendale genius for graceful yet vigorous design, and perfection of workmanship.

141. Urn and pedestal from the eating-room at No. 20 St. James's Square, London, now at the National Folk Museum, St. Fagan's Castle, Cardiff. One of a pair, carved and painted (see also Fig. 133). No design for these articles survives, but they must surely have been designed by Robert Adam, the tops of the urns having close affinities with those at Osterley. The carving is of the most beautiful and delicate quality. The frieze moulding and ram's-heads on the pedestals are identical with those of pedestals formerly at Hursley Park, Hampshire, now in the Metropolitan Museum of Art, New York. (Illustrated in E. Harris, Fig. 153.)

142. The dining-room at Saltram House, Devonshire. The National Trust. About 1780. The furniture is of carved wood painted cream with green and white ornaments, to match the room decoration. The sideboard top is of mahogany. The sideboard table is made in three sections to fit the bay, the niches of which were created by Adam by filling in two windows. The imitation Etruscan vases in the niches are of composition. The urns and pedestals were made to a drawing by Robert Adam (Soane, vol. 29, no. 159), dated 1780. The urns are lined with zinc for water, and the pedestals are fitted with bottle racks.

143. Term-pedestal. Satinwood with marquetry in mahogany, rosewood and other woods. About 1775. The baroque form of the 1770's has been overlaid with the flush-surfaced ornament typical of the middle Adam period.
Photograph supplied by Hotspur, Ltd.

144. Tripod stand in the drawing-room at Osterley Park, Middlesex. Victoria and Albert Museum. Carved and gilt. About 1777. One of the most beautiful examples of the sacrificial bowl type of tripod.

145. Tripod in the saloon at Saltram House, Devonshire. The National Trust. One of a set of four. Carved and gilt wood. The candelabra, of ormolu upon an urn of Blue John fluorspar by Matthew Boulton, was supplied in 1772 (Saltram accounts). An elegant example of Adam's 'Water Stand' or sacrificial incense-burner type of tripod, of the kind which became known in France in 1771 as 'athénienne' (see page 71).

146. Tripod-pedestal in the tapestry room at Osterley Park, Middlesex. Victoria and Albert Museum. Carved and gilt, with painted medallions. The top section is of gilt brass. One of a pair executed in accordance with Adam's design dated 1776 (Soane, vol. 17, no. 62), exhibiting much greater delicacy and refinement in the openwork carved and painted ornaments than the tripods of similar form designed three years earlier for 20 St. James's

Square (now at Alnwick, and illustrated in E. Harris, Fig. 137). In the latter tripods the pedestals are solid and of more robust character, with heavily modelled ornament. Another example of the bold solid type is Adam's drawing of a tripod-pedestal for Lady Home at 20 Portman Square, dated 1778 (Fig. 20). Adam designed several pedestals of this form, embodying familiar classical elements, but in shape only remotely resembling ancient models (see page 52).

147. Tripod-stand, carved and gilt, about 1775. A highly individual adaptation of the model established by Adam in his tripod-design for Luton (Fig. 27); of remarkable inventiveness of detail, matched by outstanding quality of craftsmanship. The volutes of the top stage, ingeniously developed from the scrolls of an Ionic column, repeat the curve of the ram's-heads which they carry.

Photograph supplied by Mallett and Son.

148. Tripod-pedestal. One of a set of four, carved, painted and gilt, about 1774. These tripods closely follow those designed by Adam for Osterley (Fig. 146), especially in the vertical semi-elliptical panels with their painted oval medallions and semi-circular ornament above, but the ornament of the open portion differs considerably. It is especially interesting to see how, in order to create a variation, the animal supports of Adam's tripod designs have been moved into the body of the pedestal from their usual position in the base. The top, with its tongue-and-dart moulding, a type never used by Adam, seems to be a later addition to the original piece. (Cf. the Osterley tripod.) The painted female figures in the medallion may be the work of Antonio Zucchi. In a bill of his to Sir Watkin Williams Wynne dated 26 September 1774 for work at 20 St. James's Square there is a mention of 'Drawings for 2 figures in wood for Trypods, £3', and there is a strong possibility that the articles came from this house.

Photograph supplied by Frank Partridge and Sons.

149. Urn and pedestal, in the library at Newby Hall, Yorkshire. Major E. R. F. Compton. One of a pair, the second piece being in the niche of the corridor. The pedestal carved, painted and gilt; the urn of alabaster. The pedestal is an example of Robert Adam's adaptation of the familiar type of ancient Roman altar or triangular pedestal, with concave sides, such as the well-known candelabrum in the Vatican Museum.[1]

The pedestal closely follows Adam's design of a 'Tripod for the Niches in the Firs Drawing Room at Apsley House', dated 1779[2] (Soane, vol. 17, no. 64). The general form, the gryphon supports and the oval painted medallion, are almost identical. Although Adam was making drawings for William Weddell at Newby Hall from 1770 to 1775, no design by Adam specifically for a pedestal and urn appears to survive, most possibly because it was never returned by the craftsman. Although Chippendale is known to have carried out work in the house, this piece does not seem to have been made by his workshop. It corresponds too closely with Adam's drawing, whereas the work of Chippendale has a strong character of its own.

150. Tripod and pedestal, from Brockenhurst House, Hants. John Aspinall, Esq. One of a pair; the pedestals carved and painted, with a painted medallion of a famous subject from Herculaneum. The tripod of gilt wood. The character of design suggests James Wyatt as the source, in his early Adamesque phase, especially in the interlace bell-flower ornament the small hoof-feet of the tripod (cf. Harris, Fig. 154) and the subject from Herculaneum,

[1] E. Harris, Fig. 77.   [2] E. Harris, Fig. 140.

which Wyatt used at Goodwood, but which, as far as is known, was never adopted by Adam.

151. Pedestal and urn, from the Etruscan room, Heveningham Hall, Suffolk. The Hon. Andrew Vanneck. One of a pair, carved and painted pale green with ornaments in the Etruscan style in terracotta and black; fitted with metal branches for candles. Designed presumably by James Wyatt about 1780–4, and painted by Biagio Rebecca, who is known to have carried out other decorations in the house. The bold and striking form and the small hoofed feet are characteristic of several articles at Heveningham, and may be taken as a mark of James Wyatt as a furniture designer.

152. Tripod candelabrum, from the dining-room, Heveningham Hall, Suffolk. The Hon. Andrew Vanneck. One of a pair, carved and painted with branches for candles. Designed presumably by James Wyatt. Although the form of the lower part corresponds closely to tripods of antique pattern by James Stuart and Robert Adam, the central column entwined with serpents is a highly original and striking feature.

153. Oval mirror, carved and gilt. About 1770. Oval mirrors are amongst the most numerous and beautiful articles designed by Adam. The earlier examples have broad frames and cresting of vigorous, bold foliage and neo-classical ornament, in this instance consisting of husks and honeysuckle.
Photograph supplied by E. T. Biggs and Son.

154. Oval mirror, carved and gilt. About 1780. In Adam's later oval mirrors the frame-mouldings became narrower, and the beautiful device of a concentric inner frame was adopted, as in the oval chair and settee-backs of this period (Plate 72).
Photograph supplied by E. T. Biggs and Son.

155. Pier-glass in the dining-room at Syon House, Middlesex. The Duke of Northumberland. Carved and gilt frame. One of a pair, executed from a design by Robert Adam dated 1764 (vol. 20, no. 14). The mirror was illustrated with other Syon furniture in *The Works*, vol. III, Plate II, mistakenly inscribed as for the Earl of Bute at Luton. This design shows the marked early Georgian influence upon which Adam depended so strongly in his early phase, especially in the 'tabernacle' shaped frame with broken sides, the term figures in profile, and the somewhat heavy strings of husks. The scrolled foliage ornament is also in Adam's bold early manner, according in scale with the scrolled ornament of the dining-room ceiling. In many articles designed by Adam, however, the ornament has been executed in bolder form than it was drawn. It thus seems possible that in some cases the lingering baroque flavour had been imparted by the craftsman through the force of tradition.

156. Pier-glass in the Etruscan room at Osterley Park, Middlesex. Victoria and Albert Museum. The frame is painted black with carved and gilt mouldings and gilt composition ornament. The crest is carved and gilt, and has a painted medallion representing Venus and Cupid. Executed to a design by Robert Adam (Soane, vol. 20, nos. 44 and 45) dated 1775. Adam designed a whole range of mirrors of this delightful type, with a crest consisting of a central motif such as an urn or medallion supported by figures. They differ greatly in detail but the general conception remains the same. The backing of part of the crest by mirror-glass is also a feature of this period. The frame is narrower and lighter than in earlier types (Fig. 155).

157. Side-table and pier-glass in the eating-room at Osterley Park, Middlesex. Victoria and

Albert Museum. The carved and gilt table, one of a pair, is of similar character to Adam's design of about 1767, shown in Plate 20, but the legs have been simplified by the omission of the clumsy square block capitals. The frieze is almost Kentian in the robust vigour of the carved decoration and in the bold scale of the key-pattern and rosettes ornament. The mirror, also of about 1767, shows an early form of a favourite Adam type having a broad oval frame and solid acanthus scrolling. Adam's palm-leaf motif at Kedleston (see Figs. 37 and 38) appears again here in the palm-leaves of the crest. The neo-classical honeysuckle ornaments and the festoons of husks have the heaviness associated with Adam's early style.

158. Side-table and pier-glass in the breakfast room at Osterley Park, Middlesex. Victoria and Albert Museum. The table, carved and gilt and with marble top is one of a pair made after an Adam design of 1777, for a wall composition (Soane, vol. 20, no. 49). The lifeless elegance and over-refinement of this late composition contrasts strongly with the vigour of the earlier piece (Fig. 157). The carved and silkwood mirror is also one of a pair made to the same design, and is an example of the tripartite type which Adam favoured after 1770. The upright divisions, shaped as terminal figures, now display that lifeless conventional quality that so often accompanies the heightening of refinement in his later works.

159. Fire-screen. One of a pair; carved and gilt, the screen panels containing water-colour paintings apparently cut from a Chinese wall-paper. About 1785. The rams'-heads and feet, and the shield-form of the screen-panels reflect Adam influence, and the piece admirably represents the spread of the Adam style to the less opulent class of furniture.
Photograph supplied by Hotspur, Ltd.

160. Candle-stand. One of a pair, carved and gilt. About 1785. A delightful example of the many objects that make use of Adam motifs and express the kind of neo-classical elegance that he favoured.
Photograph supplied by Mallett and Son.

161. Mirror. Carved and gilt. About 1775. This handsome example of the tripartite type of mirror introduced by Adam combines features of two mirror-designs in *The Works* (vol. 2, part 1, Plate 3) dated 1773, for the Earl of Derby's House, Grosvenor Square, one of which is illustrated in E. Harris, *Adam furniture*, Fig. 73. The ovals formed by husks in the upper part have been taken from one design; the term-shaped pilaster supports with medallions and balusters from another. Incidentally, the classical figure reflected in the mirror is one of a set which came from the gallery at Croome Court.
Photograph supplied by Frank Partridge and Sons.

162. Girandole. Carved and gilt base and frame, with foliage and other ornaments in moulded composition. This charming design is based on a type originating with Adam, in which a prominent horizontal member is combined with the oval glass. It appears in his design for the 'Pier-glass in the Parlour' at Kenwood (*The Works*, vol. 1, no. 2, 1774, plate VIII) and for a girandole at Apsley House (Soane, vol. 20, no. 178).[1] In the present example it is expressed with a vigorous grace absent in the latter design, which is of Adam's final period.
Photograph supplied by Mallett and Son.

163. Girandole in the long gallery at Osterley Park, Middlesex. Victoria and Albert Museum. Carved and gilt. One of a set of six. Executed with modifications from Adam's designs dated 1770 (Soane, vol. 20, nos. 36 and 37). The inverted heart-design was a motif which

[1] E. Harris, Figs. 88 and 94.

D   The Gallery at Harewood House, Yorkshire

Adam favoured occasionally; it appeared conspicuously in the cast-iron window-railings of the Adelphi buildings. The theme of female figures reclining upon the curve of the mirror frame is a feature of baroque design, which Adam might have derived from such examples as the oval mirrors of about 1750 at Woburn, which have figures similarly disposed. The house provides a compendium of various classical motifs from which Adam could have drawn inspiration.

164. Lady's writing-table, at Stourhead, Wilts. The National Trust. Kingwood, with marquetry of tulipwood, rosewood and other woods. Supplied by Thomas Chippendale the Younger about 1791. This exquisite writing-table represents the adaptation of a French type of furniture (the *bonheur du jour*) to Robert Adam's system of ornament. The English character of the piece is evident in the greater smoothness and solidity of form which it possesses, by comparison with French examples. The hand of the younger Chippendale seems to be apparent in the bold simplicity of the inlaid ornament.

165. Occasional table. Rosewood and satinwood, with marquetry of various woods. About 1775. This extremely graceful piece represents the extreme delicacy of form attained in the still popular rococo French taste during the Adam and Hepplewhite period, combined with neo-classical motifs of an urn and festoons of husks. The top is inlaid with an oval containing a bunch of flowers naturalistically executed, on a geometrical ground.
Photograph supplied by Phillips of Hitchin, Ltd.

166. Library-table in the library at Nostell Priory, Yorkshire. Lord St. Oswald. Provided by Chippendale in 1767 at a cost of £72:10:0 (Nostell accounts). Mahogany, carved. The development of Chippendale's later style is evident in this and the following plate. The descent of this piece from the kind of library-tables evolved by William Kent is apparent in the boldly formed tapering term-shaped supports, in the lion-headed capitals and in the paw feet. The ovals of husks seem to derive from the carved oval mouldings with rococo detail on the panels of desks in the style of William Vile from the 1750's. The ornament of carved festoons in the frieze is neo-classical, but retains the vigorous character of William Kent's work. The volute above the lion-heads of the pilasters is an early instance of a feature found in other pieces known to have been made by Chippendale, and there is a similarity in the piece to a design for a library-table in the *Director*, third edition, of 1762, Plate LXXXII.

167. Library-table in the gallery at Harewood House, Yorkshire.[1] The Earl of Harewood. Rosewood with marquetry and inlay of various woods. Supplied presumably by Chippendale about 1770. Together with the sideboard group (Plate 140) this magnificent piece must rank among the masterpieces of Thomas Chippendale. The treatment is now almost completely superficial, the pilasters hardly protruding beyond the surface of the piece. There is now no carved work, all the decoration being inlaid except for the ormolu mounts, which are of the highest quality. Rams'-heads with festoons take the place of the lion-masks of the typical pre-Adam library-table. Chippendale's characteristic volute ornament appears here again in the pilaster-capitals in more delicate form, and inlaid ovals now replace the carved moulding of the mid-century William Vile idiom.

168. Wine cellarette at the Royal Pavilion, Brighton. Carved mahogany, the lion-heads and feet gilt. This type is closely associated with Adam's design for a wine-cistern appearing in his drawing of a sideboard for 'the Rt. Honble. W. G. Hamilton's house at Brighton' of

[1] Note 1, p. 173.

1787 (Fig. 26). The serpentine fluting derives from the carving of ancient Roman sarcophagi, and consequently wine-cellarettes and coolers later came to be called by this name.

169. Chest-of-drawers. Mahogany with bandings and fillets of other woods. About 1790. This shows the distinctive Hepplewhite simplicity and elegance applied to an unpretentious piece of domestic furniture. The sweeping lines of the feet are characteristic. So are the pressed metal ring-handles.
Photograph supplied by Hotspur, Ltd.

170. Semi-circular pianoforte. Satinwood, inlaid. Inscribed on the keyboard panel 'W. Moore' (of Dublin, see page 122), about 1785. The present piece provides a charming instance of the semi-circular form used by Adam and Hepplewhite here applied to a newly developed type of instrument — the pianoforte. Although an adaptation of the rectangular shape of earlier small keyboard instruments, the semi-circular form is highly satisfactory functionally as well as aesthetically, because of the convenient way in which it can accommodate strings of varying lengths.

171. Grand pianoforte, at Heaton Hall, Manchester. City Art Gallery, Manchester. Satinwood, inlaid with five oval medallions on the case and two smaller medallions flanking the keyboard. Inscribed on keyboard panel: Robertus Stodart, Londini fecit. 1784, Wardour Street, Soho. The harp-like form of the case which had been used for harpsichords long before it was adopted for the larger type of piano, now achieves fresh elegance in the light woods and with the delicate decoration of a neo-classical age. The stand is neatly trimmed in the style of the day, but still retains the form of the traditional harpsichord stand, with its rather massive stretcher and carriage-bolt fastening.

172. China-cabinet at Firle Place, Sussex. The Viscountess Gage. One of a pair; mahogany with marquetry in satinwood, rosewood and other woods; from Panshanger, Hertfordshire. Here attributed to Chippendale, about 1772. The rams'-heads and husk ornaments in the pilasters with the honeysuckle ornament at the front correspond very closely with those of the library-table at Harewood (Fig. 167). The leaf-ornament and volute in the frieze are identical to those in the dressing-commode at Harewood (Fig. 121). The feet also are typical of Chippendale. Like the Harewood pieces, these cabinets must also rank among the greatest works of this craftsman.

173. Secretaire-cabinet. About 1790. Satinwood, the lower part inlaid with oval panels of partridge wood crossbanded with tulip-wood. The design is based on several features appearing in various engravings in Hepplewhite's *Guide*. The oval inlaid panels and the curved feet in one piece with the base are typical of his style, and the cornice is inlaid with a motif similar to several in the *Guide*. The vase-shaped glazing-bars of the upper part are especially beautiful. Note the high position of the loop-handles, so placed to enable the flap-front, here disguised as a pair of drawer-fronts, to be pulled down to provide the writing-surface.
Photograph supplied by Mallett and Son.

174. Secretaire at Harewood House, Yorkshire. The Earl of Harewood. Satinwood, with marquetry in various woods, the oval medallion inlaid in ivory on an ebony ground. Supplied presumably by Chippendale. About 1770–3. An English interpretation of a French type, the *secrétaire à abattant*, exhibiting extreme elegance and refinement of form. The concave pagoda-like top is of a type found in English mid-eighteenth century furniture by William Vile. It is also a not unusual feature of French originals and of much German

furniture. Unlike the French examples, which are fitted with two doors in the lower part, with drawers and a strong-box behind, this piece has a drop front in the bottom stage.

175. Bureau. Satinwood with marquetry of harewood, ebony and other woods. About 1790. The interior is veneered with amboyna, and has six drawers, pigeon holes and a central cupboard enclosed by a door painted with the figure of a Muse, in the manner of Angelica Kauffmann. The top closes by a tambour shutter. This charming piece is of a type represented by specimens at Temple Newsam, Yorkshire, and at Syon House, Middlesex. The small triangular dentils below the flutes are especially common in French furniture, but comparatively rare in English pieces.

Photograph supplied by Norman Adams.

176. An Adam and Hepplewhite interior. The drawing-room at Buscot Park, Berkshire. The National Trust and the Lord Faringdon. The house was designed by the amateur architect owner, Edward Loveden Townsend, in 1788. The neo-classical decoration is in a manner reminiscent of James Wyatt's reticent adaptation of the Adam style. Like many of Adam's drawing-rooms, the walls are hung with silk damask. The oval-back gilt chairs and the sofa are in the Adam style; the shield-back painted chairs, the small bow-fronted commode, the pair of painted side-tables (which were given by Nelson to Lady Hamilton), the Pembroke table with flower-painted border, all admirably represent the Hepplewhite phase.

Photograph supplied by A. F. Kersting.

177. Canopy bed, in the east bedroom, Harewood House, Yorkshire. The Earl of Harewood. Carved, painted and gilt. Supplied presumably by Chippendale, c. 1770. The bedposts are in some respects similar to designs by Chippendale in the *Director*, especially in the reeded posts and the square-section bases. Neo-classical influences deriving from Adam are discernible in the oval paterae ornaments of the bases, and the leaf-ornamented portion between the base and the baluster, which is a feature found in beds of the Palladian era.

The spirit of Adam is more evident in the canopy, especially in the festoon and leaf ornament, in the small-scale gilt moulding above, of a linked *ovoli* pattern, and in the crest with its honeysuckle ornament and surrounding garland of bell-flower.

INDEX

INDEX

1. The Dining-room apse at Kedleston Hall, Derbyshire, 1762.

2. 'Drawing at large of the sideboard in the nich of the Dining-room at Kedleston', by Robert Adam, 1762.

3. Design for the Painted Room at Spencer House, St. James's, London, by James Stuart, 1759.

4. Sidetable carved and gilt, in the Dining-room, Kedleston Hall, designed by Robert Adam, 1762.

5. Pier-table, carved and gilt, from Spencer House, St. James's, London, designed by James Stuart, *c.* 1759.

6. Design for a window-pier, with pier-table and tripods, attributed
to James Stuart, *c.* 1759.

7. Tripod, carved and painted, from Spencer House, St. James's,
London, designed by James Stuart, *c.* 1759.

8. Side-table, carved and painted, in The Gallery, Syon House,
c. 1761.

9. Tripod-pedestal carved, gilt and painted, and ormolu candelabrum from Spencer House, St. James's, London, designed by James Stuart, *c.* 1759.

10. Side-table, carved and gilt, at Rousham House, Oxfordshire, attributed to William Kent, *c.* 1735.

11. Side-table, carved and painted, in the Dining-room at Syon House, *c.* 1762.

12. Side-table, carved and painted, at Rousham House, attributed to William Kent, *c.* 1735.

13. Side-table, carved, gilt and painted, from Stanmer House, Brighton, *c.* 1755.

14. Design of a Sideboard-table from Chippendale's *Director*, 1762.
15. Design of a 'Table-frame for the Dining-room at Sion' by
Robert Adam, 1765.

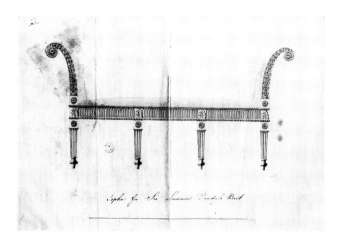

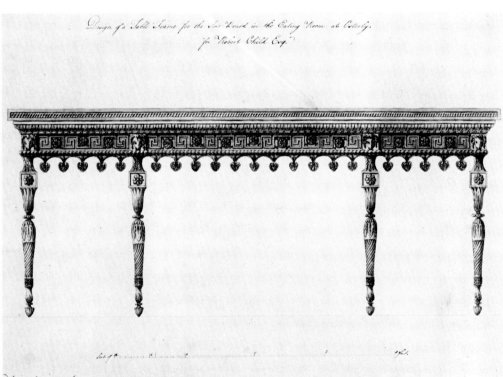

16. Design of a 'Sopha for Sir Lawrence Dundas, Bart.,' by Robert Adam, 1764.

17. 'Design of a Table Frame' for Sir Giles Farnaby, by Robert Adam, 1765.

18. 'Design of a Table frame for the Sideboard in the Eating-room at Osterley' by
Robert Adam, 1767.

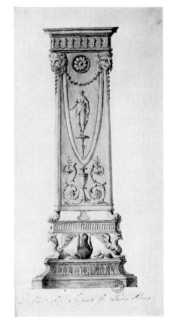

19. Design of a term-pedestal by Robert Adam, *c.* 1765.

20. Design of a tripod-pedestal by Robert Adam, 1778.

21. Design of a 'Table-frame for Sir Laurence Dundas, Baronet', by Robert Adam, 1765, executed for Moor Park and 19 Arlington Street, London.

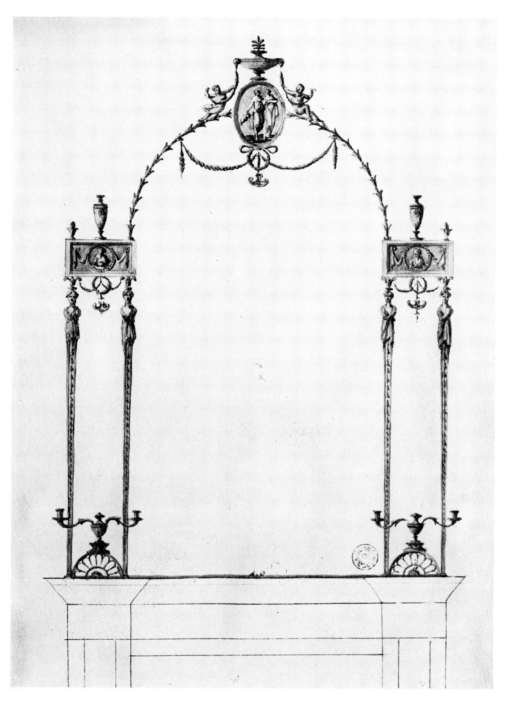

22. Design of a mirror for Apsley House, by Robert Adam, 1778.

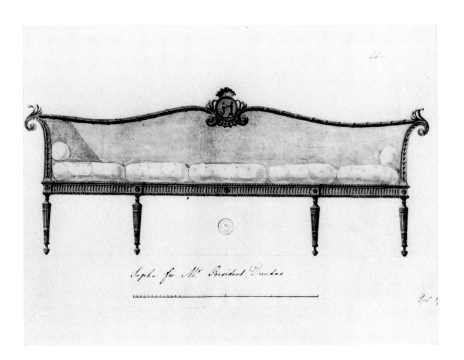

23. Design of a 'Sopha for Mr. President Dundas' by Robert Adam,
1770.
24. Design of a 'Harpsichord for the Empress of Russia'
by Robert Adam, 1776.

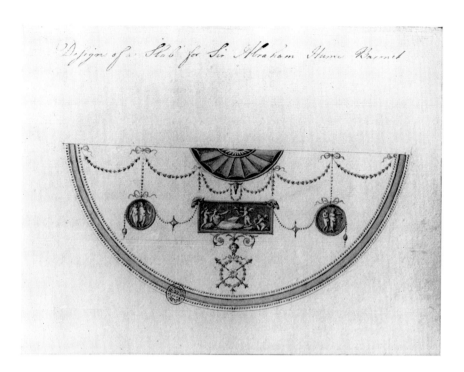

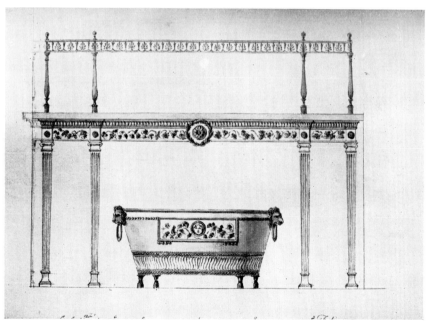

25. Design for a table-top by Robert Adam, 1779.
26. 'Design of a Sideboard Table and Wine Cistern for the Right
Honble. W. G. Hamilton's Dining Room at Brighton',
by Robert Adam, 1787.

27. Engraving in *The Works*, of a mirror, table and tripods,
for the Marquis of Bute at Luton, 1772.

28, Engraving in *The Works* of tripods, mirror and side-table, 1773.

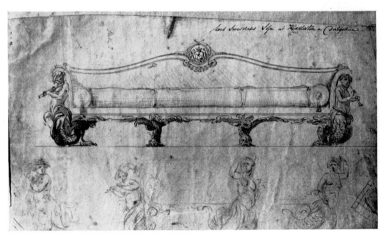

29. 'Design of a Sofa for Lord Scarsdale', by Robert Adam, 1762.

30. Design of a sofa, by John Linnell, *c.* 1762.

31. Design of 'Lord Scarsdale's Sofa at Keddlestone in Derbyshire' by John Linnell, *c.* 1762.

32. Drawing of a Triton, by John Linnell.

33. Detail of Triton end-supports of a sofa in the State Drawing Room at Kedleston Hall, by John Linnell, *c.* 1762.

34. Sofa, carved and gilt, in the State Drawing Room at Kedleston Hall, by John Linnell, *c.* 1762.

35. Sketch of a pleasure-boat by Robert Adam, *c.* 1762.
36. Design for a pier-table, by John Linnell, *c.* 1762.

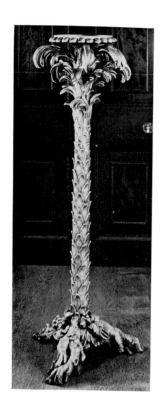

37. Torchère, carved and gilt, in the State Bedroom at Kedleston Hall, by John Linnell.
38. The State Bed, carved and gilt, at Kedleston Hall, by John Linnell, *c.* 1762.

39. The Library, Osterley Park, Middlesex, 1773.

40. The centre bay of the Gallery at Syon House, Middlesex, 1769.

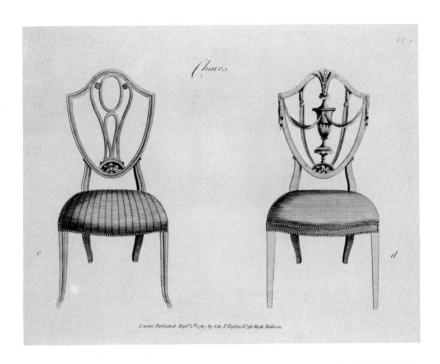

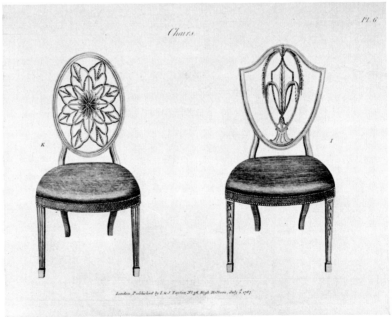

41. Designs of chairs from Hepplewhite's *Guide*, 1788 and 1794.
42. Designs for chairs from Hepplewhite's *Guide*, 1788.

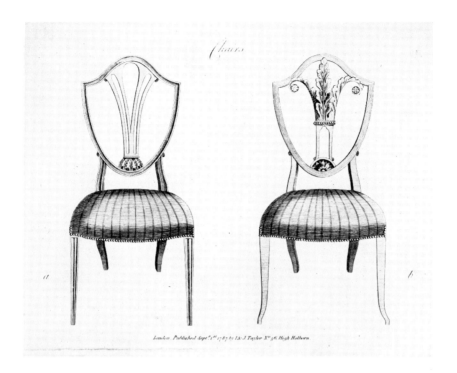

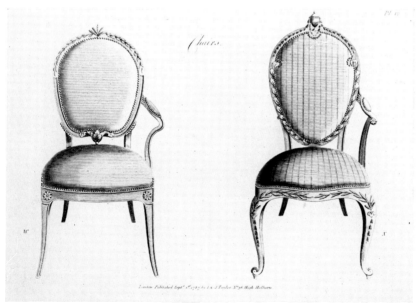

43. Designs for chairs from Hepplewhite's *Guide*, 1788.
44. Designs for chairs from Hepplewhite's *Guide*, 1788.

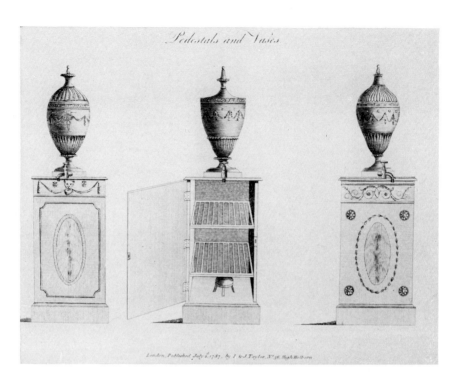

45. Designs for pedestals and vases from Hepplewhite's *Guide*, 1788 and 1794.

46. Design for a sideboard from Hepplewhite's *Guide*, 1788 and 1794.

47. Design for a Sofa from Hepplewhite's *Guide*, 1788 and 1794.
48. Design for a Chair-back settee from Hepplewhite's *Guide*, 1788 and 1794.

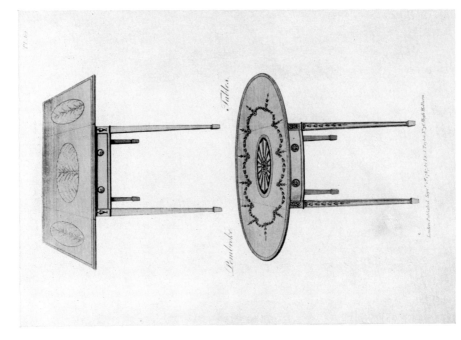

50. Designs for Pembroke tables from Hepplewhite's *Guide*, 1788 and 1794.

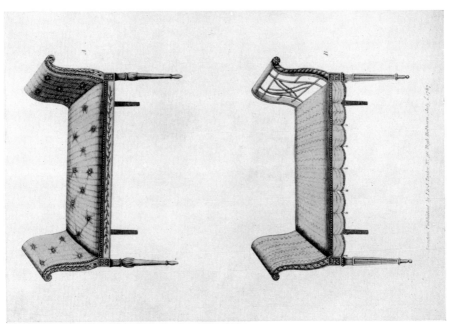

49. Designs for window-stools from Hepplewhite's *Guide*, 1788 and 1794.

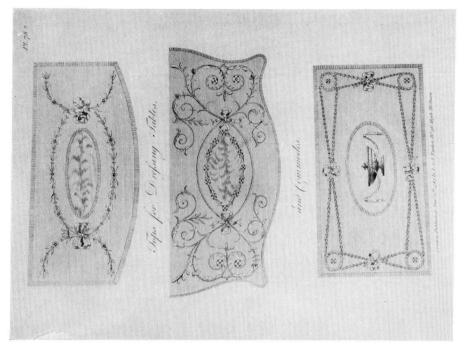

52. Designs of tops for Dressing-tables and commodes from Hepplewhite's *Guide*, 1788 and 1794.

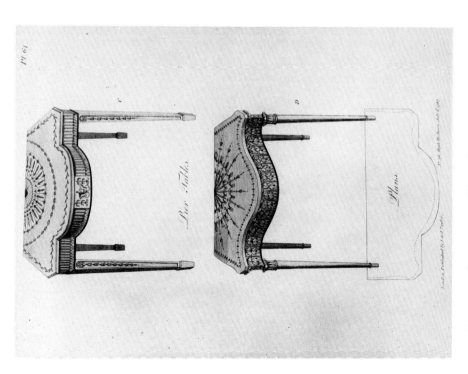

51. Designs for Pier-tables from Hepplewhite's *Guide*, 1788 and 1794.

53. Design for a 'Secretary and Bookcase' from Hepplewhite's *Guide*, 1788 and 1794.

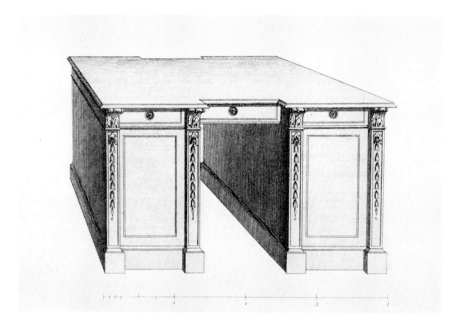

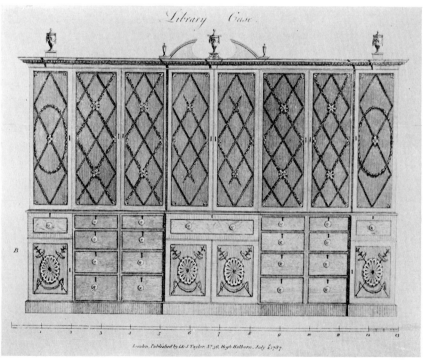

54. Design for a Library table from Hepplewhite's *Guide*, 1788 and 1794.

55. Design for a 'Library Case' from Hepplewhite's *Guide*, 1788 and 1794.

57. Armchair, carved and gilt, designed by Robert Adam for Sir Lawrence Dundas, 1764.

56. Armchair in the Gothic taste, at Alnwick Castle, designed by Robert Adam, c. 1761.

59. Chair in the Dining-room at Harewood House; supplied by Chippendale, c. 1767.

58. Armchair, mahogany, carved, from the Gallery, Croome Court, supplied by John Cobb, 1765.

61. Oval-back Armchair, carved and gilt, from the Tapestry Room, Moor Park, *c.* 1770.

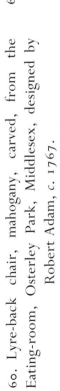

60. Lyre-back chair, mahogany, carved, from the Eating-room, Osterley Park, Middlesex, designed by Robert Adam, *c.* 1767.

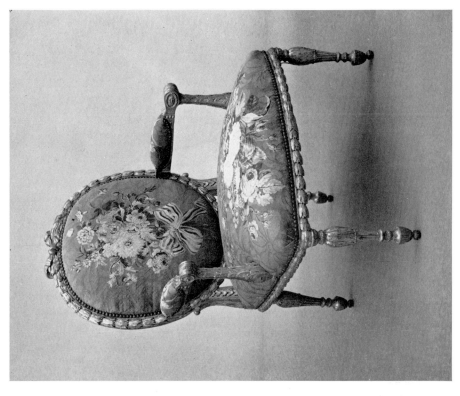

63. Oval-back armchair, carved and gilt, from the Tapestry-room, Croome Court, supplied by Ince and Mayhew, 1769.

62. Lyre-back armchair, mahogany, carved, in the Library, Nostell Priory, Yorkshire, supplied by Chippendale in 1768.

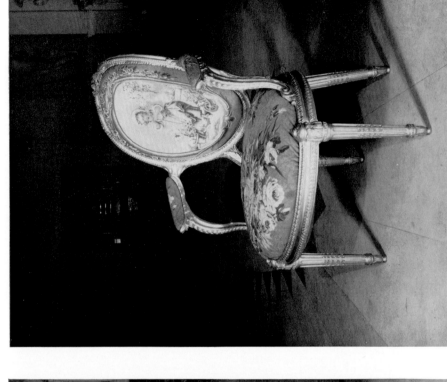

65. Oval-back armchair, carved and gilt, in the Tapestry room, Osterley Park, c. 1776.

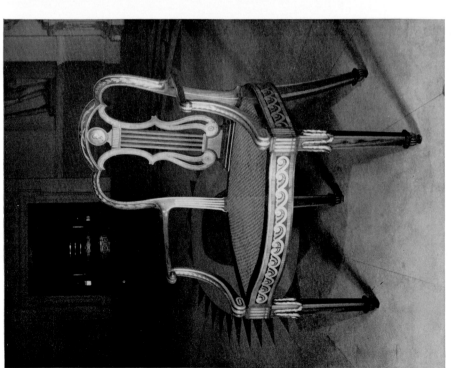

64. Lyre-back armchair, carved and gilt, in the Library, Osterley Park, c. 1773.

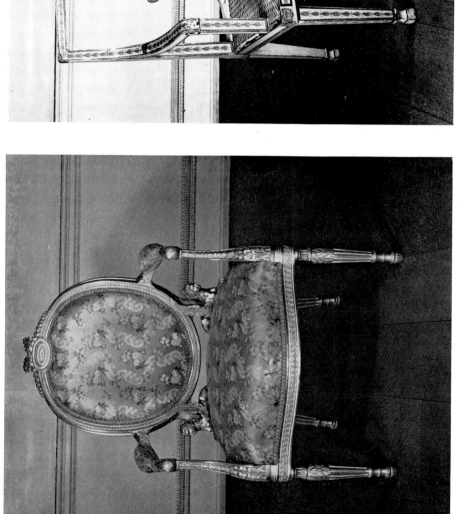

66. Oval-back armchair, carved and gilt, in the State Bedroom. Osterley Park, designed by Robert Adam, 1777.

67. Armchair, painted, in the Etruscan Room, Osterley Park, designed by Robert Adam, 1776.

68. Hall-chair, mahogany, carved, at Nostell Priory, supplied by Chippendale in 1766.

69. Chair, carved and gilt, in the Tapestry-room, Nostell Priory, supplied by Chippendale, *c.* 1771.

70. Armchair, carved and gilt, in the Music Room, Harewood House, supplied by Chippendale, *c.* 1771.

71. Armchair, carved and gilt, in the Gallery at Harewood House, supplied by Chippendale, *c.* 1773.

72. Armchair, carved and painted, *c.* 1770.

73. Chair from the Dining Room, Heveningham Hall, Suffolk, designed by James Wyatt, *c.* 1785.

74. Oval-back armchair, mahogany, carved, *c.* 1790.

75. Shield-back armchair, painted, *c.* 1790.

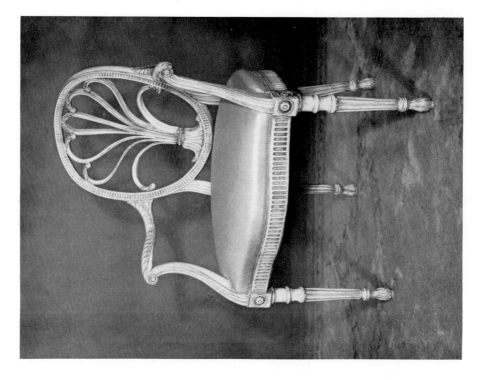

77. Oval-back chair, painted, c. 1790.

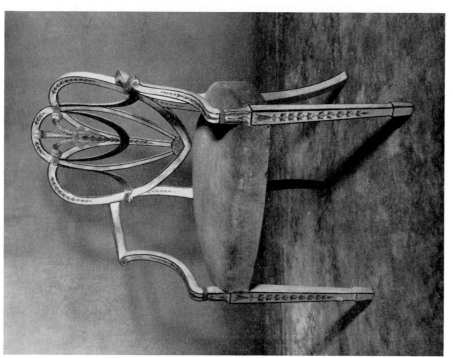

76. Shield-back armchair, painted, c. 1790.

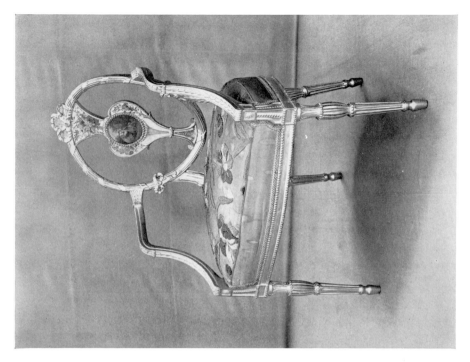

79. Oval-back armchair, carved, gilt and painted, c. 1780.

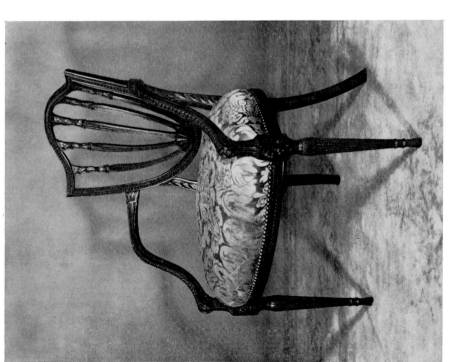

78. Shield-back armchair, mahogany, carved, c. 1790.

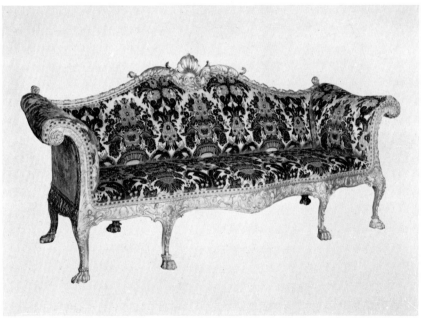

80. Sofa, carved and gilt, from Spencer House, St. James's, London, now at the Iveagh Bequest, Kenwood, designed by James Stuart, *c.* 1759.

81. Sofa, carved and gilt, designed by Robert Adam for Sir Laurence Dundas and executed for 19 Arlington Street, London, 1764.

82. Sofa, carved and gilt, from the Tapestry-room, Moor Park, presumably supplied by Samuel Norman, 1770, now at the Philadelphia Museum of Art, U.S.A.

83. Sofa, carved and gilt, in the Gallery at Syon House, *c.* 1769.

84. Confidante, carved and gilt, *c.* 1780.
85. Sofa, carved and gilt, *c.* 1785.

86. Duchesse, carved and painted, *c.* 1790.
87. Sofa, painted, *c.* 1790.

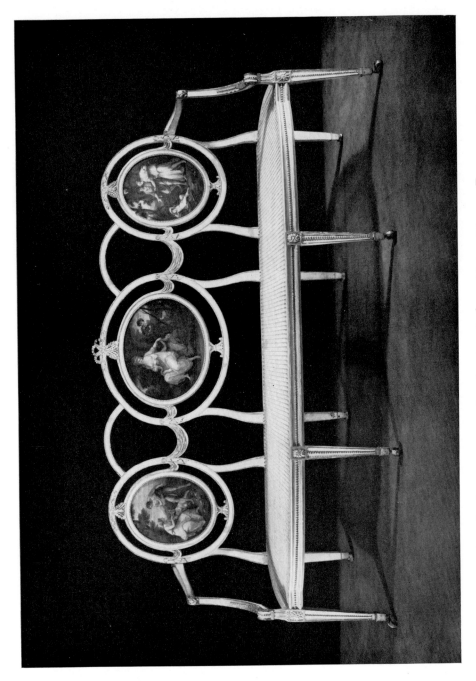

88. Chair-back settee, carved and painted, from Upton House, Essex, c. 1780.

89. Chair-back settee, mahogany, carved, *c.* 1790.

90. Window-seat, carved and gilt, *c.* 1780.
91. Window-seat, mahogany, carved, *c.* 1790.

92. The Eating-room at Osterley Park, 1767.

93. Side-table, carved and gilt, in the Drawing-room at Syon house,
designed by Robert Adam, 1765.

94. Side-table, carved and gilt, in the Music-room at Harewood
House, supplied by Chippendale, c. 1767.

95. The Ante-room at Syon House, 1762.

96. Side-table, carved and painted, in the Gallery, Syon
House, *c.* 1764.

97. Pier-table, carved and gilt, in the Saloon at Nostell
Priory, designed by Robert Adam, 1775.

98. Pier-table, carved and gilt, in the Hall at Nostell Priory, designed by Robert Adam, 1775.

99. Side-table, carved, gilt and painted, in the Tapestry-room at Osterley, designed by Robert Adam, 1775.

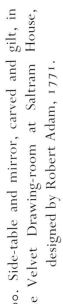

101. Side-table and mirror, carved and gilt, in the Saloon at Saltram House, 1772.

100. Side-table and mirror, carved and gilt, in the Velvet Drawing-room at Saltram House, designed by Robert Adam, 1771.

102. The Tapestry-room from Croome Court, at the Metropolitan Museum, New York, U.S.A.

103. Side-table from the Drawing room, Woodhall Park, Herts; about 1770.

104. Side-table, carved and gilt, with caryatid supports, c. 1770.

105. Side-table, carved and gilt, c. 1775.
106. Side-table, carved, painted and gilt, about 1780.

107. Side-table, carved and gilt, in the Library, Harewood
House, supplied by Chippendale, *c.* 1767.

108. Side-table, carved and gilt, in the Rose Drawing Room
at Harewood House, supplied by Chippendale, *c.* 1773.

109. The State Bedroom at Osterley Park, 1775–6.

110. Design of a console table, artist unknown.
111. Console table, carved and gilt, in the Gallery at Harewood House, supplied
by Chippendale, *c.* 1769.

112. Console table, carved and gilt, in the Green Drawing-room at Harewood House, supplied by Chippendale, c. 1772.

113. Console table, carved and gilt, from Stanmer House, Brighton, possibly designed by James Wyatt, c. 1788.

114. 'Design of a commode for Sir George Cole Brooke, Bart,'
by Robert Adam, 1771.
115. Design of a 'Commode for his Grace the Duke of Bolton'
by Robert Adam, 1773.

116. Design of a 'Commode for the second Drawing Room at Apsley House'
by Robert Adam, 1779.

117. Design for a commode from Hepplewhite's *Guide*, 1787.

118. Commode, mahogany, inlaid, in the Green Drawing Room, Harewood House, supplied by Chippendale, *c.* 1770.

119. Commode from Croome Court, supplied by Ince and Mayhew, 1765.

120. Commode, japanned green and gilt, in the State Bedroom at Nostell
Priory, supplied by Thomas Chippendale, 1771.

121. Dressing commode in the private apartments, Harewood House,
Yorkshire; supplied by Chippendale in 1773.

122. Commode in the Drawing Room, Osterley Park, Middlesex, designed by Robert Adam, 1773.

123. Bow-fronted commode, japanned black and gilt, in the State Bedroom, Osterley Park, c. 1774.

124. Commode in the State Bedroom at Woburn Abbey, supplied by
Peter Langlois, 1771.
125. Commode, mahogany, inlaid, attributed to Chippendale, about 1770;
in the Lady Lever Art Gallery.

126. Bow-fronted commode, mahogany, inlaid, in the Drawing-
room, Stourhead, presumably supplied by Thomas Chippendale
the Younger, c. 1785.

127. Bow-fronted commode, mahogany, about 1790.

128. Card-table, mahogany, inlaid, with shaped folding top,
c. 1785.

129. Card-table, satinwood and harewood, inlaid, with semi-
circular folding top, c. 1785.

130. Pembroke table, satinwood, inlaid, *c.* 1785.

131. Top of Pembroke table (Plate 130 above). Satinwood inlaid with shell and vase designs, *c.* 1785.

132. Side-table from 20 St. James's Square, London, now at Buscot Park, Berkshire. Mahogany carved, with marble tops, *c.* 1773.

133. Sideboard, carved and painted, from 20 St. James's Square, London, now at the National Folk Museum, St. Fagan's Castle, Cardiff, designed by Robert Adam, 1773.

134. Sideboard table, mahogany, from Woodhall Park, Herts.,
c. 1780.
135. Sideboard, mahogany, inlaid, *c.* 1790.

136. Sideboard, urns on pedestals and wine-cooler in the Dining-room at Harewood House, mahogany, inlaid, supplied by Chippendale, *c.* 1771.

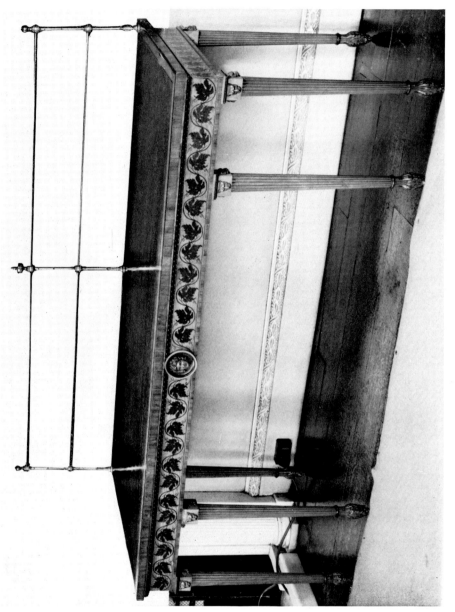

137. Sideboard, satinwood, inlaid, in the Dining-room at Newby Hall, attributed to Thomas Chippendale the Younger, c. 1788.

138. Urn and pedestal in the Dining Room at Harewood House, Yorkshire.
Supplied by Chippendale about 1770.

139. Urn and pedestal, carved and painted, in the Eating-room at Osterley Park,
Middlesex, designed by Robert Adam, c. 1767.

140. Urn and pedestal, satinwood, inlaid, in the Dining-room at Newby Hall, attributed to Thomas Chippendale the Younger, c. 1788.

141. Urns and pedestals, carved and painted, from the Eating-room, 20 St. James's Square, London, c. 1773.

142. The Dining-room at Saltram House, Devonshire, 1780.

145. Tripod in the Saloon at Saltram House, Devonshire, 1772.

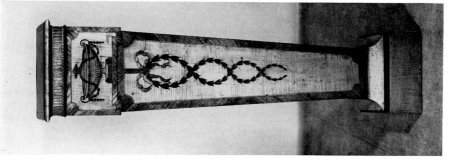

144. Tripod-stand, carved and gilt, in the Drawing-room, Osterley Park, Middlesex, c. 1777.

143. Term-pedestal, satinwood, inlaid, c. 1775.

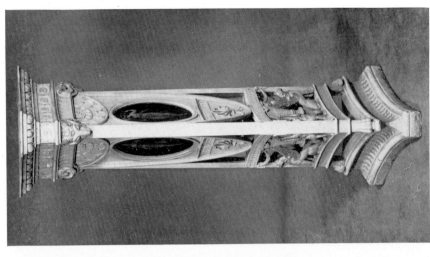

148. Tripod-pedestal, carved and gilt, 1774.

147. Tripod-stand, carved and gilt, about 1775.

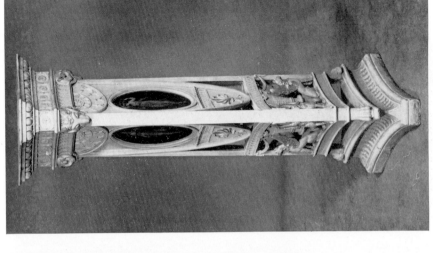

146. Tripod-pedestal, carved, gilt and painted, in the Tapestry-room, Osterley Park, Middlesex, 1776.

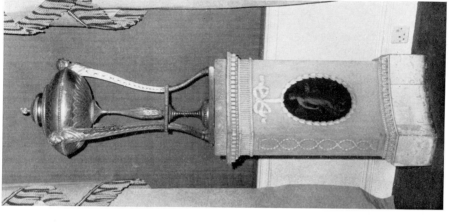

149. Urn and pedestal in the Library, Newby Hall, Yorkshire, designed by Robert Adam, 1779.

150. Tripod and pedestal, about 1780.

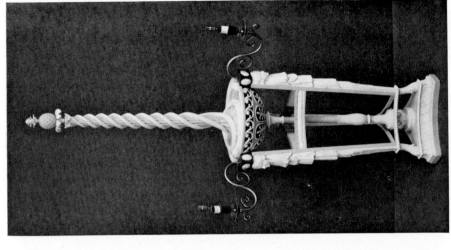

152. Tripod-candelabrum, from Heveningham Hall, Suffolk, probably designed by James Wyatt about 1784.

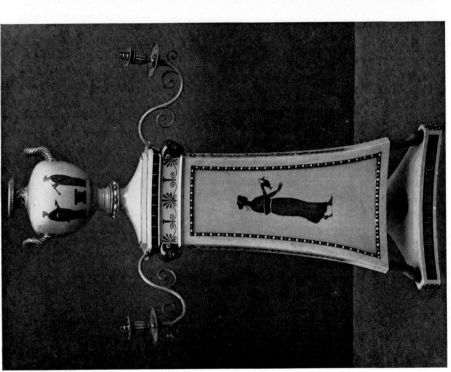

151. Pedestal and urn, from Heveningham Hall, Suffolk, probably designed by James Wyatt about 1784.

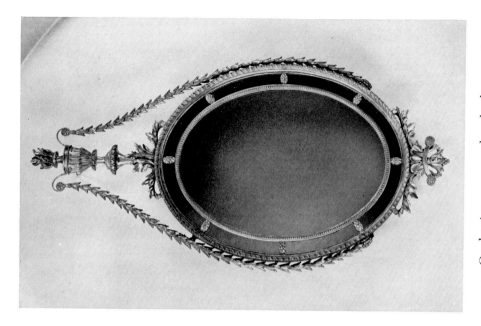

154. Oval mirror, carved and gilt, c. 1780.

153. Oval mirror, carved and gilt, c. 1770.

156. Pier-glass, carved and gilt, in the Etruscan Room, Osterley Park, Middlesex, designed by Robert Adam, 1775.

155. Pier-glass, carved and gilt, in the Dining-room, Syon House, Middlesex, designed by Robert Adam, 1764.

158. Side-table and pier-glass, carved and gilt, in the Breakfast Room, Osterley Park, Middlesex, designed by Robert Adam, 1777.

157. Side-table and oval pier-glass, carved and gilt, in the Eating-room, Osterley Park, Middlesex, c. 1767.

159. Fire-screen, carved and gilt, 1785.
160. Candle-stand, carved and gilt, *c.* 1785.

161. Mirror of tripartite form, carved and gilt, based on two designs
by Robert Adam, c. 1775.

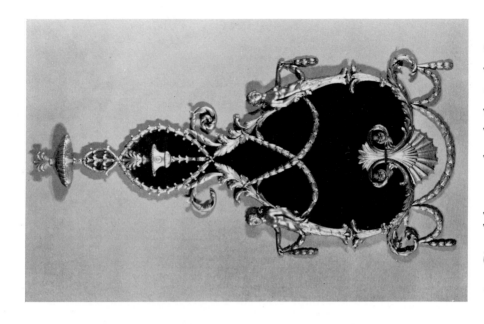

163. Girandole, carved and gilt, in the Long Gallery, Osterley Park, Middlesex, 1770.

162. Girandole, carved and gilt, c. 1774.

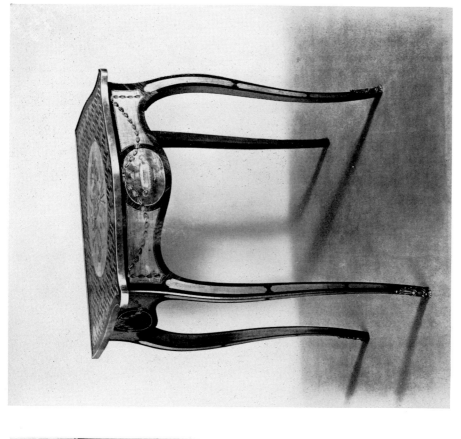

165. Occasional table in the French taste, combined with neo-classical decorative motifs. About 1775.

164. Lady's writing table, mahogany, inlaid, at Stourhead, Wiltshire, c. 1790.

166. Library table, mahogany, carved, at Nostell Priory, supplied by Chippendale, 1767.

167. Library table, mahogany, inlaid, from the Gallery, Harewood House, supplied by Chippendale, c. 1771, now at Temple Newsam House, Leeds.

168. Wine-cellarette, mahogany, carved, *c.* 1790.
169. Chest of drawers, mahogany, *c.* 1790.

170. Semi-circular pianoforte, satinwood, inlaid, inscribed
W. Moore, about 1785.
171. Grand pianoforte, Heaton Hall, Manchester, satinwood,
inlaid. Inscribed 'Robertus Stodart, Londini fecit. 1784.'

172. China-cabinet in the Saloon, Firle Place, mahogany, inlaid. Attributed to Thomas Chippendale, *c.* 1775.

173. Secretaire-cabinet, satinwood, inlaid, c. 1790.

175. Bureau, satinwood, inlaid, c. 1790.

174. Secretaire at Harewood House, satinwood, inlaid. Attributed to Thomas Chippendale, c. 1773.

176. An Adam and Hepplewhite interior: the Drawing Room at Buscot Park.

177. Canopy bed in the East Bedroom, Harewood House, Yorkshire, supplied by Chippendale about 1770.